Dream Tending

STEPHEN AIZENSTAT, PH.D.

Dream Tending by Stephen Aizenstat articulates a world alive with soul and body—exciting, rich, trustworthy guidance into dream interpretation. Readers are challenged to find their deepest truth and live their own life. A lifetime companion!

—MARION WOODMAN Jungian analyst and author of *Addiction to Perfection*

Dream Tending is a wonderfully insightful and reaable guide to the practice of dream interpretation, filled with practical exercises and affecting stories. In this book, Stephen Aizenstat brings to the field of dreams that transformation of vision that is gradually changing every field of human activity and study in our time: it breaks free from the narrow confines of the reductionist modern mind-set and awakens us to the ensouled reality of all things. It reveals dreams as an opening to the depths and expanses of the *anima mundi* itself.

—RICHARD TARNAS Professor of Philosophy and Psychology, California Institute of Integral Studies, and author of *The Passion of the Western Mind* and *Cosmos and Psyche*

The world is passionately alive, dreamed anew every instant. Stephen Aizenstat's book is an ode to this existence which he tends with great skill and care. It is filled with exercises enabling us to work our dreams by ourselves, a most difficult task requiring the guidance of a master of the craft. The book ranges from our most personal dreaming to the grand 'I have a Dream' which has spurred us to action for decades. Aizenstat teaches us to meet the dreamed beings in the way they present themselves: alive, real and full of intelligence; a healing encounter.

—ROBERT BOSNAK Jungian psychoanalyst and author of *A Little Course in Dreams* and *Tracks in the Wilderness of Dreaming*

DreamTending
Awakening to the
Healing Power of Dreams

ISBN 978-1-935528-11-1

Library of Congress Cataloging-in-Publication Data Pending

Paperback Edition 2011

Published by

Spring Journal, Inc.

627 Ursulines Street #7, New Orleans, Louisiana 70116
Ph: 504-524-5117   www.springjournalandbooks.com

Cover and Interior Design by Silverander Communications
Santa Barbara, California

Amber.   2011

"A man with no Dreams
can have no Dreams come
        True"

                              'Heaviest Fortune cookie
                                   ever"
                for   dad

        Jesse, Alia, and Elijah

IV – DREAM TENDING

CONTENTS

VI – Dream Tending

ACKNOWLEDGEMENTS

To my many colleagues through the years at the Isla Vista Human Relations Center, the Human Relations Institute, and Pacifica Graduate Institute who offered their support and made a home for me to expand my work with dreams.

To those who have offered technical and aesthetic assistance through the process of assembling this book, particularly Michael Silverander for his help in graphics and design, and Nancy Cater of Spring Journal Books who held the vision of this book along with me for many years. In addition, Lindsay Starke, Jennifer Young, and Nicole Montalbano added valuable editing suggestions along the way.

To Nancy Galindo, Heidi Townshend-Zellner, Dorinda Carr, Ross Woodman, and especially Richard Tarnas who read and offered feedback on various sections of the book. And to Marion Woodman who reviewed and commented on the text.

To Michael Taft, my editor, collaborator, and friend. It is because of his patient, diligent, and tenacious craftsmanship that this book evolved into what it is today. Our journey together has enriched the work deeply.

To the wise guardians, Barbara Biggs and Joan Chodorow, who taught me the healing power of the dream in very personal ways. And to my mentor and soul keeper, Russ Lockhart, who knows the mystery and knowledge of psyche's speech like few others.

To Joseph Campbell and James Hillman, whose bodies of work inform what I do and how I think.

To the places on the earth that I have walked and swum, especially Santa Barbara, Montana, Australia, Hawaii, Greece, and Africa. In these landscapes the voices of native teachers, the creatures, land, and seas have spoken their stories through the living images of dream.

To all of the dreamers and their dream figures who touched my soul and helped shape the craft of Dream Tending.

To my Mother and Father and their parents and grandparents, without whom the stories of the dreamtime would have never revealed themselves.

And most importantly, to Maren Tonder Hansen, my wife, whose continued love supports me to follow the calling of my heart. Her deep regard, technical expertise, and empathy for the work companions the journey of tending dreams.

INTRODUCTION

My great-grandfather was a shoe cobbler from the old country, a place called Belarus or "White Russia." His shoe repair shop in 1950s Pasadena, California was a small room on the ground floor of the old rickety house he shared with my great-grandmother. It opened to the street just a few yards from the railroad tracks, and the windows rattled when the huge locomotives thundered past. The shop had an unforgettable smell of fresh-cut leather, shoe polish, and kerosene. Shoes of every size, shape, and style were piled up in rows to the ceiling, leaving hardly any space to stand. I remember the walls were covered with little scraps of paper with parables written on them in my great-grandfather's funny handwriting.

Great-grandfather (who I called "Zadie") was so different from us. Zadie was large, had a thick Yiddish accent, and always seemed so happy. His cobbler's shop was usually crowded with people who came to sit and talk with him. He'd work on their shoes some, but mostly he asked them questions, offered advice, and told stories. He had a joke or allegory for everyone—even me. He'd ask me questions, tell me stories, and give me a penny every time I laughed. Great-grandfather was ninety-three years old the first time I looked into his eyes behind their old-time spectacles. His eyes were blue and crinkled all around the edges, and the skin around them scrunched up even more as he laughed and laughed. His hands smelled like shoe leather and the borscht he had for lunch. He made me feel completely grown up and ready for adventure. I had never felt such belonging.

I was just six years old when he died and I don't remember the funeral. There wasn't much talk about him after that. It was easy to see that my father, his grandson, had loved him, but at the same time my dad seemed uncomfortable and even ashamed whenever he was mentioned. My family, like every family I knew, was from a world far different from the long-ago village. We grew up with the Cold War, the H-bomb, and Sputnik. It was our duty to do well in school, go to college, and study science and math in order to beat the Russians at everything. There was little room for remembering the quaint oddities of an old man from a completely different time, and so eventually I stopped thinking about him.

Twenty years later, I had become a psychologist interested in dreams. The 1960s had radically opened up the field of psychology, and I had eagerly joined in the revolution. I went to workshops and lectures of every kind, and gradually learned that dreams were something more than just a chaotic rehashing of our daytime life. During that time, I was at a dream workshop and remembered a dream I had about my great-grandfather.

In the dream I heard his voice. He told me to go to a house where there was a wooden chest, and inside this chest was a book that contained my whole future. This dream was different from any I had had before. It was not so much a dream as it was a commandment from the other side. I was shook up, but also aware of the warmth I felt for my nearly forgotten great-grandfather.

Excited, I called home that afternoon and asked my mom and dad if they knew anything about a wooden chest and a book. Neither had a clue what I was talking about. Not wanting to let this go, it occurred to me to contact my great aunt, Zadie's sister. She was always a bit odd, but she was one of my favorite relatives. I called her and told her about my dream. Incredibly, she said she knew just what I was talking about and told me to come right over.

When we were sitting together in her living room, she asked me what I remembered about her older brother. I told her my memories and all that had been shared with me, which wasn't much. She then pointed to a wooden chest covered with an embroidered cloth and flower-filled vases. "Stephen, in that chest is a book that will give you the answers to everything you are searching for. I have saved it all these years, waiting for the person who would come to find it. Now it's yours."

Crossing the room, she opened the chest and handed me the book. Strange hieroglyphs covered its worn red cloth cover. My aunt explained that the book was written in Yiddish and that it ran from right to left and back to front. Turning the book over, I opened it and saw something I never expected. On the first page there was a photograph of my great-grandfather with his wife at his side. He was dressed in a grey flannel suit, and those amazing eyes I remembered from childhood were staring at me.

"Your father's grandfather was a revered tzaddik," my great aunt told me. "The people you remember seeing in his shop were there to ask him questions about life, to hear his stories, and to listen to his teachings." She described him as a man who was learned, but not in the ways of the university. My great-grandfather, it turns out, was steeped in the oral tradition from the elders of his country and others. "This book is called Der Shooster, which means 'The Shoe Cobbler,'" she said. "It's a book about him."

I looked at the photo again, and I was filled with pride and a sense of belonging to a lineage I had never imagined existed.

What had been a source of embarrassment for my family was now flooding me with something essential, something wise. I felt my great-grandfather's presence in my blood, his heart beating in my chest. The force of his character strengthened my own. It was my turn to open the book and read the story that would forever change my life.

In the following months I had the book translated into English. I located a woman in New York City, who lived in a Jewish neighborhood not far from where Zadie had lived when he first arrived in this country. Every thirty days or so, I received about a dozen pages of typed text. For over a year, as the translation continued to arrive, I experienced the revelation of my inheritance, yet it took me much longer before I began to truly realize the depth and meaning of my great-grandfather's teachings. It came as a shock to me that this man, whom my family had always seen as a fossil from the past, was the storehouse of the very knowledge I needed to encounter the future.

The Dream Tending Vision

When I began my work as a therapist, psychology was enjoying a tremendous boom in popularity, boldly striding into new areas of research. Living in California, I was exposed to every possible form of therapy, from the rational and straight-laced, to the far out and unusual. I tried them all, seeing for myself what seemed to work and what did not. I had the great pleasure of learning personally from some of the greatest teachers and thinkers of the 20th Century, such as Frederick Perls, Robert Johnson, James Hillman, Marion Woodman, Carl Rogers, Virginia Satir, Gregory Bateson, and Joseph Campbell, as well as many gifted analysts, native teachers, and others.

But there was always something missing for me, until I had the dream about my great-grandfather. Even then it took me a long time to appreciate his teachings, because many of them were deceptively simple, such as, "There is life in the shoe leather." At first I didn't know what to do with an aphorism like that, but slowly, as I began to understand, these teachings transformed me from the inside out. I realized that my interest in psychotherapy was the continuation of my family lineage in a new, more modern, form. Using his seemingly simple idea that everything in the world is alive, I began treating dreams as having a life of their own. That's when something began happening in my professional psychotherapy practice that I hadn't seen happen with the other forms of therapy I was utilizing. People's lives began to turn around.

At first, I was a little skeptical. Was what I was doing simply the next "therapy of the month"? The culture was flooded with dubious cures for every possible affliction, the bookstores buried under an avalanche of self-help books, and it seemed like most of them disappeared as fast as they caught on. I didn't want to be the source of another well-intentioned but ineffective therapy. I have to admit that sometimes the idea that dream figures are alive sounded more like a hallucination than a contribution to the practice of serious psychotherapy.

Yet the more deeply I listened to dream figures, the more my clients experienced a positive change in their lives. Sometimes in just a single session, making contact with a particularly potent living dream image transformed someone's addiction or opened new heights of intimacy in a couple's relationship. As their dreams came alive, so did each person's own sense of self worth. Not only were serious problems worked through, but an authentic life emerged, one informed by the truth of what existed at the inner core of each individual.

Personally and professionally, my life has been shaped by my relationship to the living figures of the dreamtime. I now experience life in the world as if it were a dream. This does not imply that things seem more distant, surreal, or disconnected. Just the opposite, in fact. Dreams keep my imagination active and vital. Living with this quality of mind brings me closer to everything and everyone around me. I feel more present, more aware, more engaged. I experience the world as burgeoning with color and texture.

Remember as children when we had access to the miracle of our imaginations? How wonderful it was to explore the world as a place of magic and mystery? For most of us, school and society very quickly trained us away from our imaginations and into the business of making a living.

We travel many paths, looking for the ones that will take us back to the place of imagination and dreams. We all know that there are many wrong turns, many detours. The demands of family and work leave us no time or energy to touch the living dreamtime. Sometimes a new love will break us out of our stale patterns for a few weeks, yet this is usually only a faint echo of the magic we once knew. Other times we get caught in the seduction of drugs, with their false promise of giving us back our long lost creative lives. And so we continue relentlessly searching for the originality with which we were born, longing to remember the living images of our dreams.

"Keep the dream alive" is more than a romantic ideal. I am convinced that tending dreams holds great promise for the future. I believe that the DNA of our individual and planetary evolution is coded in the images of dreams. Combine this conviction with the idea that dream images not only live within us, but they exist all around us, in every animal, plant, and object of this world. My great-grandfather's teaching echoes an old yet new idea: that, in a certain way, everything is dreaming. If we allow ourselves even a few minutes a day free from distraction, we will certainly begin to encounter this lush and expansive dream life. We need only learn how to listen to the living images of dreams.

The system that I have developed to work with living dream images is called "Dream Tending." Dream Tending uses techniques that I have tested on myself, my family, my peers, my clients, and thousands of university and workshop students from around the world for over thirty years. I have carefully weeded out anything that didn't seem to bear fruit and have poured further energy into developing the concepts and exercises that I've seen repeatedly helping people.

I look forward to sharing Dream Tending with you.

Chapter One

THE LIVING IMAGE

Dream Tending is a life practice that healers, storytellers, and poets have known by many different names for thousands of years. Passed on through the generations, the art of tending living dream images emerges in a culture when the call to⟩ ²⁰¹²⁷ see the natural world as alive is urgent. Then, after a while, the teachings are forgotten and go underground once more. My great-grandfather understood this at a time when people were in desperate need of the life-affirming power of the dream. I believe I picked up the nearly forgotten threads of knowledge three generations later, as a small boy in his cobbler's shop. As years passed and the culture again suffered the pangs of separation from the wellspring of internal nature, I felt the awakening of this craft within me.

Dream Tending, as I would name this calling, did not appear to me as a fully formed vision. The craft came to me out of both necessity and destiny. My early struggles with dyslexia meant that I had to find alternative learning skills simply to survive. Belonging to my great-grandfather's lineage was a matter of fate, but what was most formative in the revelation of Dream Tending was the journey of discovery itself. It was not a direct route, not a ⟩ straight path to the wisdom that dreams are alive and the images ⟋

in them are as real as you or I. It was, in fact, just the opposite. It was a circuitous expedition, clumsy at times, often not conscious, yet always underneath I felt pushed by a force, as if the journey was guided by the living images of dreams themselves.

Connecting to the living images of dreams opened me to a life abundant with possibility. These living images, dismissed as irrelevant in our society, became teachers and guides shaping my life. I discovered that they exist at the core of our being. We are born into their presence. They live with us always, making visit upon visit each night. Living below conscious awareness, they significantly influence our behavior and temperament, animate our life, offer warning when needed, and inspire our work.

THE JOURNEY TO THE LIVING IMAGE

When I was a kid, I dreamed of becoming a doctor. Of course the adults in my family and community assumed *all* of us kids would become either doctors or lawyers, and so we were continually pushed in those directions. Thinking about it now, I'm not sure whether the dream of becoming a doctor was actually theirs or mine. But in any case, I worked very hard in high school, kept up my grades, and got accepted into the premed program at UCLA, at the time my definition of heaven.

The college experience, however, turned out to be far from what I anticipated. I was no longer among a group of teenagers who just happened to go to the same high school. I was in a group of high-achievers from around the nation and the world. These teenagers were the cream of the crop. I found myself in hardcore chemistry, biology, and calculus classes and surrounded by serious and dedicated students who seemed to have a much better idea of what was going on than I did. By the time we got our first round of test scores back, I realized that I was falling behind. I was serious and dedicated too, but these subjects didn't come naturally to me. Furthermore I found I didn't really enjoy them at all.

I hadn't expected college to be easy, though, so I dug in and tried harder. I spent night after night in the library, studying until they shut the doors behind me and turned out the lights. And still, when test day rolled around, the exams might as well have been written in a foreign language. I got Ds across the board. It was a very hard time for me.

One day in biology lab we were going to be tested on our knowledge of the anatomical structure of the brain. Like the other students I had on my white lab coat and was standing in front of my slab, ready to lift an animal brain out of its jar of formaldehyde solution, plop it on the table, and begin cutting it up. Standing there looking at that brain, I found myself overcome with nausea, panicky at the thought of what I was supposed to do next. I knew that I wasn't going to be able to find and identify all the little structures in that mass of flesh.

As I was stood there trying to pull myself together, the teacher's assistant asked me to follow him out into the hallway. I had no idea what he wanted, or why he would interrupt me right at that moment, but I didn't mind escaping that room full of brains. When we got in the hall, he took a deep breath, let it out in a sigh, then looked me right in the face. "Steve, let me ask you something. Do you see anybody here like you? What I mean is, when you talk to your classmates do any of them seem interested in the stuff you're interested in? Do you really belong here?"

I didn't know what to say. On one hand, I had spent my whole life preparing for medical school. All my plans, all the dreams the family had for me, revolved around becoming a doctor. So at that moment, I felt an urge to dismiss his questions and get back to business. On the other hand, deep down I knew that he was absolutely right. None of the people in the premed program were anything like me.

Then, in the nicest way possible, he asked, "Have you ever explored the other side of the campus?" I had no idea what he was talking about. I didn't even know there was another side of the campus. I said, "no." He explained that the north side of campus was where the humanities programs were located, and that I might want to go up there and take a little walk around.

And so not returning to the brain waiting for dissection in the classroom and feeling very confused, I hiked from the medical school to the humanities hall. Right away I could tell that the people there were different. They were hanging out in the sculpture garden, seemingly relaxed and open. I heard people talking about art, literature, and the issues of the day. Instead of the tense, focused, getting-things-done atmosphere of the premed students, people who were talking about philosophy, politics, love, and life surrounded me. Even the landscape was different. Instead of cold concrete laboratories, there were trees and gardens, brick and ivy.

It had never occurred to me that college could be about anything but science. I couldn't believe that you could get college credit for using your imagination, entertaining ideas, and valuing human experience. My secret life of fantasy, politics, art, literature, and especially dreams (that I now understand to have been inspired in me by Zadie and that I had kept hidden from everyone else while growing up) stirred a re-awakening within me. I was able to see these things as something that people actually *valued.* I dropped out of premed and enrolled in a sampling of liberal arts classes, just to find out what I was really interested in, which turned out to be political science and psychology. That was where my exploration of the living images in dreams began in earnest.

REDISCOVERING THE LIVING IMAGE

When I started reading about psychology, particularly about dreams, something came alive inside me. The reading list in Psych 101 included Freud's *On the Interpretation of Dreams*, in which he suggests that dream images are more than what they appear to be. He said they are representations of latent wishes or repressed aggressive sexual drives, which are too disturbing for the conscious mind to encounter directly. Freud developed a reductive method of getting to the meaning of this repressed material, called "association" or "free association." To associate means to find the hidden connections between a dream image and past experience.

Allow me to illustrate this with an example. If there were a lion in a dream, we might think of a trip to the zoo, where we saw a lion. We might also remember something from *National Geographic* about lions in Africa. This might then remind us of a boss who was particularly mean-spirited. Which might further remind us of our aggressive father. We might even remember a specific incident in which our father punished us too harshly which would then remind us of our own pent-up rage. So using association, we would reduce the dream image back to an early scene in our life which evoked unexpressed feelings of rage. This rage was the repressed material that the dream was masking.

I learned that the task of a good Freudian was to "play detective" and use association to uncover this hidden material in a dream. This was a concept that I could readily relate to. At the time I was trying to find meaning in practically everything around me, seeing the "deeper truth" in all that existed, even in existence itself. This was the late 1960s, when psychoanalysis was all the rage. From Woody Allen to John Lennon (and his encounter with primal therapy), the whole idea was that our early experiences with our neurotic parents totally shape who we are. That year at college we all became "wannabe" Freudians. We ransacked our dreams for the keys from our past that would free us from our neuroses. I used to sit on the steps of Royce Hall at UCLA, stroking my beard, analyzing my friends' dreams. The psychiatrist was definitely "in."

Then in my second year, the human potential movement hit like a tidal wave. In my psych and sociology classes we were now reading Jung's *Collected Works*, Maslow's *Toward a Psychology of Being*, and Campbell's *The Hero with a Thousand Faces*. Back at the dorm we were into authors like Theodore Roszak, Betty Friedan, Allen Ginsberg, Norman Mailer, and every existential French or German philosopher we could get our hands on. Just as the 1960s opened up the culture in general, this period also exploded the field of psychology. The 1950s lab-rat-in-a-maze, behaviorism, and shock treatment model of mental health gave way to the expression of feelings and creativity, the humanistic psychologies of Transactional Analysis *(I'm OK, You're OK)*, Psychosynthesis, Gestalt Therapy, and Carl Rogers' work on empathy. Now we understood the images in dreams in a completely new way. They were no longer just literal references to our personal history—stories about how messed up our relationships were with Mom and Dad. Instead they pointed to something much bigger than our personal egos.

The genius behind this viewpoint was Carl Jung. Jung felt that dream images are much more than just repressed infantile wishes and drives. They originate, he said, in the collective human psyche and can represent universal *archetypes*. That is, dream images are similar to the characters and themes found in fairy tales, mythology, religion, and world literature. They are archetypal in that they can tell us something of the grand story in which we live.

From Jung's point of view, the method of association is not the only way to work with dreams. Instead, Jung developed a process called *amplification*, in which we discover a dream image's connections to universal cultural themes. For example, to amplify the dream image of a lion, we would note that lions represent royalty or nobility, like Richard the Lionheart, or *The Lion King*, or the zodiac sign of Leo. Lions are also fierce protectors, presiding over home and palace alike as guardians at the gates. And in many mythologies, lions symbolize the heart.

Perhaps when we *associated* to the lion image in our dream in the example above, we found that it was a stand-in for our own infantile rage. However, when we take the same image and *amplify* it, the lion now points to something regal, noble, fierce, or big-hearted in our nature. Using amplification we expand the image to its full stature as an archetype, and then see how that archetypal motif is currently active in our lives.

This obviously takes us in a much different direction than association. Amplification opens us up to the great teachings that are alive and active in dream images. These stories tell us about the perils of our situation, the potential positive outcomes, strategic teachings, and the collective wisdom of generations past. As the great mythologist Joseph Campbell said, dreams are like myths. A myth is a story that expresses something meaningful about a culture, from origins to values to sanctioned social interactions. Every night the dreaming psyche is generating something of our own personal mythology, informing us about our origins, values, and so on. A single dream image, amplified through literature and mythology, can offer us tremendous insight into our lives.

When Jung's ideas hit our campus with full force, they were as revolutionary as the times. No longer was I playing psychiatrist on the Royce Hall steps, analyzing dreams as neurotic patterns of early childhood. Even in our psychology classes we passionately discussed everything from the *Tibetan Book of the Dead* to *A Midsummer Night's Dream*, from *Siddhartha* to *Alice in Wonderland*, and their relationship to human behavior and dreams. Everything for me became a quest to understand how dream images worked in both the popular imagination and our own lives.

I was learning to live within dreams, as if I were participating in a great play. At this time we began to stretch beyond Jung's grand concept of amplification. I was living in an artists' commune in Santa Monica surrounded by professional actors, musicians, artists, dancers, and a few surfers, exploring the frontiers of "liquid theater," using improvisation to act out dream images on stage. Watching my friends perform at the Mark Taper Forum in downtown Los Angeles, it was suddenly obvious that dream figures are actually alive and interactive. Watching a person improvise being a prowling lion onstage, I experienced the actor actually taking on and inhabiting the living archetypal presence of the lion. When I witnessed the embodiment of Lion, it became clear that dreamwork was about more than just the mythology of Lion; it was also about the direct experience of the figures. Rather than going off to a library and only studying these images' history in some dusty encyclopedia of mythology, it was now possible to talk to them, dance with them, argue with them, live with them. Yet as dream images came alive to me through the arts, I was still struggling to understand conceptually what I was learning in my direct experience.

ANIMATING THE LIVING IMAGE

Around this time I heard of the work of James Hillman. One night my friend Richard Tarnas and I were at Esalen in Big Sur, walking under a brilliant sky full of stars and talking about new directions in psychotherapy. Rick handed me a book by Hillman and said, "You have to read this." After only the first few pages, I realized that Hillman was talking about dream images in just the way I was experiencing them. As a twenty-two-year-old self-proclaimed Jungian, I saw it as remarkable synchronicity that Dr. Hillman would be giving a talk in nearby San Francisco a few days hence. So I hitchhiked to the Bay Area and crashed the conference to attend his lecture.

Hillman cut an impressive figure. Tall, thin, and fit, he had intense eyes that reminded me of a hawk. In a roomful of California new-agers, he brought the discriminating intellect of a European scholar and cut right through our fuzzy, feel-good thinking with the sharp sword of erudition and experience. His *profound scholarly knowledge* ideas set the room on fire. I listened enraptured as Hillman described in depth, detail, and scholarship the view of dream images that I had been blindly groping towards.

James Hillman had been one of Jung's senior students, and his work took up where Jung's had left off. He said that dream images were more than signs pointing to some answer, as Freud said, or symbols representing a meaning, like Jung. They were also phenomenal, like living animals, and had presence, place, and body. He said that dream images are actually "persons of the soul" and "necessary angels." They are demons, djinn, and gods who show us our fate and await a response from us.

In his way of looking at dreams, we needed to go beyond association and amplification to a new process called *animation.* In animation, we look for ways of experiencing dream images in their living, embodied reality. For example, the lion, rather than just referring to our childhood rage or the universal archetype of nobility, now takes on a physical existence, actually present in the room, on the prowl, roaring with its fanged mouth, lashing its tail and licking its huge, furry paws. Furthermore, this is not like watching a lion in a movie, because in Hillman's animation we are able to actually interact with the lion, talk to it, ask it questions, pet its fur, hear what it has to say, and follow it through its habitat. It's a full-immersion, interactive experience.

Inspired by what I was learning, in the 1970s I co-founded a school of depth psychology dedicated to the exploration of the living images that was the forerunner to Pacifica Graduate Institute. One of our first presenters was a Jungian, Marion Woodman. Students crammed into a bare room lit by an anemic light bulb to drink in her lively energy and encyclopedic understanding of dream images. Her view fit very well with Hillman's—essentially, that dream images exist both in spirit and in matter and as such are expressions of both body and soul, psyche and soma, and allow us to connect with ourselves in both realms. Marion Woodman helped me understand dream images as even more concrete, even more embodied. It was somewhere around this time that I finally grasped the most basic concept of all my future dreamwork, that *dreams are alive.*

In conclusion, the process of Dream Tending stands on the shoulders of giants. From Freud's association, to Jung's amplification, to the animation of Hillman and Woodman, as well as from my personal experiences with indigenous teachers of dreams worldwide, and with direct inspiration from my great-grandfather's teachings, I have developed Dream Tending.

ASSOCIATION, AMPLIFICATION, ANIMATION

In order to begin Dream Tending, we need to be familiar with the three methods of dreamwork that we have looked at: association, amplification, and animation. In this book, we will spend the majority of our time learning techniques of animation. Yet I have found that the other two methods come in handy often enough that it is important to be proficient with them as well.

These three techniques have a natural sequence, which also happens to be both their historical order in modern psychology and their order of psychic "depth." Association comes first, and is closest to the ego; then comes amplification, which has its home deeper in the psyche; and then animation, which arises from the deepest level of the psyche. Actually these processes are not hierarchical, however, it is useful here at the beginning to see them in this sequence.

Learning Dream Tending is not just reading about ideas. It is also experiential, because a real feel for the material can only develop through actually working with living dream images. The teaching points in this book can be thought of as support for direct interaction with living images, which is offered in the exercises. Living images are where the action is, and what our work is about. Along with each teaching point, I invite you to experiment with the material in an exercise.

EXERCISE: *Association, Amplification, Animation*

Choose an image from your dreams that has really gotten your attention recently. It may be a character, like a person or a creature, or it could even be something like an ocean, a forest, a rock, a building, or another object. Whatever image you choose, notice what aspects of it get your attention and seem to stay with you in the time since you had the dream. Write a description of the dream figure, being as concrete and specific as possible.

Now, work with the image using *association*. Let your mind spontaneously connect the dream image to any events, feelings, ideas, or scenes from personal history that come up. Let one association lead to the next. Do not worry about getting the "right" answer. Just let one impression connect to the next, over and over. You can write down these associations in a dream journal as they spontaneously occur to you.

Observe where this process of association takes you. Take special note of any childhood experiences that come up. From the point of view of the personal unconscious, such a memory may be the root of your dream image, and offers an important insight into why this particular image is occurring now in your dreams.

Once you have completed the process of association, you are ready to give *amplification* a try. In this method, you correlate the dream image to symbols, archetypes, and figures from mythology, fairy tales, literature, theater, and other forms of cultural expression. You are looking for universal themes that connect to the dream image. For example, the image of a horse may be related to the mythological flying horse, Pegasus, or Burak, the eagle-winged horse that carried Mohammed on his journey to heaven. The dream image of an ocean may be amplified into the Source of Life or the place of the Night Sea Journey. Include contemporary as well as historical themes or characters. A character from a novel, a movie star, or a contemporary political figure may be a current representation of a cultural archetype.

There is no limit to how many archetypes the image can be amplified into. You may find that your dream images relate to an ancient Japanese myth as well as a modern Hollywood movie, to a poem from Medieval Spain as well as the poetry of a pop song. These amplifications are not contradictory; rather, they weave together to form a rich and complex understanding of the dream image. You might continue to discover the image's network of archetypal connections for many years, always deepening your intimacy with it.

For now, write in your dream journal what you have learned about the image through the process of amplification. How does this expanded view of the image offer insight into your present life circumstances?

Once you have completed the processes of association and amplification, you are ready to move on to the practice of *animation*. This is the core practice of Dream Tending, and something that you will be doing in virtually every exercise in this book. To animate an image, you bring it to life in the here and now, rather than associating to the past or amplifying it into a myth or story.

Start by imagining the figure present in the room with you. See it clearly in your mind's eye. Even if it is wispy or indistinct, pay attention to any little bit of the image you can mentally see. Imagine for a moment that it has a life of its own, separate from all your associations and amplifications. Seeing it as a living entity, existing in its own right, what do you notice about what it is doing and how it is moving? How is it interacting with you? How does it affect you? Write your discoveries in your journal.

You have now associated, amplified, and animated a dream image. Read and compare the entries you made for each method. What happened to the image in each of these processes? What surprised you? How has each of these experiences affected you? What have you learned from each process? How has each of the methods increased your intimacy with the dream image?

Learning to Work with Living Images

Dream images are alive and embodied. This is the fundamental insight at the heart of Dream Tending and is at the heart of our work. The rest of this chapter will be dedicated to learning the skills of animating living dream images. In Part I, I will show how to prepare for Dream Tending. In Part II, I will cover the basic skill set, which includes accessing the archetypal ego, asking the core questions, and using language to vivify images. This will give us solid ground upon which to enter Part III, "Hosting the Guest," which introduces us to a series of more advanced skills. Then in Part IV, "From Relationship to Revelation," we will learn ways to interact with dream images on even deeper and more rewarding levels.

Part I: Preparation— Entering the Realm of the Living Dream

When I listened to my great-grandfather tell his stories, I was transported from his little shoe shop in Pasadena to another world. With him, my imagination was completely active and open. He put me into a dreamlike state of mind, in which the images from his stories sprang to life in my mind's eye. This state of mind turns out to be crucial to Dream Tending. I have found that there are four attitudinal qualities to prepare us to hear dreams in this dreamlike manner. We must:

1) Meet the Dream in the Way of the Dream

2) Open Body Awareness

3) Become Present in the Here and Now

4) Engage the Dream in an Attitude of Not Knowing

These attitudinal qualities set the stage for dream images to come to life and reveal themselves.

1. Meet the Dream in the Way of the Dream

One of the most useful watchwords I have discovered is that "a dream loves a dream." This means that when we approach an image with an open, accepting, dreamlike attitude, it comes to life.

In the actuality of the dreamtime, everyone experiences dreams as alive. When we are dreaming, the characters and action seem as real as anything else in our lives. It is only when we wake up, remember them with our conscious mind, and write them down in our dream journals that they can become static and dead.

To explain away an image is to lose contact with an important visitor. Most folks who listen to a dream try to figure it out mentally. They look for what it "means." This is a trap. Dreams are not a product of the logical mind, and when a dream is met in the way of rational thought, images get folded, spindled, and mutilated to suit the rational mind.

When we approach dreams with an agenda to interpret or judge, the living image becomes stagnant, fixed, and eventually dies. For example, to interpret the dream image of a giraffe as a phallic symbol misses its actuality as an image in the inner landscape of our dream life.

It is crucial to sidestep the ego's desire to understand, make meaning, and dominate. A dream needs to be met in the way of the dream. This is particularly the case when we have an immediate idea of what a dream "means." When this happens it is very hard to find the patience to center ourselves, let go of our explanation, and then connect to the reality of the living dreamtime. So an attitude of wonderment, curiosity, and presence is a necessary first response to a living image.

2. Open Body Awareness

There is a line from Mary Oliver's poem "Wild Geese" that informs all my dreamwork:

"You only have to let the soft animal of your body
love what it loves."

When I work from my "animal body," greeting dream images in an embodied way, they in turn respond to me in the same way. It's as if a dream image is actually a kind of person or animal with a body of its own, albeit imaginal. Images have life force and walk about on legs of their own. Even the non-creature dream entities, like clouds or airplanes or houses, are living, personified presences of the dreamtime. They too have a vitality that blossoms into visibility when met body-to-body.

To meet images in an embodied way, I pay particular attention to the feelings running through me as I encounter an image. I take the time to listen to what is happening in my corporeal experience. It pays to be patient, because often when I try to tune into my body and feelings, the "knower" is the first on the scene. He scrambles to figure things out, take control, offer an opinion. When he shows up, I instantly lose the immediacy of contact with my body. So over the years, I have learned to simply say hello to the "knower" and let him pass by. Then after quieting down, I bring awareness back to the immediacy of my animal body. Connected to my instinctual sensitivities, I am now ready to make body-to-body contact with the living embodied images of the dreamtime.

3. Become Present in the Here and Now

A third attitude for preparing ourselves to work with living images is to get anchored in the here and now, to come into the present moment. A dream image is always here, always now—always ready to connect in the eternal timeless Now of the dream.

I have never heard of anyone having a dream in the past tense. They are always in the present. Therefore it is helpful to become centered in the present moment as a way to enter the dreamtime.

Think of meeting a friend at the park. When I am preoccupied with the demands of the day, I bring nothing with me but a cluttered mind. The interaction is stale and dull. I have not made the effort to bring myself mentally to the meeting, and so neither of us comes to life. We both remain trapped inside a compulsive mind and a deadened body. Sound familiar? It hurts to realize how often we are nothing more than a head, floating in the future and past, disconnected from our body.

Now imagine the opposite. Maybe on the walk through the park to meet my friend, I opened my aesthetic eye to the sensual riot of flowers and took deep, full breaths of the fresh scent from the trees. The sensual richness of the world displaced past regrets and future worries, and centered me in the luxuriant, beautiful Now. When I meet my friend I am awake, receptive, grounded, fluid, interactive. Rooted in present time, I listen in a different way. My friend feels this and engages me with his presence, attention, and openness. Rather then just a check-in, we have a rich, fulfilling experience.

This is exactly the attitude to take with a living image. When we let go of our past and future concerns and simply meet the image in the eternal Now, we create an appropriate environment for good Dream Tending.

4. Engage the Dream in an Attitude of Not Knowing

The first encounter with a living dream can create a sense of being overwhelmed or confused. This is especially true when we depend solely on the rational mind for explanation and meaning. Dreams can be complex, bizarre, confusing, and yet seem to have profound import. When feeling overwhelmed or confused, I have found it quite helpful to reframe this experience as a positive state of "not knowing." Not knowing means that we allow ourselves the comfort of not having all the answers about a dream. We give ourselves the luxury of taking the dream at face value, without struggling to unravel its knots. At its best, an attitude of not knowing is expansive, related, and attuned to the living actuality of dreams. Contrary to feelings of confusion, not knowing creates more room for the dream to present itself and for us to encounter it.

For example, let's imagine a dream in which we find ourselves on a tropical island with a clear pond filled with colorful koi. Around us, swarms of fire ants are on the move. As the dream progresses, we are attacked by a snarling wolf. Presented with such a dream, it would only be natural to wonder what it all means. Any Jungian or Freudian would salivate at a dream like this! There is so much to make out of it. To find some answers would feel reassuring and insightful and remove any unpleasant sense of confusion. We could speculate forever about the possible implications. Yet for all our supposed insights, there is that which remains undeniably, unmistakably, and unchangeably true: a wolf with fangs is prowling, red ants are marching, and brightly colored fish are swimming. The dream itself is a *fact*. Everything else is conjecture.

However clever our explanations of dreams, they actually take us away from the clarity and reality of the dream itself. They are an attempt to deal with our own anxiety and confusion about such a compelling occurrence. If we become more comfortable with not knowing, we won't be so motivated to explain away our dreams. In the long run it is much more satisfying and rich to sit with the mystery, wonder, and sometimes, even bizarreness of a dream. In not knowing, dreams stay fresh, alive, interactive, and surprising.

To experience the presence of living images in all of their wonder and possibility, we start out with these four fundamental attitudes: meet the dream in the way of the dream, open our body awareness, become present in the here and now, and engage the dream in an attitude of not-knowing. These four orienting attitudes bring us into relationship with the living reality that the dreaming psyche is presenting.

EXERCISE:
Entering the Realm of the Living Dream

Select a vivid dream to work with. Sometimes this is an obvious choice; perhaps the dream you had last night was so compelling that it hasn't let go of you all day. Or maybe there is a dream from the past that has continued to come into your thoughts again and again. Whatever dream you choose, or whichever dream chooses you, write or draw it in detail before going further.

When you are ready, find a quiet place and get settled. Reconnect with your body in whatever way you know. You may want to pay attention to your breathing. Notice how you begin to relax and deepen into your body sensations. Allow any thoughts that arise to gently pass through your mind, like clouds floating easily through the sky. Return to your breath. Allow your mind to clear and let go of any interpretations of the dream that you might be considering. Relax in your chair or couch. Take a few moments to feel your presence in the room.

Next read the text of the dream aloud to yourself or take a few moments to really witness the sketch that you have drawn. See the entire dream in your mind's eye, just as you saw it the first time you dreamt it. Imagine that you are in the theater of dream, participating in a live performance.

Notice carefully how entering this dream theater makes you feel. What emotions come up? What physical sensations arise in your body? Write down your observations in your journal.

By bringing yourself into the dream in an active and responsive way, in present time, you begin to open to the consciousness of the dream. You leave your daytime world ever so slightly behind, and begin to walk into the dream world. You are meeting the dream in the way of the dream. Begin to move forward, further and further into the dream. It is no longer an inanimate object that you are going to pick apart. You begin to see it as it really is—a living reality that is here and now.

Now close your eyes and notice your breathing. As you bring your focus to your body, observe where you are feeling tight. Allow your inhaling to naturally deepen, then bring your awareness back to the dream. Notice what you observe and write it down.

LEARNING TO WORK WITH LIVING IMAGES— PART II: THE BASIC SKILL SET

Contacting the Archetypal Ego

Once we have entered the realm of the dream, it is helpful to contact a part of ourselves that I call the "archetypal ego." This more essential self is located in the depth of our being, not in our heads, and is often referred to as our true nature, or the authentic self. This is somewhat different from what Jung called the archetype of the Self. Aligned with the archetypal ego, we have a much greater ability to tend to living images. From this center place, we have the capacity to witness without feeling compelled to act, and the images thus begin to interact with us more freely.

Dream Tending depends on our ability to sustain contact with the archetypal ego. It invites and engages with the animated spark alive within dream figures. Through this deep contact, dream figures come to life and reveal themselves as embodied entities and we gain access to the innate intelligence of these animated images.

My experience is that connecting to the archetypal ego is easier to understand conceptually than to actually do. But I have specifically developed Dream Tending exercises to help you get the hang of it. Like learning most new activities, it's a matter of doing the exercises and keeping an open mind.

EXERCISE: *Contacting the Archetypal Ego*

To connect to the archetypal ego, identify a dream image that touches you emotionally. Sometimes it happens that the first image invites a second dream image into your awareness. If a second dream image shows up, stick to this new image and let the original one go. Spend time exploring this image. Use the skills of animation that you have learned to vivify the image and watch its activity. Meet the figure in the way of the dream. Notice what is particular about it.

Now enter more deeply into a relationship with this figure. Engage in a dialogue, either mentally or by writing it down. As you interact with the figure, notice how your connection to your breath, your heart, and your core deepens. Now imagine the figure alongside of you. Feel your feet on the ground, your breath deepening still further, and your heartfelt awareness broadening. From this awareness, you are now ready to meet the dream in the way of your animal body. You have engaged the archetypal ego, or what some call the authentic self. This is the desired state of awareness from which to continue tending the dream.

One way to help you connect with the archetypal ego is to discover a gesture associated with it. You may make some kind of gesture with your hands when remembering a dream. Notice this gesture, and before you start to work with a dream, repeat the gesture. Then exaggerate the movement, making it bigger in order to open up its range and feeling. You most likely will feel something new come forward from inside, perhaps an awareness of an inner depth. Bring forward your awareness of what you are experiencing from this more intimate place. How are you now engaging your body and your feelings?

Another trick involves any sound you might find yourself making when remembering a dream. Repeat the sound, using no words, just the pure sound, and allow it to move you into your body experience. Ask yourself what sensation you are connecting with and whether it is an experience that is familiar to you. Is this a place that you have known for a long time? Is it a place you visited before? If yes, then let your body experience take you back to the body memory of that quality of experience. What do you notice here? As you further tune into these feelings, what do you discover? Do you have a sense of belonging? Home ground? Allow yourself some time to deepen into this aspect of yourself, the archetypal ego.

It is here, at this more essential level of your personhood, that you will find the mode of being to meet the living dream in the way of the dream. Anchor here and reapproach the dream that you are tending. From this quality of being, what are you noticing about the dream images as they come forward? Keep watching with your open heart and animal body. As the dream images walk about, let what happens happen and simply take note. Stay with it. Don't do anything. Become present and stay patient.

When you feel ready, acknowledge what you have witnessed, say good-bye, and find transition from this experience. Write down what you have observed and what you have experienced.

Asking the Core Questions

Anchored in the archetypal ego, we are now in *anima* country, the wild place of the dreamtime. We are beyond the constructed, civilized, mental landscapes of modernity. Here we are open to the visitation of living images. We experience the world and ourselves in a different way. We do not know what is going to happen before it does.

Surprise is a big part of the joy of working with living dream images. When I am tending dreams, people often ask me how I know what is going to happen next, and my answer is, simply, "I don't." They look puzzled and ask, "Well if you don't, then who does?" It is the dream images themselves that know what is coming next.

There are two questions that are the fundamental pillars of the Dream Tending system and distinguish Dream Tending from all other methods of dreamwork. Simple as they may first appear, these questions shatter decades of cultural conditioning, breaking through the prevailing zeitgeist of reductive literalism.

These questions are "Who is visiting now?" and "What is happening here?" These questions replace the more familiar "What does this dream mean?" or "Why did this happen?" It is really very simple. This tiny change in orientation shifts our consciousness completely. No longer are we playing detective, trying to solve a puzzle with our logical mind.

When we ask, "Who" we invite the living image into active dialogue. It is similar to meeting a new person; we wonder who they are, not what they "mean." Getting interested in the person

(Who is visiting now?) invites him or her to come forward and encourages open expression. Interrogating a visitor (What do you mean?) creates defensiveness and stops friendly interaction.

The question "What is happening here?" evokes curiosity. We wonder about the activity of the dream figure and notice how it interacts with us. When we get curious about what is going on in the dream (What is happening?), the dream figure also gets interested and comes to life. Cross-examining persons of a dream (Why are you here?) makes them clam up, just as any of us would.

In orienting around the "Who?" and the "What is happening?" we trade in our critical, cynical minds for body wisdom and instinctual curiosity. Imagine for a moment that a powerful ambassador visits you in a dream. He is a high-ranking official in an international peace delegation operating through the United Nations. In the dream he is touring a remote African village devastated by drought, orchestrating some kind of humanitarian aid program. Upon awakening we consider the "humanitarian aspect" of ourselves and perhaps connect to how this humanitarian impulse in us has not been active in recent months. In fact we remember that we wanted to make a donation to Habitat for Humanity, but have forgotten to do so. We feel secure that we have now understood the dream's meaning, decoded its message, and solved its riddle. Yet this is the reasoning mind at work, jumping to conclusions, making sense, and taking action. We have completely lost our direct connection to the dream ambassador who originally visited us. The figure no longer exists as a living entity in the psyche, but has been reduced to a trite symbol, dispensing safe and obvious observations about our ego.

When we use the two orienting questions of "Who is visiting now?" and "What is happening here?" with this image, however, we generate a very different outcome. When we get personally interested in this dream ambassador, he becomes an imaginal presence in the room along with us. We sit down and take the time to get to know him, to befriend him, and to engage him in conversation. He senses our interest and begins to open up more completely about what he is doing. We learn from his talent, commitment, and intelligence. The appropriate starting place is "Who are you?".

Discovering who is visiting involves paying attention to how this image engages in his particular activity in the dream (What is happening?). By observing what he is doing, we slow down the process and allow ourselves time to get curious and specific about his actions. By noticing how events are unfolding in the dream and how this main figure is interacting with other images, we gain more information about the image. We are tending the ambassador as a living image. This is part of why I call this activity Dream Tending, not Dream Dissection. We tend our relationship with a dream figure as we tend our relationship with a friend. The figure is engaged in his own activity in the here and now. Our curiosity is about him as a person and what he is up to, not about what he signifies about our own ego.

EXERCISE: *Asking the Core Questions*

Choose a dream that has an identifiable figure (whether person or creature) in it. Tell or write the dream as it actually occurred, noting as much detail as possible.

Take the time you need to center into your archetypal ego and use skills that you have learned so far to animate the image. As it comes to life in the room, get curious. Let go of the tendency to make meaning. Instead ask the questions "Who is visiting now?" and "What is happening here?" and allow the dream image to answer in whatever way it wishes. This might take a long time, which you will want to fill with lots of ideas about the figure. Let go of all these thoughts. Simply be patient and allow the figure to answer these questions in its own time.

The task is not to make sense out of what you are witnessing. Do not play detective, interrogate, or cross-examine. Rather, gather information by allowing the figure itself to unfold in front of you. Your work is to observe like a naturalist would, noticing the activity and particularity of the figure itself. What is he doing now? What is she up to? How is he moving about in the room? How is she interacting with the other dream figures with you?

Pay particular attention to any odd or unique behavior. This figure may not have a physical shape, but instead may present itself through a voice, or even a feeling, form, or color. The important thing is to notice what or who comes forward to greet you. Even if this image is frightening, stick with it as well as you can. Often difficult dream figures prove to be the most important to get to know.

You are not being asked to figure anything out. You are not using your rational mind at all. Rather you are open to your sense of discovery. You are curious about who is visiting now. Return again and again to the orienting questions "Who is visiting now?" and "What is happening here?". As you conclude your interaction, write down what you have experienced.

Using Language to Vivify Dream Images

To complete our basic skill set, we must make a few changes in the language we use to talk about dreams. There are four simple verbal changes that will help us to allow dream images to achieve their full expression and vitality. I particularly like these methods because they are easy, yet have a profound effect on our dreamwork.

Most of us have encountered forms of language that have a deadening effect on experience. Much of our language today is devoid of beauty, grace, and style. Bureaucratic, business, and institutional language tends to be dry and confusing, and is usually enough to make me want to fall asleep. Abstract academic language can also suck the life out of even the most interesting topic. We only have to imagine our wildest love affair described in the language of a lawyer, the turgid prose of a government pamphlet, or—dare I say?—the flat, clinical utterances of a therapist, to instantly feel how such language can turn whatever it touches to dust.

When we describe our dreams however, we are naturally drawn to using vivid and stimulating language. With a few minor adjustments we can make this even more effective. As I mentioned, there are four linguistic changes that make a big difference when working with living images. They are straightforward and structural; no artistry is required for them to work.

First and foremost is to talk about a dream *in the present tense.* As I mentioned earlier, I have never met anyone who had a dream in the past tense. When we have a dream, it always takes place Now, in the eternal present. Yet when we talk about our dreams, we tend to talk about them in the past tense.

If we talk about them instead in the present tense, they come alive and the images animate quickly. When expressed in present tense, the figures seem to be in the room right along with us. For example, when we remember a dream of being chased through a forest by a bear, we change it from "A bear chased me through the forest" to "A bear chases me through the forest." Notice how different this feels right away.

Second, it is helpful to talk about dreams using verbs ending in "-ing." So, for example, we would change "A bear chases me" to "A bear *is chasing* me." These "-ing" verbs bring the action of the dream even more into immediate experience.

Third, we can *remove all articles* (meaning "a," "an," and "the") from the telling of a dream. Articles tend to reduce the image from a specific character with an independent identity to a generic class of beings. For example, in the dream image just mentioned, we take out "a" and "the" so it reads simply, "*Bear* is chasing me through *forest*." Notice how this no longer indicates just a class of animals called bears, and instead now indicates a discrete, individual bear. The forest, too, has been linguistically transformed into a unique entity.

The last change is to write the names of the dream characters *using capital letters* to give them the status of proper nouns. For example, we change the noun "bear" to the name "Bear." This completes the transformation of the living image to an individual character with its own life, experience, and most importantly, *name*. In the example the description becomes "*Bear* is chasing me through *Forest*."

These four linguistic moves bring energy and individuality to our expression of dreams. We started with a dead report of a past occurrence—"A bear chased me through a forest"—and ended up with something much more alive—"Bear is chasing me through Forest." Notice how without the articles, and using capitals, "-ing" verbs, and the present tense, we can feel the uniqueness and immediacy of these two dream images much more sharply.

Who is visiting now? Bear is visiting now. Forest is visiting now. And Bear is chasing me through Forest! I feel their vitality and I sense the spark of life within them.

EXERCISE: *Using Language to Vivify Dream Images*

> This exercise is short and easy. Take the dream you've been working with so far and write or tell it again, making these four changes: 1) use the present tense, 2) change the verbs

to use the "-ing" ending, 3) take out all the articles ("a," "an," and "the"), and 4) write the names of the primary dream characters using capital letters.

These four techniques will bring the dream into the room in present time and the image will further animate. Notice that as the dream image comes alive into the room with you, your own body opens up in new ways and with a new awareness. Also notice that as the living image wakes up, it reveals more of itself. Observe, get interested, and take note.

LEARNING TO WORK WITH LIVING IMAGES—PART III: RELATIONSHIP SKILLS

One day I overheard an interesting conversation coming from the back bedroom of my home. My six-year-old daughter, Alia, was talking to her friend about the plight of a baby chipmunk. It was her urgent tone of voice that first caught my ear. The chipmunk apparently lived in the yard outside her bedroom. The weather had turned cold in the last few days, and there were few acorns. To make things worse, the chipmunk's parents were nowhere to be seen. The baby was clearly in danger.

Next I overheard Alia's friend comforting her with advice about the chipmunk. She made it clear that everything was going to be OK and offered a number of useful suggestions about how to help the creature. As the hours passed, they discussed whether or not the chipmunk was scared, how to make it feel better now that it was missing its mommy, and what it might want to eat. Did it like candy bars? Did it want to be petted, or did it need a blanket? Where would it prefer to sleep? Do chipmunks sleep all night?

Finally, toward evening, I knocked on Alia's door to announce dinner. "Come in," she said. When I did, I was astonished to find that Alia was all alone in there. There was no friend, and even the chipmunk was imaginary. Neither of these beings existed in objective reality. They were figures from the dreamtime whom Alia, in her childhood innocence, had hosted so well.

In our Dream Tending work so far, we have learned basic skills to animate the living images of dreams. When we do this we find ourselves in the midst of living beings who are present and active in the room with us in the Now. Like Alia, we want to be a good host to these images we have invited into our lives. Hosting is an ancient and beautiful art, requiring a sensitive and active engagement with the guest. If we host our images well, they will feel comfortable and friendly and perhaps disposed to reveal a good deal more about themselves. We can then engage our senses to encounter them more fully.

Hosting the Guest

I have found three qualities of hosting that are particularly helpful when tending dreams. First, hosting entails seeing to the comfort and needs of the guest. We imagine what they may want and think about how to provide it for them. A host is gracious and responsive.

Second, hosting requires an ability to create beauty and atmosphere. To feel comfortable, the guest needs a sense of being received in a secure and appealing place, a setting where they feel a sense of belonging. We take the time to create a beautiful, welcoming, appropriate, well-arranged space for the meeting. We set the table, put out the good silverware, light the fire in the fireplace, and place vases of fresh flowers around the room. We adjust the lighting and the music to comfortable levels.

Third, to host well is to know something about the guest. We need to know what interests her, what is going on in her life, what she may be excited to talk about. If we don't know these things in advance, we ask the guest about herself in order to learn. Most people love to talk about themselves, and it is no different when the dream guest is a whale, a spaceship, or an insect. Conversation is a good way to tune into his wants and needs, likes and dislikes.

When we take pains to host living images, they feel welcomed and will share a tremendous amount with us. Hosting the image allows us to establish a long-term relationship with an image and be able to go very deep with it. I have found that the more I host (rather than interrogate or dissect) a living dream figure, the more rewarded and satisfied I feel. No longer are we two strangers passing in the night. Instead, we get to know each other as long-term friends.

A fragment of a poem by Kabir (in Robert Bly's translation) highlights this aspect of hosting dream images:

> *Kabir says, Listen, my friend:*
> *There is one thing in the world that satisfies,*
> *And that is a meeting with the Guest.*

EXERCISE: *Hosting the Guest*

Choose a dream figure that you have been working with for a while, or select another that is particularly active at the moment. In silent imagination, invite the figure into relationship with you. Relax, become receptive, and imagine that you are asking the figure into your home, to join you in conversation.

Now greet the figure in whatever way makes sense to you. One way or another, say hello and welcome the image into your presence. Ask the dream figure, "How are you?" Take the time to listen to the response.

Don't make up in your mind ahead of time about what you are going to say next. First, really listen to what you hear, and see what you see, then let your response originate from the curiosity that comes from what the dream figure says and does.

Be patient. Become interested in what is happening, not what this interaction means. As a host, keep your focus on the wellbeing of the dream figure. This interaction is at least as much about the image as it is about you, perhaps more. What occurs to you as the next part of your greeting? Do or say this now.

Get curious about what the image is doing. Ask the question, "What is happening here?" and watch the figure's activities in relation to you. If other images from the dream have entered the room, which may happen because of the friendly atmosphere you have created, observe those interactions as well. Take the time to witness. There is no hurry. Hosting is about creating the space to feel secure and open. Settle into the ambience.

If the dream figure leaves the room for a time, wait for it to return. If it is gone for a long time, you might turn to another image for a while. When your original guest returns, bring your attention back to it. Patience is required to sustain a friendly connection. Continue your conversation and interaction. Do not ask the figure too many questions about how to solve your personal problems or pump it for information about yourself. That would be rude. Instead just observe with interest what the figure is up to now. Stay curious. Ask it questions about itself.

What do you see or hear from the image? Is it asking for something more? As a good host, how do you respond?

How does the image respond in turn? Go back and forth in dialogue from a place of caring. You are mindfully hosting the image. Take your time and enjoy your deepening friendship. Do not lead the image or talk for it. Remain open to the spontaneity of the conversation. Watch for any surprises.

Sustaining Relationship with an Image by Using the Senses

Once we make friends with a guest, we need to sustain that relationship, whether in life or in Dream Tending. In other words, for better or worse, we are stuck with them and are now part of the same dreamtime. Whether a Wise Elder offers important teachings or a Vampire frightens with a thirst for blood, the image is here now. We have hosted it, and now is the time to deepen our engagement.

One way to increase our contact with the figure is through the use of our senses. When we listen more attentively, see more precisely, even touch, taste, and smell more fully, we bolster our connection with the living image. Of course, we cannot literally touch or taste an image, but we can get a clear sense of doing so by imagining just what the texture or scent of a figure might be. As we open our senses to an image, we experience it as a three-dimensional, fully detailed, living figure. If we are working with the image of Horse, we feel its smooth, thick horsehair, see its huge, soft eyes, and smell its undeniable horsey-ness. The image comes to life, walking on four legs and swishing its tail. As we contact the dream animal in this sensory way, we feel that Horse is actually in the room with us. As Horse embodies, it begins to assert its autonomy, its will.

To go even further with this, we look at Horse with an eye for the details. How is this dream horse different from any other horse that we have seen before? We notice everything we can: the color of its coat, its particular markings, the shape of its head, and so on. Often these details become the source of its name: Painted Pony, White Stallion, Red Tail. All these details give individuality to Horse, who is now standing, walking, galloping in the room along with us.

Before we move into the exercise, let's imagine how this kind of engagement might unfold with a dream figure that is not a person or an animal. For example, in a dream image of Ocean, we use our sense of smell to pick up the strong scent of the sea. We touch the salty water to feel its texture and temperature. We imagine tasting the water to see what that might be like.

Looking more closely at Ocean, we see if it is aqua blue, emerald green, or steely gray. We notice how this particular ocean is different from others. By not giving in to interpretations like Ocean as a "body of tears" or as the source of all life, We invite Ocean to come to life, present and embodied. Particularity keeps us in direct, experiential contact with this dream image of Ocean visiting now. Using our senses of touch, taste, smell, sight, and hearing, we bring our instinctual body into relationship with the living image as an embodied entity.

EXERCISE: *Sustaining Relationship with an Image by Using the Senses*

> Use the Dream Tending skills that you have learned thus far to bring yourself into a present-centered, embodied relationship with an image. Notice the quality of contact that you experience with this image. Notice how you are interacting with it. How are you in relationship? Most likely, you are watching the image, observing what it is up to. Again notice the quality of your body experience here at this stage of relationship. Bring your attention to the depth of emotion and the range of motion of the dream image. Write about this in your journal.

To begin, turn away from the image and spend a few moments awakening your senses. A simple way to do this is to look around the room in a mindful way. Focus your attention on the object that captures your attention with its beauty, its form, its texture, its brightness, or some other sensory quality.

Now close you eyes, quiet down, and listen to the sounds in the room. What do you hear? Perhaps you hear the hum of a fan, the chirp of birdsong from outside, or traffic noise from the street.

Then bring your awareness to your sense of smell. What does the room smell like? Can you differentiate various scents? Notice how the flowers or plants have a different scent than that of the carpet or the furniture. Is there a particular odor from the furnace or heater? If a window is open, can you make out the fragrance drifting into the room from outside?

Now open your eyes and notice how you see differently, with sensitivity for color, shades of light, and detail. Notice how much more acutely you hear and smell the world around you.

Turn back to the image that is in the room with you and use your activated senses to engage it. What do you become aware of? Next, imagine that you reach out and touch the image. Notice the texture, the hot or cold qualities, and the contours of the image. As the image becomes more real and present to your imagination, use your sense of smell. Close your eyes and really breathe in its particular smell. Take your time. Let the scent come to you. What do you smell?

Now, with eyes still closed, listen. Really listen, as if you could hear the sound of silence. Be patient. At first you may only hear the external sounds around you. Let those sounds deepen your sense of hearing. What do you hear from the image? Does it make a sound when it moves? Does it have its own call? Do you hear purring, chirping, or words? Is there a soft hum or a piercing noise that comes from it? Follow whatever sound you are hearing, stay with it for some time, and make note of what you are hearing and any changes that are occurring. Bring these recollections back with you as you open your eyes.

With activated senses, continue to engage the image. What do you notice about the embodied presence of the image? In this state of heightened sense awareness, take your time and follow the image as it continues in its activity. Note anything about this image that is unique or distinctive. What makes it particular, unlike any other image? What do you notice about your own body experience? Write down your findings in as much detail as possible, as well as your reflections about them.

LEARNING TO WORK WITH LIVING IMAGES— PART IV: FROM RELATIONSHIP TO REVELATION

The Portals of Soul

As our Dream Tending evolves and our relationship with the living image deepens, a new and important possibility arises: the capacity for revelation. Living images contain many surprising insights and secrets that reveal themselves under the right conditions. We do not manufacture revelation. It happens naturally when we are attuned to living images in an embodied and receptive way. For an image to reveal something essential, it must exist in a field of acceptance, positive regard, and openness.

A few years ago I took a journey to Australia, the land of the aboriginal dreamtime. As I explored the outback, I encountered what were, for me, many out-of-the-ordinary creatures. One day while walking with my son through a rainforest, I found myself face to face with a koala bear curled around the branch of a eucalyptus tree only a few feet away. I looked at this remarkable creature for a long time, much longer than I had looked at a wild animal before. As I continued to watch him, the way I was seeing started to change.

First, I was surprised to be in the presence of such an unfamiliar, yet delightful being. He was certainly as appealing as any of those cuddly stuffed toy koalas that I grew up with. As time passed however, something more interesting began to unfold. As I felt more comfortable, I became more receptive and patient, and my way of looking at Koala deepened.

I saw the soft, gray-brown fur that covered Koala's tiny round body, and the small, cupped ears that flared out from both sides of his wide head. His sharp claws and strong legs were perfect for climbing the almost-vertical branches of the eucalyptus tree. I saw the extraordinary beauty that made this creature a particular, unique, individual Koala Bear.

Then I realized that Koala's beady black eyes were *looking intently right back at me.* As we looked into each other's eyes, I experienced a warm feeling of relationship and compassion. I felt that Koala and I belonged to the same community of beings.

It was then that I became aware of my breathing: a kind of breathing that seemed to come from the very source of breath itself. I felt part of something larger than myself. I felt at home. I stopped being a self-conscious observer of a strange animal and instead became an active participant in a very old dance between like-minded creatures. As Koala and I saw into and beyond each other, I found myself doing an amazing thing. I introduced Koala to my son, who was standing beside me. It was as if Koala were an old friend of mine. It seemed perfectly natural, in fact *required*, to introduce him to my family.

In those moments Koala, my son, and I shared a primal recognition of life knowing life. I felt, for a time, the living and breathing reality of that which sources all life, that which I have come to know as "the dreaming."

As Dream Tenders we can set the stage for revelation by bringing the qualities of subtle perception and deep listening into our interactions with images. By subtle perception, I mean a kind of seeing in which we are aware of both our peripheral vision and our focused, core vision at the same time. It is a kind of total seeing that we do with both very relaxed and very alert eyes. To view a dream image in this way is like walking in the woods and seeing the uniqueness of particular trees and simultaneously witnessing the forest in its totality. When we do this, the living image often will reveal its innermost self, its soul.

In addition to subtle perception, it is also important to engage in deep listening. Deep listening, as we touched upon in the art of hosting, is a kind of hearing without the impulse to know or respond. Often this is somewhat difficult to do. Usually we have already prepared a response before a person has even finished her sentence. Obviously this way of listening does not allow for the fullest consideration and understanding of the other. Even if you do not speak, but there is a constant stream of mental responses to a dream figure, the revelatory process will likely come to an end.

We accomplish deep listening by emptying our minds of all responses. To listen carefully without reacting allows a dream figure to continue its activities uninterrupted and to reveal from the inside out what it has to say. When we listen to a living image in this way, its revelation is not conditioned by our expectations, judgments, or agendas.

Once we shift our mode of seeing and listening to subtle perception and deep listening, there is one additional move we can make to witness revelation. The eyes have always been known as the portals of the soul, and this is true for dream figures as well. With the permission of a living image, and making sure that we are not forcing anything, we can gently gaze into its eyes. It is crucial to remain soft, relaxed, and open when we do this. If the living image is open to such contact, and we have shifted into the alternate modes of perception, then looking into the figure's eyes can open up a world of revelation.

I would like to emphasize the delicate nature of this eye-to-eye meeting. It is important not to barge into the eyes of a dream figure, demanding it reveal some sacred truth to you. This process is not about surging forward on the Hero's Journey, vorpal sword in hand. We are not on a quest for the Grail, nor are we thieves, plundering a roomful of treasure.

The one thing we do gain is a profound and intimate connection with the dream image. Within the eyes of a dream figure, we find a well of timelessness and presence. We surrender to another kind of consciousness, a subtle mode of connection, requiring finesse, patience, sensitivity, and spaciousness.

With extended practice of looking into the eyes of a dream image, we will occasionally make contact with other images residing in the inner realms of this awareness, such as ancestor figures and guardian animals. This can be a tremendously rewarding experience. I have found that looking gently and mindfully into the eyes of a dream figure changes people. Entering the portals of the soul opens us ever more deeply into our own soul life and to the mysteries of the dreamtime.

EXERCISE: *The Portals of Soul*

Identify an image that you have already befriended, and that also has eyes. Sometimes it is too difficult at first if the dream image doesn't have literal eyes, such as the figure of a mountain or a river, but eventually it will be possible to look into the eye of a storm, a hole in a tree, and so on.

Once you have found the image, approach it. Connect to your archetypal self. As you do this, notice how the image responds. You will most likely see the image turning to face you. If not, wait a few minutes and try again. If it just does not want to face you, then let go of your work with this image for today, and begin again with another one.

If you have found a figure that wants to face you, ask permission to look directly into its eyes. Once you feel some form of assent, imagine its eyes as the portals of its soul. Continuing to feel connected to your ground of being, allow yourself to be received by the eyes of this figure. Do not go into this with the need to know or the need to find an answer. Rather, feel received and allow yourself to travel deep inside the figure. Pause here. Take in this experience and become aware of your state of being. What has shifted? How are you breathing?

If you feel comfortable, come back to the image and repeat the above exercise. Asking permission again, feel received through the portal of the eyes of the image. This time, notice who or what greets you here. What do you become aware of? What feelings are evoked in you? Linger here for awhile and notice everything that arises.

Now begin the journey back into your body, into your presence. Make a note of what you have experienced. Even if what has happened does not make immediate sense to you, write it down so you can consider it at another time. Make sure to acknowledge the figure that you have spent time with and have been part of. You have entered the inner landscape of soul. Take the time in this experience to breathe. You may want to watch for ways this figure shows up in subsequent dreams.

The Intelligent Image

At this point in our work, we are ready to go even further in our relationship with living images. This will not take any new techniques or tools, but simply requires knowing what to look for, which is that *living images have their own intelligence.* The intelligence of living images is perhaps the most surprising and important revelation I have experienced over the years. Just as my great-grandfather taught, all phenomena in the world have a quality of mind. "All things speak their story," he said. My experience with living images fully confirms this revolutionary idea.

Intelligence lives in the images of the dreaming psyche, available night after night. This "brainpower" is embedded in the image itself. It is not something we make up about the image, nor is this intelligence located in a pre-existing system of early family or symbolic explanation. When we rush in too quickly with our bright ideas of what the image means, we rob it of its native intelligence and replace it with our own, which may not be as illuminating. We want to hear its knowledge, not ours.

Great discoveries and new possibilities present themselves each night through our living dream images. Einstein had a dream that explained the entire theory of relativity. He then spent the rest of his life giving expression to the wisdom of this extraordinary dream. Ingmar Bergman said that his films depicted images from his dreams. The brilliant physicist Niels Bohr said that his model of the atom appeared to him in a dreamlike experience.

Countless others in the fields of music, science, literature, cinema, architecture, and the arts have reported similar findings.

This intelligent quality of images is one of the best-kept secrets of dreamwork, yet we all have had some experience of this. We often wake up knowing that "something important" happened in our dreams. On occasion we even have a hint of the images talking to us with an intelligence that seems to come from somewhere else.

I remember having a dream of sitting in a classroom, while a dream teacher was explaining the "next evolution of psychological thought." She drew elaborate images on her chalkboard, each one like a seed bursting with psychological insight and new possibilities. I was so excited when I woke up that I was flooded with grandiosity and thought, "Move over, Freud, the new paradigm has arrived!" That may or may not have been the case, but I will never know because I never wrote this dream teaching down. How many opportunities like this do we waste in the course of our lives? I would wager that there are hundreds of occasions for each person where this sort of dream intelligence is squandered.

Personally and culturally, I believe that the intelligent image is one of our most under-utilized resources. When images come to life, they offer us perspective, innovation, and insight. Tree knows the intelligence of the tree; Bear knows the ways of the bear; just as the dream image of Rock knows the "mind" and qualities of rocks. Even the Intruder, who is a most threatening dream image at first, brings intelligence beyond our own. The key is to take the time to listen to the images speaking on their own behalf.

Over millions of years, human beings evolved the capacity to dream, to imagine, and to envision. Before we even learned to talk, there were images. For most of human history, it was these images of mind, not written language, which appeared on the walls of caves or were displayed on ancestral masks. The dreaming psyche is the source of an expansive, primal knowledge.

When we experience the intelligence of the living image it is powerful and exciting. What we considered out of the question, beyond our reach, and impossible to know is active in the living images, waiting to be known. Connecting to our imaginal intelligence opens the doors that lead to our fullest capacities. The following Dream Tending exercise opens our ability to access this intelligence of living images.

EXERCISE: *The Intelligent Image*

Begin by making physical and mental space for this exercise. Create a place in your home or office that provides you the needed space to receive all that arises and offers a way of paying respect to the wisdom of the image. This kind of regard is always a good first step when working with dream figures.

Next, come into relationship with your deep psyche by using the tools that you know: center yourself in the here and now, connect to your body, activate your senses, observe with particularity, and follow your curiosity.

At first, experiencing imaginal intelligence might feel unfamiliar and perhaps uncomfortable. To feel secure in this new territory, stay focused on the now-familiar question, "Who is visiting now?"

Ask the question again, but this time to the dream figure itself. Practice deep listening so you might hear if any response is forthcoming. Check in with your body, open your posture and breath. Become more receptive with each breath, and bring your attention to what originates from within the living image, allowing yourself to become ever more image-centered. As the image animates, what are you hearing, feeling, seeing? Do not wait for some lightning bolt of knowledge to illuminate you. Even if all you get is just a fragment or two, or little words, or phrases, or pictures, write these down.

Do not be afraid to make-believe. Often the unfamiliar feels as if it is not really true, not really happening. The key here is to experiment. Particular phrases or emotions, even those of little apparent consequence, may lead you to a new dimension of awareness. The dream figure may further animate. Get curious.

What intelligence comes forward now? Remember that you are not in search of an answer, but rather an experience of what the image is revealing. Write down anything you perceive. It may not make sense at first and it may not be in a rational order or sequence. This is to be expected.

Fill your journal with sketches, words, impressions, and feelings. Put these on the page in circles, starbursts, or any other shape. Like a puzzle, the separate parts may not form a complete picture right away, so be patient and in a few minutes come back to the page. Take a few steps away and look down and see it as a whole using soft eyes, then focused eyes. Notice without judgment, opinion, or expectation what has appeared. Let it come forward and make sense of itself to you. Let its intelligence find you. Do you notice any pattern emerging?

At this point, do nothing. Do not take action for at least an hour. Give the process time to gestate and settle. Stay aware. Various insights may arise over the next hour. Keep a record of these insights. Before you leave the process, remember to pay tribute in some way to the dream figure that has shared its wisdom with you.

The Evolving Image

We have now experienced dream images as real, embodied, and having intelligences of their own. In the realm of the living dream, we have witnessed the actuality of the figures as they come in and out of visibility, and we have even looked into their souls. As we do all this, we eventually realize that dream images evolve and dissolve over time. This fact has consequences in the practice of Dream Tending and impacts our self-understanding.

When an image transforms in shape, style, or character, we are affected. Imagine that a dream image of a vagabond appears one night, and afterward we do some Dream Tending with this figure. As our relationship with the dream image deepens, the figure we now call Vagabond also changes. The next night he visits again, this time as a potent Guide. In active imagination, we may follow him about or listen to what he knows of unfamiliar places. Three months go by until he appears again. This time Vagabond appears as a Teacher, humble yet wise. The image itself has evolved from Vagabond, to Guide, to Teacher. And because we are in relationship with him, we too have changed. Like in any meaningful relationship of which we are a part, when our partner shifts in consciousness, so do we.

Images themselves evolve first and our experience with them can be seen as a consequence of their individuation process. As the French scholar, philosopher, and mystic Henri Corbin wrote, "It is not we who individuate, but the image." When a living image individuates, we are affected in turn. Living images, particularly those who carry the intelligence of the ancestors, are at the core of our personal maturation. As they open to their own depth, we open to ours. As they gain substance, vitality, and significance, so do we. As we witness their changes, we understand the forces that influence our behavior. We feel the support for what is new and possible inside of us. And most importantly, as images shape-shift, we see into the possibilities of our own transformation.

Dream images lead the way, with intelligence and intention of their own. It is good to know the changes that they are going through, because it gives us clues about our own imminent development.

EXERCISE: *The Evolving Image*

Select an image that you have been tending. Write down all that your remember about the first time you saw this image, in as much descriptive detail as possible. You may want to make a sketch of it as well.

Next see the image as it occurs now in your mind's eye. The image has probably changed from its first appearance. Notice what physical, emotional, or attitudinal qualities have changed. How is the activity of the image different from when it first appeared? List these differences.

Once your list is complete, notice how you feel about the changes in the image. Are you pleased, pained, fearful, or surprised? Write spontaneously about your feelings.

It is also possible to access the organic evolution of living images by working in a completely different way and in another medium. At night, put a box of crayons and individual sheets of paper on the table by your bed. In the morning, draw your feelings in color, form, and texture. Imagine that you are an impressionist painter. You are not after literal representation, just the impressions that the dream images make.

After seven days, take the individual paintings you have made and spread them on the floor. Now arrange and rearrange them in any way that the color and design seem to fit together. In this mosaic you may see that Tuesday's dream painting connects with Saturday's expression, and so on. After a while you will have a full story in images. You will notice a pattern that emerges from your work. How is this montage of images moving through you now? There is no need to act. Rather, become aware of how the life force as expressed in images is moving and evolving through you.

You have gained insight into the movement of the dreaming psyche, and in turn you have looked into what is orchestrating your own becoming.

The Love of an Image

I remember working with veteran Dream Tenders at a retreat on the deck of a beach house in Malibu. They had gathered there to deepen their Dream Tending skills and get supervision in their clinical dreamwork with others. I was returning from a month-long vacation in which I had spent a lot of time walking the wilderness, engaging deeply in my own dream life, and practicing meditation.

As the retreat began, I noticed something different happening in me. Something touched me in a way I hadn't felt before. When I began working with the Dream Tenders, the living images presented themselves in a new way. I didn't need to use any Dream Tending skills at all with them. Instead it was just a matter of being present with the images and allowing them in turn to bring the Dream Tenders and me into a deeper quality of presence. As we were preparing to tend to the images, I realized that they were already tending to us. Getting ready to host the living figures of the dreamtime, it was suddenly clear that we were already being hosted by them.

At a certain point in our work with dreams, the images will come and touch us directly. On these occasions when we sit with them in mindful relationship, without using any of our skills, the living images will appear extremely vivid and intense. When living images present themselves in such a strong way, it is as if life itself is pouring out through them. They are like portals to the source of life, connecting us to the process of creation. Because life is basically compassionate, when we experience images in this way, we feel a sense of love and caring.

EXERCISE: *The Love of an Image*

Choose a dream that you have already tended and invite it into your awareness. As it is going about its business, notice your place in the activated field of imagination. Allow the "energetic field" to sharpen your senses of sight, smell, and hearing. Drop into your archetypal ego, your authenticity, and acute perception.

Next, locate an object or a sound, either inside the room or outside the window. As you have practiced in previous exercises, listen to the wind move through the trees, or pick up the scent of a flower in the room, or let the beauty of something in the room open your aesthetic sense. In whatever ways that you know, contact the immediacy of the moment. Connect to your breath even more deeply and become as still and mindful as possible. As thoughts arise, simply notice them and let them pass by. Return to an inner place of things being just as they are.

Now bring this quality of being and perception to the dream figure. Do nothing in particular. Notice from your still center who is visiting now and what they are up to at the moment. Continue being present. Bring your awareness to how you are being received by the dream image. How is it opening to you? What do you notice about its pace? Has it slowed down?

As you experience the deepening presence of the dream figure, do not attend to it in ways that you have previously learned. Let go of earlier associations or connections to the image, and instead allow its living presence to further open your own. Experience the wonder of this encounter as you would a wordless meeting with a beloved friend.

Open your heart further as you feel met by this familiar image of the dreamtime. In what way do you feel cared for? Do you feel connected to something larger than the two of you? How are you experiencing the love generated by the intimate heart-to-heart relationship between you and the image?

Chapter Two

WORKING WITH NIGHTMARES

As a young man in Belarus, my great-grandfather lived under the constant threat of violence. All across the country, religious zealots and political tyrants whipped the townspeople into mobs that attacked Jews. The Jews' own neighbors, the same people they may have been talking to the day before, destroyed their businesses, burned their synagogues, dragged them out of their homes, and chased them off, turning a stable community into a mass of terrified refugees. These pogroms often blossomed into all-out massacres, with dead and wounded bodies littering the streets. Randomly and without warning, someone my great-grandfather knew or loved could be attacked, raped, or murdered at any time, anywhere. There was no way of knowing.

Faced with the possibility of destruction, Zadie looked within himself for answers. Pushing aside his fears, sorrow, despair, and an almost overwhelming sense of helplessness, he dug deeper and found something else—a fire of anger and indignation at the hypocrisy of the so-called religious people. It was this flame of indignation that gave him the personal strength he required. He saved what money he could, organized what was left of his life, and left Belarus in 1903 to make the journey that would hopefully lead him to a life of freedom in a new world. This indignation also gave him the courage he would need to arrive as a foreigner in an unknown country, not speaking a word of English, and with few contacts and no job.

Because my great-grandfather had witnessed so much persecution at the hands of religious people, he completely rejected all forms of organized religion as nothing more than systems of social oppression and justifications for greed. These feelings led him to attend the communist meetings then popular in New York City. Eventually he realized that, unlike the communists, he was not an atheist. He believed that beneath the rational mind there exists a spirit that feeds our essential humanity and is part of a larger spiritual truth. This belief in the wild, beautiful, brilliant life force that is the essence of all things became the truth that guided his entire life.

In later years, people coming to his shop telling him of their nightmares (whether those of the daytime or the night) found him to be an unshakable support and in him, boundless compassion. His eyes had seen true nightmares, and he told them how he had learned to look such horrific images in the face and find the strength to stand up to them and even to find wisdom in them. He helped people realize that nightmares are simply the life force revealing itself in its most raw, wild, and threatening form. I have never forgotten this part of his teaching or his towering example of its truth.

Nightmares — The Most Alive of Dream Images

There are many theories about the origins and function of nightmares. Sometimes they are said to symbolize everything from unsettled aspects of our personality to early traumatic experiences that exist just below the surface of consciousness. Nightmares may symbolize acute dysfunction in our relationships, the onset of illness, or reactions to movies we watched just before going to bed. Other times they may be graphic reminders of environmental destruction, like the consequences of global warming and acid rain, or societal dysfunction like the devastation of war. Whatever the cause of nightmares, we always experience them as a real and terrifying threat to survival.

Everyone experiences nightmares. The question is, how do we deal with them? When we feel terrified, overwhelmed, helpless, and alone, what can we do to work with these difficult images? Sometimes we try to simply ignore them. We deny their existence or attempt to explain them away. Soon enough, however, we discover the futility of such approaches. While nightmares can sometimes be put off for a short time, sooner or later they return, and often their encore is even scarier than their original appearance. And our helplessness and isolation increase each time they show up.

Nightmares may allow themselves to be pushed out of consciousness, but that does not mean they are forgotten. Just below the surface of awareness, we still carry the terrifying images of the dream into the next day. The slightest reminders of the nightmare can shake us up. Somebody might look at us in a menacing way, say something critical, or accidentally push up against us and—boom!—we feel anew the horror of last night's dream visitation.

The simple fact is that nightmares cannot be ignored, forgotten, or explained away. I have found it imperative not to avoid the intolerable, but instead to find the strength and skill needed to go face-to-face, toe-to-toe, with the "terribles" of the night.

We can learn how to work constructively with nightmares using a six-step process I have developed that is a natural extension of the ideas of animation we learned in the first chapter.

They are:

1) Connect to Your Strength and Find Supportive Figures.

2) Stand Your Ground and Gain Knowledge.

3) Make the "Stop" and Create Separation.

4) Discover the True Nature of the Figure.

5) Establish Relationship with the Figure.

6) Experience the Vitality of the Imagination.

The exercises for each step will build on the preceding ones. Together they offer a comprehensive system to effectively tend to the demons of the night. In addition, the process will open ways of finding value in what is our most challenging relationship with the dreaming psyche—our encounters with the horrifying images of nightmares.

THE SIX-STEP SYSTEM OF WORKING WITH NIGHTMARES

Step 1—Connect to Your Strength and Find Supportive Figures

The first step in the Dream Tending system of working with nightmares teaches us two simple and effective things we can do to prepare to confront our most frightening dreams.

First, we need to find the inner strength and support to face the intolerable. To confront an attack by a poisonous viper, to face a devastating tidal wave, to cope with paralyzed legs, or to deal with a menacing intruder, we must anchor ourselves in our core capacities. We connect ourselves to the deeper well of personal strength, the archetypal ego.

In order to connect with ourselves, we get centered. As we have learned, there are a number of ways to do this. Becoming mindful of the breath is probably the easiest and most effective.

Getting out of a disconnected, busy mind and into a grounded body quickly increases our feelings of personal strength.

Another method is to notice how our body is responding to a nightmare. We notice where we are tight or constricted and then exaggerate that experience. Then we create the opposite gesture. For example, if the stomach or jaw muscles are clamped down, we first intensify this by intentionally clamping them down harder, then we release and soften the muscles. This tightening-then-releasing move always allows them to relax. The feeling of connecting with our strength grows as we come back into a conscious relationship with the body.

So part one of this step is to get centered by meditating on the breath or by doing the muscle relaxation technique. Part two of this step is to find our dream friends. When working with nightmares, going it alone is not a productive path. Instead we develop supportive relationships, both inside and outside of the dream. Inside the dream, there are often figures who function as allies, quite willing to accompany us in the hard work to follow. In the awake world, supportive friends or trained dream guides can really make a difference in dealing with nightmares. Asking for help is not a sign of weakness. On the contrary, gathering allies or consulting with experts in the field is a tradition that goes back thousands of years. In any epic struggle, the warrior of the heart needs trusted companions to accompany him or her along the way.

In order to do this with dream images, we write down a nightmare and then look closely for any figures with whom we can make friends. Marginal figures might not look all that helpful to begin with, but they will probably be quite helpful given a little attention. Tending them as shown in Chapter One will awaken these images and allow them to guide and protect us in our work with nightmares.

Let me illustrate how a colleague of mine, Bob, began working with his nightmares by getting centered and connecting with allies. As a child, Bob became terrified each night just thinking about going to bed. He felt anxious and feared the return of threatening monsters. Now thirty-eight, every month or so Bob still woke up terrified and sweating, pursued by an ugly creature in his dreams. The recurring image had evolved over the years into a predatory half-animal, half-Terminator killing machine. Bob was desperate to put an end to these nightmares. He was constantly on edge and always extremely anxious. In awake-life, the smallest stimuli would make him panic. His energy became depleted, and he retreated from social interaction, becoming increasingly isolated.

Bob had worked with these nightmares for years in an attempt to stop the assault. With the help of a therapist, he began to understand how these dreams related to his life. He saw how his abusive father had entered his nightmares in the form of this Terminator figure. Yet this understanding didn't stop the attack of the beast-machine at night. Desperate for an explanation, Bob consulted countless dream dictionaries. He asked his doctor for medicines that could make him sleep. The sleeping pills helped a little, but after a number of months the nightmare came back to terrorize him.

This horrific figure had now plagued Bob for over half his life. From the perspective of Dream Tending, Bob had failed to encounter Terminator Beast as a living actuality, an autonomous figure of the dreaming psyche. He needed to see it not only as a symbol of his past, but also as a living image of his present. The first steps for Bob were to find ways to connect to his personal strength, and then to inner supportive dream figures.

In order to connect with his personal strength, Bob centered himself by following his breath. Next, Bob carefully explored the nightmares themselves by writing them down. He found the figure of a lost dog hiding in the margins of each nightmare. At first Bob had paid no attention to this dog because he was preoccupied by the overwhelming presence of Terminator Beast. This black Labrador was wandering about in the wastelands, as Bob put it. He tended the dog figure, and as he did so it changed into a powerful Doberman pinscher. It was just what Bob needed to accompany him in his confrontation with Terminator Beast. Once this first step of the Dream Tending system was accomplished, Bob had the beginnings of what was required to successfully encounter Terminator Beast of his nightmares.

Your images will be different from Bob's, yet the skill set remains the same. To start your work of tending to nightmares, use the following exercise to connect to your strength and find supportive figures.

EXERCISE: *Connect to Your Strength and Find Supportive Figures*

> Identify a nightmare image that has recently come into your dreams. If more than one pushes forward, choose the image that has been around for a longer time.
>
> For now, put this image to one side. Before working with it, it is necessary to get centered. For the series of exercises in this chapter you will need your whole body engaged. Either enter into a meditation that you are familiar with, or use the following: close your eyes and feel the floor come up and meet the bottom of your feet. Imagine roots growing down from your feet, through the floor and into the earth. Breathe into and activate these roots. Get a sense of deep connection.
>
> Now locate a dream figure who feels supportive, kind, and nurturing. Imagine him or her sitting next to you. If a dream

figure does not come to mind, then imagine a supportive friend and notice his or her smile. Breathe.

Grounded now, and with this supportive figure beside you, you may feel safe to turn toward the nightmarish image. Notice the size of the figure, its placement in the room, and its activity. Pause. How are you feeling? Notice how big and powerful the image is compared to you. It makes sense that you will first experience a wave of fear. This is a normal response. Allow time to pass. Hang in there.

Turn toward your supportive figure once again and drink in its care and helpfulness. Re-center yourself and wait until you feel calm and whole again. When you are ready, turn again to face the intolerable image. Simply witness it without expectation. Do nothing else, just observe. Take note of its activity. Has it left the room? If so, be patient. Nine times out of ten, it will return within a very short time. Keep observing.

Before going on, take stock of your encounter with this nightmare image. Most of the time, this kind of engagement is perfectly constructive, however, there are times when it is not advisable. For example, if the image has a direct link to genocide in your family history, or if the fear implicates childhood abuse or something equally serious, stop here and work with a professional who is familiar with such matters. If you feel yourself getting overwhelmed or terrified beyond control, seek help to work with this image.

Assuming that you feel comfortable working with this image, return to your breath. Find your center again and then tune into your supportive friend. Once you have found your strength, look at the image with a more active interest. How is this monster unique? What particular features can you identify? Notice the image's size and power in the room. Has it become less threatening? If so, continue. If not, stay here for a moment and look again to your support figure, regroup, and repeat this exercise.

Step 2—Stand Your Ground and Gain Knowledge

The second step in the Dream Tending system of working with a nightmarish image is to stand our ground and gain knowledge about it. A terrorist dream figure often cannot remain so terrible when we stand our ground. When it sees us as a formidable opponent, it may begin to transform. It is then that we can learn something essential about it. The same is true with virtually all nightmare images, like tidal waves, earthquakes, menacing animals, threatening aliens, and so on.

So step two consists of standing our ground and gaining knowledge. Let's take these in order.

First, we establish our rightful position in relation to the threatening dream figure. Nightmare images must be shown in no uncertain terms that we can stand up for ourselves and fight back when necessary. Standing our ground and rooting deeply prevents us from being blown away by the fury of an approaching tornado, vaporized by a nuclear explosion, murdered by a vengeful mob, or dismembered by a monster.

Think of confronting a bully. We must first find our "fire in the belly," our guts, in order to stand tall and gain the bully's respect. The bully needs to know that we are here now, firmly rooted, ready for the engagement.

We also literally talk back in a direct way to the threatening figure. We find a quality of voice, a gesture, and the words that allow us to tell it that we are not afraid and will not be moved. Only then will the threatening image take notice of us.

So in part one of this step we stand firm, and then express ourselves as having enough strength to make the threat back off.

Doing this makes it possible to do part two of this step, which is to observe the particularity of the image in order to gain knowledge about it. The important thing here is to stand firm and to watch the figure closely.

As we have learned in the previous chapter, living images of dreams carry innate intelligences of their own. This is easier to notice when figures appear wise, like an image of Elder Sage. Yet it is also true when figures appear harsh, like a Cruel Henchman or a looming Lightning Storm. Countless times I have seen how some of the most horrific and destructive images contain valuable teachings. Here we get very specific about the qualities, activities, desires, and all other particularities of the figure in order to connect with this knowledge.

Nightmare figures may not always wait patiently for us to observe them. It is important to seize the opportunity when it arises. Every bit of knowledge we can ferret out allows us to work more effectively with them.

In Bob's case, he learned the hard way that Terminator Beast had only one thing in mind: to find, attack, and destroy him. Terrified, Bob would find hiding places in the dream landscape, like a cave or a space under a fallen tree. In his nightmares he would sometimes succumb to fear and claw a foxhole out of the ground with his bloodied fingernails. Bob would do whatever it took in order to avoid the burning of Terminator Beast's fire on his skin, smelling its fetid odor, or hearing its blood-curdling snarl.

As the months and years passed, without any long-term relief of the attacks, Bob was losing his will to survive. He became increasingly paralyzed and quiet in all areas of his awake life. Bob needed a way of facing Terminator Beast without being destroyed.

In step one of his Dream Tending work, Bob had built his inner strength and located a companion, Doberman, to support him in confronting Terminator Beast. Now Bob went further. He found his voice and gave expression to his terrible rage. He stood his ground and fought fire with fire. He told Terminator Beast in no uncertain terms that he would no longer allow it to frighten and control him.

To his surprise, the nightmare image began to change and evolve. This did not happen all at once, but over the course of many dreamwork sessions. As Bob continued to hold his ground and pay very close attention, the figure transmuted. As the months passed, the first hints of the knowledge this figure possessed began to appear.

Let's try this step now.

EXERCISE: *Stand Your Ground and Gain Knowledge*

In this exercise, it is important to sustain engagement with the repugnant image that you are working with. Do not avoid it. Go toward the image, not away from it. Listen for the figure's characteristic sound or speech. Does it have a roar, a menacing voice, a hysterical scream, or an intense hiss? Identify the quality of this sound.

Look away from the image. Turn your chair, if need be. Now try to imitate the sound of the nightmare figure. Do it out loud, as loud as you can. You may want to open your throat and relax your stomach to let the sound come from deep inside you. This can be uncomfortable, but it is extremely helpful. The figure needs to understand that you are powerful and able to fight.

You are not out to destroy or annihilate the figure; just the opposite, actually. You are here to have a conversation, and so you need to firmly stand your ground. The sound you are making will fire up your courage and at the same time get the figure's attention. Once it knows that it is not in complete control any longer, it will be more ready to meet you half way and have a conversation. Stay with this process until you notice that the figure seems to be more available.

Either out loud or in your journal, explicitly tell the figure that you are not out to destroy or annihilate it. Once it feels more tolerant of you and your intentions, it becomes much easier to work with. You can become more interactive and ask it the questions you would ask any other dream figure. Who are you? What are you up to?

Now you are going to add another process designed to help you gather information about the figure. Draw three columns on a sheet of paper. In the first column, make a list of all the people you know, or characters in movies, who have something in common with this image. For example, your friend Sam may have a mean streak, or Jane may be intrusive at times, and so on. List about ten people who personify particular aspects of this difficult image. In the second column, list how they use this behavior to control you. Sam may intimidate you and Jane may manipulate you. In the third column, list what each of these behaviors is "stealing" from you. For example, Sam's intimidation may be robbing you of your personal power, and Jane's manipulation may be robbing you of your sense of safety, and so forth. Take the time to fill in these three columns thoughtfully.

Once you have completed this list, notice what you have learned about the figure: how it operates, how it creates fear, how it stays in control, and how you pay the price. Take a moment to reflect on what you have learned, and write a paragraph about it.

As you gain knowledge about the figure, you may notice the beginnings of a transformation in the figure itself. Simply witness what is occurring. You will certainly want to watch for any changes in the figure in the dreams that follow in the nights to come.

Step 3—Make the "Stop" and Create Separation

Now that we have gained some ground, it is time to transform our relationship with the nightmare image completely and reclaim our sense of personal authority. Here we learn how to stop the instinctive fear response of fight or flight.

Of course, fear is a reasonable response to a dangerous situation. Yet when we are afraid of recurring nightmares, we become paralyzed, unable to respond effectively to what is arising. In these circumstances, it is important to break the cycle of fear and reclaim our power.

Nightmare images gather much of our vital energy into themselves, leaving little room for positive images. Furthermore, we spend a lot of our remaining energy trying to avoid thinking about them. To reclaim our authority, we must take back some of the energy that is vested in the frightening image. We can then become less frightened and avoidant when we encounter things that remind us of the nightmare.

There are many ways of confronting our fear, but I have found that most of us first attempt to talk our way out of it. Frankly, I feel that this is the least effective method of all. It is far better to find some form of *physical expression* to stop the cycle of fear. We need some kind of concrete interruption to break the chain. For example, taking a cold shower or going for a swim are body-centered activities that can put a stop to the automatic fear reaction. Anything physical helps, whether it is shooting basketball, going for a walk, or doing yoga. These interrupt our fearful thoughts for at least a few hours and give us the time and opportunity to work constructively with the nightmare. No longer in a spiral of panic, we have the room and presence of mind to engage the figure.

The second part of this step is to create separation between the figure and us. Nightmare figures are often trying to catch us or attack us somehow, and we need a way to keep them at a safe distance. Usually, just verbally ordering them to stay back will do the trick, as long as we order the figure strongly enough and repeatedly. Once it actually stops its assault, we will then have gained some breathing room and a measure of safety.

Let's check back in with the example of Bob. After finding his personal strength and a supportive companion, Bob was standing tall and engaging the creature. The monster that had been untouchable, unapproachable, and relentlessly aggressive, now slowed down and became smaller. Bob was creating the conditions that would allow him to get to know who he was dealing with. Bob was making progress. But—and there is almost always a "but"—as Bob gained in confidence and courage, so did the figure. Terminator Beast, fearing for its existence, fought back with determination.

When the next round of nightmares came, Bob's fear hit like a cyclone. He needed another tool to break the cycle of paralyzing fear in order to continue his work with the nightmare. Once the locomotive of fear starts rolling down the track, it's hard to get off the train.

In order to create some kind of physical interruption of the fear cycle, Bob began to go swimming in the ocean every day. The cold seawater cleansed ideas of the monster from his mind and the activity centered him in his body. Bob had found his "Stop."

Next, it was time for him to create separation from the figure in active imagination. When it came toward him, slobbering and snapping its jaws, Bob didn't shrink in terror. Instead he stayed in his body, gathered support from the Doberman beside him, and commanded Terminator Beast, "Back off!" It kept coming, but not so fast or confident. Summoning all his power, again Bob ordered it to "Stop."

Terminator Beast came to a halt. It was not vanquished, nor did it disappear, but for the very first time it wasn't in charge of the dream or of Bob. He had reclaimed much of his power that up to this point had been stolen by Terminator Beast.

Let's practice using this method in the following exercise.

EXERCISE: *Make the "Stop" and Create Separation*

At this point in working with your nightmare, find some physical activity you can do that interrupts the cycle of fear and rumination. Allow this activity to completely remove the nightmare from your thoughts, and ground you in your body and present-time experience. You have now made the "Stop."

Once you have accomplished that, you are ready to create separation from the figure. Your feeling of personal strength will have grown somewhat because of making the "Stop." Connect to your strength now and turn your attention to the ground of the dream setting. Feel your feet grow roots into the landscape of the dream setting and pull strength from the source.

Imagine your ally standing next to you now. Turn to the threatening figure and say, "Stop!" Do it again with more force. Other statements may feel more appropriate like "Get out!" or "Leave me alone!" Find the assertion that works most effectively for you. You may also make some kind of stopping gesture, like that of a policeman, when you do this.

Now watch the figure. It will come at you again, but stand your ground. Do not run away. Your first wave of fear is natural. Let it ripple through you, but remain firm. If you are not already doing so, actually stand up. Assert your words once again with more volume, and make your gesture if you are doing that. Repeat this several times with authority.

Now say to the figure, "I am here now, and I will not be killed." Say this three times. Then simply say, "I am here now." Look again at the figure closely. What do you notice? How has it changed?

Most likely there will be some small shift in its appearance or behavior. Look at the expression in its face (if it has one), or its body language, or the landscape. What aspect has calmed down, even just a little? Follow that.

As long as the figure is still, keep witnessing it. Is the figure getting more related, less automatic, less psychopathic? If so, get curious about what you are seeing. Stay rooted firmly in your strength as you allow yourself to observe. Often the monster will attempt to attack once again. If this happens, meet this assault with another command to stop. Each time you take this action, asserting yourself will get easier, and the figure will become more responsive to your commands. There has been a shift in the power relationship.

Notice how you are now feeling. In what ways have you reclaimed your sense of personal authority? How has the figure or situation responded? What has changed in your interaction with it? Write this down in your journal and keep track of these interactions.

Your curiosity, not your fear, will provide the strength you need to sustain this process. Notice how your power increases as the energy in the image decreases. Watch for the time when there is a reversal in orientation. When does the once life-threatening dream figure stop attacking you and instead help you assert yourself against external opposition? Mark this day in your dream journal. It is a day of independence.

Step 4—Discover the True Nature of the Figure

As our work with nightmares continues, another aspect of the figure reveals itself. At this stage we see for the first time the "humanity" of the nightmare image. This is the breakthrough. When this takes place, we discover anew how each living dream image is part of the natural order. This is not a romantic fantasy, but simply a manifestation of the organic nature of dream images.

This is the step where I have seen the most amazing transformations happen. Sometimes the image that scares us the most turns out to be extraordinarily valuable. As we engage with these powerful figures, they lose some of their destructive intensity. Their stranglehold on our lives gives way to positive regard. No longer compelled to act out in destructive ways, the nightmarish images can deepen into their true nature. This shift is a reflection of their ability to grow out of their need to be menacing and terrifying. As they mature, we can see their value and access it.

This does not mean that all nightmare images become angelic. However, when any image unfolds, it begins to reveal itself from the inside out. Even the terrifying, monomaniacal Tyrant will become more dimensional, more available for relationship.

Individuation is inherent to living images. This is particularly the case with nightmarish images. The images of the horrific are particularly potent, active, and alive. In dream after dream, the horrific images vibrate with the intensity of the life force. For example, Terminator Beast in Bob's dream life pulsed with intense "psychic libido."

In Bob's case, discovering what was particular about the figure depotentiated it and Bob was then able to watch Terminator Beast go through its changes, evolve, and reveal something of its true self.

As time went on, Bob saw Terminator Beast was more than just a representation of a past abusive aggressor (his father) or aspects of his own unexpressed aggression. He now saw that Terminator Beast was a storehouse of knowledge and mastery in its own right. When put to constructive use, it was not a killer, but a valuable companion. Terminator Beast had innate knowledge about the power of conviction, the strength of determination, and the certainty of purpose. For Bob there was tremendous value in discovering these positive qualities. He used Terminator Beast's skills to confront the challenges in his life, and he allied himself with the dream figure to encounter other demons that arose in his dreams. They could mess with Bob, but no one messed with Terminator Beast. Bob, alone, was still intimidated by aggressive colleagues or frightening dream figures but not so when Terminator Beast stood beside him. For Bob, the value of developing a relationship with the embodied nightmare image was profound.

Here I would like to underscore a key insight. To discover the value in threatening images requires both patience and persistence. Patience requires all the inner strength we have cultivated so far. Persistence means sustaining the determination to stay on the scene, repeating the Dream Tending work with the figures until they are ready to change. It is by repeatedly engaging the figure over time that the magic begins to happen. With patience and persistence, a nightmare image may show itself as a wise elder or an ancestral spirit. In fact, this nightmarish figure may have been trapped in the form of a monster for many generations. Just as in a fairy tale or myth, the figure may have been waiting for release into its next incarnation. These types of meaningful surprises are in store for us when we are patient and persistent in our work.

I have noticed that when tending strong images our patience is tested in several ways. Sometimes, as we attend to the figure, it will suddenly get up and leave the room, or simply disappear all together. Other times, when we get close to making contact with what is essential in the image, it shape-shifts into something different. It may be that this is the image's last line of defense, or perhaps the image is still too hot to handle.

Whatever the case, it is important not to get thrown off by such maneuvers. If the figure leaves the room, wait a few moments and turn your attention to something else. Then look back and discover where it is situated now. If the image shape-shifts, sit tight and wait for its original form to return. What is crucial is to be patient and persistent. Stand firm, anchor, and watch for the true nature of the image to reveal itself.

In this next exercise, you will learn to engage the nightmare figure with patience and persistence, and to see into its true nature. It is here that the essential value of the nightmare begins to reveal itself.

EXERCISE: *Discover the True Nature of the Figure*

Turn once again to the nightmarish figure that you have been working with. What is it doing now in the room? Has it changed in any way? Take notice.

If you were to say something to the figure, what would that be? Say this to it now. Do not expect a response or an answer, yet notice what comes back your way. It might be a gesture, a sound, or something more. Again, speak your mind. Say what you need to say directly to the figure.

Do nothing more at this point. You do not need to "integrate the figure back into your personality." While this is a common practice in some forms of dreamwork, it is the opposite of the Dream Tending approach. You are to recognize its autonomy, stand your ground, and engage in an ongoing relationship with it. Continue to look it in the eye, say what you need to say, and gather knowledge about what intelligence is at work in the essential body of the figure.

Your work now is to continue the conversation with the figure. The key here is to remain patient and persistent, even if this stage takes a long while to unfold. You might notice that the figure may at times turn away, walk out of the room, or even disappear. Stay with it, take a breath, focus on another figure for a while, and then bring your attention back to the difficult image. Nine times out of ten, the figure will return and make contact with you again. Stand firm. Say your piece, listen to what comes back from the figure, and respond yet again. Repeat this sequence many times over.

Notice how as you engage the figure, your fear and anxiety diminish. Also notice how the figure changes, becoming less forceful and threatening. As this process continues, become particularly aware of increasing your own stature and reclaiming your personal power in relation to the figure. What is it like to regain some control in this situation? How is it to be in a responsive rather than a reactive mode? Do you notice a difference between feeling like a powerless victim and feeling more secure, potent, and engaged? What begins to reveal itself from the inside of the image? What do you begin to recognize as the essential nature of the image? Remain patient and notice what comes forward. What greets you and extends itself to you? Who are you coming into contact with now? How is this of value?

Step 5—Establish Relationship with the Figure

The most peculiar, harshest, and scariest images are in many ways the most authentic of all dream figures. They do not conform to our conventional ideas or concepts of how an image should look or behave. They have not been domesticated or homogenized by cultural norms. Often we experience such terrifying images as more primal than other more familiar and refined images. Freud recognized long ago that the most stark, raw, and uncivilized images are closer to our "primary process"—meaning, the core of our being. They have not been cloaked, revised, and filtered, or made tolerable and civil by our minds. They can therefore provide access to our unique person-hood. It's as if they hold the code to who we are and who we are meant to be.

When we tend to these core images, we open the doors to our true sense of self. Their very oddity mirrors back our individ-uality. From the point of view of the dreaming psyche, the night-mare pulls us out of "business as usual" and places us in an alto-gether different context. During an encounter with an intolerable image, our bodies are awake, energized, and alert. The image itself demands new methods of dealing with the horror lurking in the psyche. It makes us discover unique ways of responding. We are pushed to access new abilities, find new resources, and expand our boundaries. So nightmares, paradoxically, touch our authenticity.

There are many ways to discover our uniqueness through nightmares. The process that I have developed for this purpose is called "art dialogue." It involves further witnessing the dream image as we have done, yet with an additional intention. In art dialogue, we establish an ongoing relationship and interaction with the nightmare image. Using artistic expression, we engage the image and actively encourage a response over time. As in making a friend or tending to a family member, as we become more familiar with this image, we seek conversation and a more intimate relationship. Initiating contact and listening for a response opens the way to new discoveries. In art dialogue with the image, it will reveal something of our uniqueness to us.

To see an example of this, let's return to Bob's relationship with the dream image of Terminator Beast. In step four, Bob discovered that by standing firm and patiently dialoguing with the figure—this time adding sketches to his dialogues—he found a source of determination and courage. As Terminator Beast became present and embodied, it became a warrior/companion informing and supporting Bob in his life. The way in which this newly-evolving image operated was unique in Bob's experience. In his dreamwork, Bob observed the half-machine-half-animal figure manifest qualities of power that were previously unknown to Bob. Terminator Beast did not use the tactics of violence that Bob had been subjected to as a child. Nor was the figure using threat and terror to express its authority. This more evolved, embodied dream figure was assertive not aggressive, firm not violating and fully present not intimidating. All of these ways of being were new to Bob. It was as if the pull of the future was now showing itself to Bob rather than the influence of a torturous past.

As a further example, I knew a woman named Joan who had a recurring nightmare of falling. For her, sleep was not a time of rest because her fists would clench, her shoulders would knot, and her stomach would contort in a vice-like grip. She woke up each morning exhausted and paralyzed with fear.

Her falling nightmares had been part of her life since she was a little girl and had had many variations. Sometimes she would see herself going over a cliff on a bike or in a car. Other times, the ground would open up and she would fall into a bottomless chasm. Joan was terrorized by feeling out of control in the fall itself and by the fear that she would be broken on the sharp rocks below and die.

Joan tried everything that she could think of to prevent or avoid the fall. She would stay up late at night and wait until exhaustion took her into sleep. She would put soft pillows all around her in bed "to break the fall." In her desperation, she tried anything she could think of to stop the repeating image of the uncontrollable fall. Explanations like "falling in esteem," "falling down on her job," "falling out of favor with her friends," and "falling out of love" were instructive, even insightful. Yet the nightmares didn't stop. There was no explaining them away.

Then Joan learned the Dream Tending way to work with nightmares. She needed to get into relationship with the falling dream and learn something more about its meaning than just catastrophe. Joan wanted to understand how falling was connected to her core sense of purpose. She began by mobilizing inner resources to gain strength, she became curious, and she gathered knowledge, just as we have already learned.

Joan was gaining ground, but at this point something more was required. She needed to embrace the fall in a safe way. The act of falling itself needed to be transformed into an expression of her unique talents. So Joan began using the art dialogue technique. For five nights, the falling dream plagued her in her sleep, and each morning she reached over to her bedside table and used crayons to draw impressions of the fall. Images of whirlwinds and downward spirals, colored black, silver, and blue came pouring out of her. Each night the terrifying feeling of falling would take place, and every morning Joan would express her experience in her drawings. Later in the day, Joan would get to know her pictures through art dialogue. She would write a story not *about* the dream images, but directly *to* them. Back and forth, she wrote, acting out her own part and then the part of the nightmare image. At the end of five days, Joan and the fall felt like companions. They had gotten to know each other and were in art dialogue.

Like Alice falling into Wonderland, or Persephone's descent into the Underworld, Joan learned how to use the nightmare of falling to make a journey into abundant places of her inner psychic landscape. There she found new dream companions, creative resources, and inner wisdom. Rather than being caught in a never-ending cycle of falling, Joan learned through art dialogue how to use her relationship to the nightmare to access her true character.

EXERCISE: *Establish Relationship with the Figure*

To continue with the nightmare you have been tending, sketch or somehow artistically express the dream that has been so torturous for you. Get very detailed about its most frightening aspects. When you hit your fear response, stop. Take a few minutes, return to your breath, align with your body, get your strength, then return to your journal and continue to depict the qualities of the nightmare.

Do not figure anything out. The idea is to give expression in a conscious way to that which has been so terrifying. Go slowly with this activity. There is no value in getting re-traumatized. One step at a time is the most constructive approach.

Art dialogue brings the nightmare image into a horizontal relationship, instead of allowing it to be an overwhelming presence threatening your very existence. Again, use your strength to keep the image separate from you and in relationship to you. Similar to sitting with a friend who is possessed by rage, keep your footing, your certainty, and your persistence. Trust that the figure will weaken, like a hurricane when it hits land. The nightmarish image also wants to find its true sense of being, which exists below its storm and fury.

Once the true nature of the horror reveals itself, get curious. Do not take this opportunity to dominate or destroy, as appealing as this may be for you. Instead, get very interested, pay attention, write a long dialogue between yourself and the image, or write an open letter to it. Wait for a response. When you hear something coming back your way, record it in your journal. Also feel free to draw the image. Again, wait for a response. Let the pictorial reply of the image come to you. Notice if you hear a voice or see an artistic expression that emanates from deep within the dream figure.

Art dialogue is allowing what has not been seen or heard to come into visibility. Perhaps you will discover something that has never before been expressed. Listen with care and patience. What is revealed that is new and essential?

Step 6—Experience the Vitality of the Imagination

By now it is apparent that nightmare figures are often the most fascinating and creative of all images. By keeping us off balance and uprooting us from our complacency, they juice the vital forces of our imagination. Of course it doesn't always feel good to be out of our comfort zone, yet the intensity of nightmare images opens realms of the imagination we might otherwise never explore. Even Bob's Terminator Beast—a hybrid image of machine and beast—is the product of an artistic, creative (one could even say poetic) dreaming psyche. For Joan as well, the terror of her falling nightmare opened up her creativity in a new way.

If you think about it, images of the horrific function as gateways to other worlds in many mediums as well. In tales of horror, at theme parks, and in drama, it is the weird, malicious, and frightful figures who guide us to the outer realms of fantasy. Think how fascinating a horror movie can be. For example, the creature in the movie *Alien* is far more interesting than any of the human characters. Godzilla, too, steals the show and grips our attention with its bizarre, grotesque appearance. Terrifying images ignite our creativity like no others.

So in this step we are going to work with the creativity of the nightmare figure, and use this to fire up our own imagination. This will pump our creative juices and also allow us to appreciate the brilliance and wonder of these difficult images. The key is to come face to face, toe to toe, and body to body with the image, engaging the most fascinating aspects of the nightmare figure using our imagination. To walk through the portal into the realm of the imagination, we need the eyes, ears, and sensibilities of its indigenous inhabitant, the nightmare image itself. My experience is that people are often astonished at the sheer brilliance and creative vitality that exists at the core of their nightmares.

EXERCISE: *Experience the Vitality of the Imagination*

First, face away from the terrifying image. You are now strong enough to allow this nightmare to face your back. With the image behind you, connect to your sense of self. Do this in ways that you have learned thus far: befriend a supportive image, engage your core strength through breath or gesture, and so on.

When you feel connected to your core, turn back around and face the nightmare image. Witness the activity that is taking place in the scene all around it. Keep your distance. Observe what is revealing itself. Do not try to fix or rescue what you are watching. Do not run away to seek shelter from it, either. Rather, remain connected to your core and witness the action. Anchor. Get curious. Breath. Keep the activity at arm's length.

The activity in this psychic landscape may pick up speed and intensify. Just let it do so. Continue to watch without doing. If it helps, imagine that you are viewing a dramatic enactment, and that it is your time to simply witness this action. In this theater of the horrific you just watch the nightmare as it plays out upon the stage. Notice the intricacy of the performance, the intelligence of the presentation as well as its qualities of horror and terror. Get fascinated by how incredibly ingenious this enactment actually is.

Continue to allow the dread of the nightmarish image to arise within you. Notice how it invites your fascination. See it as it sees you, and pretend to take on some nightmarish qualities of your own. Relate to it through fiendish gestures, with devilish eyes, and with mischievous interest. As you further engage, notice how your imagination comes to life. What gets juiced inside of you? What additional images come forward in your mind's eye?

Now let go. Let go of reason and rationality for a moment, and let the intelligence and fluidity of your creative mind come forward and take in the situation anew. What surprises you? Who and what shows up now?

After some time, write or draw what the imaginative psyche has revealed. Ask yourself when was the last time you felt so deeply immersed in this kind of artistic process. What do you notice about yourself when you are in this creative flow? What knowledge arises? And as the portal of imagination opens, what realms of the inner life do you connect to? In this never-ending story of creative life, stimulated by the nightmarish image, what comes awake? As the veil of the intolerable gets lifted and you cultivate the capacity for engagement, what imaginal intelligence can you offer back to the world?

Chapter Three

Applying Living Images
to Major Life Challenges

My great-grandfather was a practical man. He worked with his hands to fix people's shoes, mostly cutting and sewing leather. His tools were glue, nails, brushes and hammers. Simple. His wisdom was equally as simple. I remember sitting in his shop watching as people young and old brought him their stories. They talked to him, sometimes complaining about money, jobs, or children, and he would just listen. He listened in a way that came from deep within his heart, a listening that could reach out to touch theirs. His listening presence filled the room with hope; calm replaced fear; and each person found something they had lost.

Three generations later, I aspire to follow in his ways. For me the alchemist's gold is not only found in concepts and ideas, but in pragmatically and effectively coping with life's everyday challenges. I have found that dream images open people up to new ways of living, and we need only pay attention to the deep resources of our dreams in order to gain their help to transform some of our most difficult afflictions.

The power of the living image can be directly applied to painful life dilemmas. Addiction, dysfunction in relationships, trouble in the workplace, and separation from our true vocation are challenges most of us face at various times in the course of our lives. In this chapter, we will look at each of these troubled areas in turn and explore how Dream Tending—in the practical spirit of my great-grandfather—can help us embrace and heal them.

ADDICTION: SPIRIT IN THE BOTTLE

I once had a client named Joel, who had a recurring dream that a flock of vultures was attacking him. The vultures sank their talons into his skin, tore at his flesh with their hooked beaks, and crashed into him with their sharp wings and bony bodies. These awful dream vultures visited Joel almost every night, terrorizing him and giving him no peace. Most nights he woke up terrified, panicked, and sweating.

Joel had come to my office desperate. He was an alcoholic and his life was going from bad to hopeless. There seemed to be no time he wasn't drunk; he was hiding bottles at home and at work; he couldn't remember whole events or conversations. His wife was threatening to leave him, and his boss was giving him one last chance. Beyond the nightmare of what his life was becoming, even his sleep was now disturbed by this recurring nightmare of vultures. His sponsor in Alcoholics Anonymous referred him to me, one of the "dream experts" in town, to see if I could at least help him with his nightmares.

In addition to the tried and true methods of addiction treatment—which include comprehensive family histories, medical reviews, treatment programs, and continuing contact with a sponsor—Dream Tending offers a powerful source of assistance. As a companion practice to these therapies it is highly effective, often giving the individual a kind of leverage with an addiction that he or she didn't have before. Frankly, when a person hits bottom, looking to dreams for guidance isn't that peculiar an idea. It's a matter of re-discovering that "there's no place like home," meaning that the most important answers are right inside us.

Addiction is a fierce and relentless affliction. Slowly over decades, or quickly in just a few months, it can destroy a life. Treatment requires serious psychological, behavioral, and spiritual intervention. Dream Tending skills are enormously helpful in all of these areas.

Like Joel, many of us have experienced addiction. Besides drugs and alcohol, overconsumption of food, gambling, sex addiction, and obsessive shopping are some of the out-of-control behaviors that can kidnap our lives. Whatever the type, all addictions are accompanied by living dream images. The dream figure gives a face to the addiction, tells us something about the disease, and also points the way to the cure.

In this section, we will learn to apply Dream Tending skills as an additional treatment for dealing with addiction. I have developed a practical, five-step approach that draws on a number of skills presented in the previous chapters. This system is a potent weapon against a titanic adversary. I want to emphasize that *this method works in real-life, real-world situations* and—in tandem with Alcoholics Anonymous or other programs—has helped many people in the throes of addiction to break free.

The method consists of five steps:

1) Identifying the Addiction and Naming the Image

2) Using Association and Amplification to Relate the Dream Image to the Addiction

3) Stopping the Compulsion

4) Befriending the Image

5) Finding the True Nature of the Image

These steps are arranged in a logical sequence, although as in all dreamwork they may actually unfold in a different order for each individual. This system draws on the skills we have already learned, and applies them here to a specific life challenge in very concrete ways. Most of the skills used in this system will be familiar, and yet the details of their implementation have been adapted for working with addiction.

We start by identifying and giving a name to the addictive behavior.

Step 1—Identifying the Addiction and Naming the Image

This first step is a simple but important one. It is crucial that we identify the addiction that is ruling our lives. Clearly, before we can engage the dream image related to the syndrome, we have to know what we are looking for. Acknowledging that we are caught in an addiction is the first order of business.

Once we are clear about the fact of the addiction, we can then look at our dreams and find an image that seems to relate to the addiction. Often there will be an image that displays some kind of addictive or compulsive behavior of its own. It may be out of control, obsessive, or driven in some way.

Having identified the addiction and a dream image that relates to it, we then *name the image*. We do this exactly as we did in Chapter One. Learning the name of the image will allow us to begin tending the image in earnest. Of course we would rather take another drink, shoot up, or place a thousand dollars on red—anything other than naming the addiction and the images surrounding it. But, if not now, when? Let's jump right in.

EXERCISE:
Identifying the Addiction and Naming the Image

Have a frank and honest coming to terms with yourself. Answer the question, "What am I addicted to?" It may help to think in terms of dreams, by reframing this question and asking, "What nightmare am I currently living? How is my life like a bad dream?" Get very direct and practical, and ask yourself, "How is this addiction operating in my life? What are the costs to me personally and professionally? From one to ten, how powerful is the addiction at this point in time?". Write down the answers to these questions in your journal.

Follow this self-appraisal by surveying your nighttime dreams. Which dreams seem to represent the addiction that you are experiencing? If it is not immediately apparent, ask yourself, "What images have a compulsive quality about them? What images recur again and again? What images feel out of control?" . These are likely to be images representing your addiction. From these, choose one to work with in this exercise. It may be the most out-of-control image, the most seductive, or perhaps the one that seems the most nightmarish.

Once you have found an image that is connected to your addiction, it is time to name it. This is important, but the process need not be elaborate or convoluted. Joel simply named his image Vulture. So name your image, and speak this name aloud.

Now just sit for a while with this image. Allow it to come into your awareness and observe its activity. Do nothing else with it for now.

Step 2—Using Association and Amplification to Relate the Dream Image to the Addiction

In the second step, we use association and amplification to understand how the image relates to the addiction. We learned the methods of association and amplification in Chapter One, but let's review them here.

In *association*, we look for ways that the dream image relates to something in our everyday life. Association opens up the dream, calls out the issues it speaks to, and shows how it relates to our personal circumstances. If we have a dream of our real-life alcoholic father, for example, this is an obvious association to a cause of our addiction. It is amazing how much of the obvious we lock away in the vault of denial. Association is a key to that vault.

Amplification takes the image and expands it to its archetypal dimensions. The previous dream image of an alcoholic father, for example, might be amplified as the mythic figure Chronos, the father-monster who devoured his children. This connection functions as a dose of reality from the mythological realm, pointing to the pain of a dysfunctional relationship that may be driving us to drink.

When addiction is part of our family history and there is a predisposition toward self-destructive behavior, dream images act like emergency sirens, warning us in no uncertain terms that the addiction is now a threat to our life. Association to these dream images brings immediate attention to the situation. Dream images alert us to the threat by dragging what's hidden in the closet out into the open. By first associating with the images, we make certain that we are not missing the obvious facts that the psyche is confronting us with. When we next amplify these images, we explore their deeper significance and give them more weight and value.

Let's return to Joel's story to see how he used association and amplification to make the link between his addictive behaviors and those images that appeared in his dreams. For Joel, the nightmare Vulture was not some concept he read about in a book. It was a monster that attacked him when he closed his eyes to sleep, threatening his health and sanity.

Using methods of association, Joel viewed Vulture as representing the constant "attack" of his addiction. Other interpretations are possible, of course. One person might see the Vulture as representing uncontrollable compulsions, or the ravaging of vital body organs by alcohol poisoning. For another, this hostile dream image might be interpreted as an abusive person from the past, like a parent, relative, or employer; or it could be a picture of some type of post-traumatic disorder. These are all ways of associating with the dream image and gaining a sense of how it is connected to the pattern of addiction.

As months of dream work continued, Joel went beyond this direct association into the wider symbolic realm of amplification. He made the link between Vulture and the myth of Prometheus, whom the gods punish by having his liver torn out and eaten for eternity by a vulture. This archetypal image depicted the terrifying consequences Joel faced in his alcohol addiction. To see his life being taken from him, devoured by his addiction, and to see himself caught in the never-ending cycle of helpless victimization, rocked Joel to his core. Through the process of amplification, the story of Prometheus offered precise warning, honed over thousands of years of human history. Its promise of liver damage and eternal suffering sobered Joel at least for the moment.

In this second exercise, we will associate and then amplify the images that represent the addictive process.

EXERCISE: *Using Association and Amplification to Relate the Dream Image to the Addiction*

For this exercise, use the image that you named in the last exercise. Watch it closely. What is it doing now? Use your Dream Tending skills to witness its activity.

Notice any associations that you may have in relation to this image. How does it represent the circumstances in your life at the moment? Using the addiction image as a point of reference, can you identify family circumstances, early childhood trauma, or an addictive syndrome that was occurring when you were growing up? As you explore these associations, does the image become more vibrant? Where in your body do you feel the effects of its activity?

Now change the channel. You are going to *amplify* the image, which requires you to open your imagination. What stories, legends, fairy tales, or myths can you connect to the image? These could even be movies, modern books, Internet memes, or other ideas from the culture at large. See how the addiction image is reflected in these bigger, more universal stories.

Once you have connected the dream image to a "bigger" story, you can use the story to gain understanding of the image. What more does the story tell you about the dream image? How does the activity of the image relate to this story? Notice how the dream image informs you about your situation.

Step 3—Stopping the Compulsion

Joel found that associating and amplifying Vulture provided him with information about it. However, while going down the path of interpretation may bring useful understanding and even temporary relief from an aggressive image, the image is only pacified, not engaged. It does not die, as we might hope for an image of something destructive. It simply retreats for a brief time. The living image is still lurking in the psyche, biding time.

Although association and amplification were helping, Joel was not attending to the living image of Vulture in its actual presence and activity. Without engaging the living image, he was still missing the opportunity to peer into Vulture's intelligence, discover its essential inner nature, and befriend it. The essence of Dream Tending is to move beyond ideas and symbols into the living reality of the dream image. To go in this direction, however, Joel would need to do something that he found next to impossible. He would need to stop his compulsive drinking.

In addition to work with treatment programs, we need to use the Dream Tending technique of *animation* to deal with the powerful images of addiction. In the last chapter, we learned how to animate images of nightmares. These are the same skills that I believe are necessary to work with the dream images of the addiction process. Addiction images are a kind of nightmare, however the images inherent to addictive syndromes have special features not found in common nightmares. Their primary distinguishing characteristic is extremely repetitive behavior. Addictive images are often out of control, and they carry us along in their obsession and compulsivity.

Once the compulsive behavior grips us, it takes on a life of its own. Trapped in this whirlwind, we are caught up in an intense swirl of accelerating speed, which is very hard to interrupt, so we must stop it before it gets started. Then we will be able to constructively engage the root image living at the core of the addiction. I have found that compulsivity and genuine curiosity cannot exist in the mind at the same time. Based on this powerful idea, I have developed a four-part process to stop compulsive behavior.

1) *Find an Interruption.* This means doing something that will short circuit the cycle of compulsive behavior. It does not need to be complicated. In fact, the simpler, the better. For example, taking a cold shower, pounding the bed with a tennis racket, or shouting "Stop!" as loudly as possible all work. Anything that breaks up our mental obsession and halts the compulsive activity creates the all-important interruption.

2) *Hold the opposites.* Compulsion has two sides to it: one side constructive, and the other side destructive. For example, drinking provides stress relief and a warm buzz, yet too much drinking causes blackouts, destructive behavior, and illness. So our compulsions are composed of interesting polarities. Here we uncover these opposites and hold them in our minds, mentally embracing both sides of the compulsion. This will open the middle ground of opportunity and curiosity.

3) *Get curious about the image.* It is nearly impossible to be filled with curiosity and compulsivity at the same time. One cancels out the other. The more curiosity we have about an image, the less compulsion there is to fuel the addiction.

Furthermore, curiosity helps us learn about an image: its origins, its knowledge, and its desires. From the point of view of Dream Tending much of the crucial information about the addiction lives in the image itself. Moving towards curiosity creates a positive feedback loop. When we slow down compulsivity, there is room to get curious and learn more about the image. As we do so, we become less anxious and more relaxed, which in turn furthers our interest in the more subtle aspects of the image. Curiosity is our friend. It halts the obsessive drive and returns us to healthy patterns of interaction.

4) *Take action.* We make a concrete action in the real world on behalf of what we become curious about. For instance, when

we get curious about a particular figure in a dream, we might want to place an object representing it on an altar in our home. Another action might be to clean the house of stuff that has outlived its usefulness. The nature of the action is not as important as the intention behind it. Taking action on behalf of our curiosity affirms our ability to follow an alternative instinct and putting a stop to the addictive compulsivity.

There is an interesting neurological principle at work in this fourth part. Recent studies by Nobel prizewinner Eric Kandel and others have shown that taking some concrete action in the real world, no matter what it is, actually builds new synapses— connections between brain cells—that begin to cement in place our new condition. This suggests that every time we make even a momentary stride forward in our recovery process, we should do something physical to help fix it in place. That way, little by little, our dreamwork moves us inexorably out of compulsion.

Each time we go through this four-part process of stopping the compulsion, we gain a little ground in the struggle with the addiction. I have used this compulsion-stopping system with a large number of clients and students and have had impressive results. Let's try these methods now in an exercise.

EXERCISE: *Stopping the Compulsion*

> Begin by anchoring yourself and finding the support of your breath, and an allied dream figure. Now turn to face the addictive image as it presents itself in the here and now. This is where we add our new four-part process.
>
> *1) Find an Interruption*—That is, do anything that you can think of, from taking a cold shower to yelling out loud, in order to stop your mind from spinning into old associations or anticipating future consequences. Get into your body and stop the mental activity surrounding the addiction.

2) **Hold the Opposites**—Identify the polarity at work in the compulsive aspect of the image. Now extend out your hands in both directions. Imagine holding the two poles of the image's compulsion in your two hands. Hold the positive aspect on the right and the destructive aspect on the left. Then see you and your curiosity located in the center position, between these two extremes. Now look again at the image and begin to gather information about it from here. Has it changed in any way? How has the image broken out of its compulsivity?

3) **Get Curious about the Image**—As usual, do not try to analyze or figure out anything. Pay very close attention to the activity of the image. See what it does, what it likes, how it moves, where it goes, and so on. Most especially, discover any activity of the image that is compulsive or out of control. Is it controlled by any blind urges, impulses, or drives? Do not interact with it at this point, just gather information about what you observe. You want to keep some distance from the whirlwind of compulsivity.

4) **Take Action**—Respond to this exercise by taking one concrete action in the world. Do something tangible on behalf of this dreamwork exercise. It does not have to be a big or seemingly important action. Something simple, direct, and achievable is best.

Write in your journal what you have learned about the image.

Step 4—Befriending the Image

Stopping compulsivity, as we did in the last step, provides a temporary release from the grip of the addictive image. Since we are now out on parole, so to speak, a new kind of relationship to the image becomes possible.

It is time to stand our ground and face the image of our addiction directly. By standing up for ourselves, we turn the tables and can look directly into the image to discover its essence. When we do this, we gain an understanding of its true character, as well as any helpful knowledge it may possess. This knowledge is important because it shows us the way out of the syndrome. It also sets in motion a new phase, in which we can befriend the image, and in which we gain some measure of power back for ourselves.

As Joel's dreamwork progressed over the months, he came to understand that Vulture represented more than his addictive behavior. He realized that Vulture in one form or another had been around for as long as he could remember. The creature had tormented him since he was a little boy. Throughout his life, Joel had used all his ingenuity and energy to figure out ways to avoid Vulture. But no matter how hard he had struggled to keep Vulture out of his life, he had often experienced the menacing bird personified in other people. Sometimes Vulture had shown itself in public figures or in the characters in movies. Even more brutally, Joel had seen Vulture in his love relationships. His partners had sometimes taken on Vulture's characteristics and unintentionally played its destructive role, to his great dismay.

Now that Joel was actively fighting alcohol addiction, Vulture was loose in his dreams. Psychological explanations, interpretations, and associations brought only temporary relief. Like the need for the next drink, Vulture just kept coming back. Between Joel's attempts to flee from the raptor and deal with the intensity of the image, Joel was worn out and depleted. He desperately needed a way out of the war zone, a safe haven. I showed him that by standing his ground and facing Vulture, he could gain a deeper understanding of who Vulture was, what it wanted and what was required to come to terms with it.

Joel found the courage to stand his ground in front of Vulture. Then he could actually begin to observe the image more closely. He watched Vulture's activities and how it interacted with other figures.

As Joel noticed the figure in its particularity, a curious thing happened. Vulture's dominance began to lessen. The dream bird became smaller, less aggressive, and eventually began to change. After almost three months of Dream Tending with the image, Joel realized something dramatic: *in many ways Vulture was like him.* Joel realized that the demonic monster that had been persecuting him in his dreams was actually quite a bit like he was—aggressive on the outside, fearful and anxious on the inside. And not only that, but Vulture also reminded him of his parents and even grandparents. It had been around long before he was born.

By standing firm and having a good look at the creature, Joel now saw that Vulture was more familiar than he could have previously imagined. Because it spanned many generations of his family, Vulture had a sense of immortality about it, as if it were timeless. The problem was that it never changed or evolved over time. It was frozen in attack mode for generation after generation, constantly wreaking havoc.

This new information about Vulture brought Joel into a closer relationship with it. Joe's empathy for Vulture allowed him to accept Vulture's presence. He moved into an on-going relationship with the figure rather than fearing, resenting, and avoiding it. This was the beginning of Joel's recovery from addiction.

As they became friends, he noticed that the aggressive tendencies of the image began to diminish. Its need to dominate and possess lessened. Joel changed his end of the relationship, too. He learned that he was not out to exterminate the figure. By befriending Vulture, Joel gained the very knowledge he needed to begin to free himself from the addiction.

In this next exercise we will learn to come face to face with the dream figure at the center of the addictive behavior, and make friends with it.

EXERCISE: *Befriending the Image*

Now it is time to directly face the dream image at the center of your addiction. With a figure such as this, however, you will need to do what seems like the impossible: look at the figure and see the ways in which it is like you. Be ready to face what perhaps will be a big and difficult irony. Discover how you are similar to the very figure that you have done everything to avoid and even destroy.

As you look directly at the figure, what do you recognize? Notice how the figure seems to know you in essential ways. In what ways are you the same? Experience your feelings in this recognition. If embarrassment or humiliation comes up for you, acknowledge this. It is natural. You are facing the one whom all your life you have hated, who has tormented you, and who has created massive dysfunction.

Write about this in your journal. Then do something expressive with your body: move, make sounds, run, or cry. Get your feelings out of your system. Release. When you are ready, return to the image. Begin the process of really getting to know each other. In your journal write a dialogue back and forth. Take both parts. Write to each other as kin. You have a lot of catching up to do. Then watch your dreams over the next weeks.

Step 5—Finding the True Nature of the Image

Animated images are always more than what they first appear to be. In step five, we venture to the energetic presence that exists at the core of the image itself. Using our skills of animation we find the spirit or spark that enlivens the image. This psychic essence is the nutritious substance that we crave when caught in an addictive behavior. In other words, the substance of an addiction is just a stand-in for what we really want, which is the powerful psychic juice at the core of the image. It is not the literal alcohol, gambling, or drugs that we crave, so much as the pure food of spirit hidden within the image.

It is not enough to know this intellectually. That would be like talking about food to stop ourselves from starving. We do not find fulfillment in concepts, but in finding and experiencing the spiritual root alive at the center of images of addiction. We cannot be sated until we taste it.

After Joel deepened his relationship to Vulture, he had a dream in which his grandmother appeared. She had always been a force to be reckoned with. Joel had met her just a few times when he was very young, but he remembered many family stories about her. She had been an activist, a suffragette from Tennessee, working for women's rights. She had written political commentary for the newspaper, which in the South at the turn of the century was both bold and dangerous. She was credited with helping to get the 19th Amendment through Congress, which guaranteed women's constitutional right to vote. She had been a woman inspired and driven by the passion of her conviction.

Joel's father had had a really hard time with his mother (Joel's grandmother) and had been embarrassed at school by peers who had mocked her and accused him of supporting women's rights, a position the group of teenage boys found ridiculous.

Joel's father had also felt inadequate because he could not measure up to the force of his mother's character. Like her, he was a good writer, but he never published a word. To deal with the pain, he had started to drink when he was sixteen. By the time Joel was a teenager, his dad had become a full-blown alcoholic.

To tend a dream is to follow the images where they will go and discover whom and with what they interact. For Joel, it was first Vulture, then Joel as Vulture, then Grandmother, then Father, and then back to himself. Joel got curious about certain traits that they all shared in common. Each of them had lots of intensity, drive, and an ability to attack. For his Grandmother, this energy had been put to good use. It was probably this passion that had enabled her to work for women's rights, against long odds and tremendous opposition. Vulture energy certainly seemed present in her determination, her insistence, and her aggressive drive. She had expressed Vulture's power in a potent and constructive fashion. This was not the case for Joel's dad. The creative passion of Joel's grandmother had become a stabbing knife of anguish for his dad. He had not been able to handle Vulture's intensity and turned to alcohol to dull the sharp edge of shame and pain. Like his father, Joel used drinking to stop the hurt.

Alcoholism runs in families. It has a psychological and biological predisposition that can be transmitted genetically. As Joel worked with the figure, he focused on this trans-generational quality. This is when, at last, Vulture became more than a destructive predator. Too hot to handle by his father, the essence of Vulture was in fact the "spirit in the bottle" long denied. When denied or repressed, Vulture created severe disturbance in Joel and manifested in his addiction to alcohol. What's more, when denied or neglected by Joel, Vulture lay in waiting, poised to wreak devastation in the next generation. When befriended, Vulture began to show its creative aspect in Joel's life, just as it had long ago with his grandmother.

You might see a part of your personal story in Joel's struggle with addiction. Recovery is a lifelong process. It requires continued work in treatment programs, support, perseverance, diligence, and help from higher powers. Dream Tending offers access to the realm of the dreaming spirits. These spirit-like images offer support and unconditional acceptance, essential to the process of recovery. In many cultures, the figures of this realm are experienced as mythic gods or deities. For me they are simple yet profound living images of the dreamtime. Our challenge is to look them in the eye, tend to them, and to sustain our relationship with them. To do so takes time, compassion, and force of character. Like good friendships, the attention we invest is rewarded in kind with love and care.

In this last exercise, we will learn how to find and recover the spirit at the very heart of the addiction.

EXERCISE: *Finding the True Nature of the Image*

Begin by looking again at the dream image that you have been working with. By now it should be less menacing and intense. List its characteristics as you see them now. What other dream images or living persons does this list of attributes remind you of? As they come to mind, continue adding new characteristics to your list. Once your list is created, make a composite of the primary qualities. What transcendent aspect comes forward when you consider your list as a whole?

Give a name to this transcendent aspect, or what you are calling this "spirit-like" quality.

Find an object, like a stone, figurine, or shell that in some way depicts the spirit. You can also make a picture or sculpt a figure in clay. Put this object in a special place in your home. Choose the setting with care. You will come back to it time and again. To sustain your relationship with the figure, it is important to establish a private area that will not be disturbed by others. From the outset, appreciate that, as in any relationship, you will go through phases of getting close and taking distance. This is natural.

Now write a letter of commitment to this composite dream image, this essential figure. Sign this agreement, affirming that you will take time each day to make contact. Be realistic. It is important that you follow through with consistency. Begin with once a day for two weeks, then you can re-commit. Working with addiction is always a "one day at a time" process.

Pause. You need to feel acknowledged by the figure itself. Close your eyes, and in active imagination check this out. Do you have an agreement between the two of you to be in relationship? If not, repeat the above. This is a time to use the force of your personal power. You want an ongoing relationship of mutual regard, so be persistent until the dream figure acknowledges, accepts, and agrees to meet you in this way.

Once this commitment is established, observe the activity of the figure. Is it bigger or smaller than the last time you met? What is its attitude toward you, and yours toward it? For the first few days, do nothing more than notice, listen, and record your experiences in your journal.

Watch the figure animate. As it goes through its "recovery" and comes into vitality as a living image, notice what other aspects come to life. Do you see a glimmer in its eye? Or if it is an object or a landscape, do you see a part of it that begins to illuminate in some way? Do you see a different quality of color or light radiating from inside it? If so, bring your interest to this aspect. What does it tell you of the spirit of this being? How do you experience this essential spirit originating from inside the figure or the spirit of place originating from the object or landscape?

After a week or so, determine what comes to life in you as a result of being in direct contact with the figure and its spirit. Take time to really explore this. What attitude, feeling, or new behavior has come forward in you as a result of sustaining this relationship? You now must give form to this new spirit in you and offer it back to the dream figure. You can do this by crafting a poem, making an art piece, taking an action in the world, playing music, dancing, or engaging in some other form of expression. Place your offering next to the image. If it is a performance piece, take the time to share it with the figure. Notice how this is received and how the dream image is affected. Now notice how the relationship between the two of you is impacted. Remain open. What comes back to you from the dream figure? Does the figure act in any way like a muse? What are you inspired to do or express in your life? Do it.

The End of Addiction

When Joel discovered the essence of Vulture, it radically changed his life. In conjunction with other treatments for alcohol addiction, Joel had found a relationship to his "spirit" through his relationship with a nightmare image that had seemed like just another awful symptom of his disease. Over time, Vulture evolved, individuated, and became as strong an ally for Joel as it had been a nemesis.

With Vulture at his side, Joel discovered and recovered his true inheritance, hidden all these years. Like his grandmother,

Joel began to write. Starting with poems about the work he was doing with images, he soon started writing essays, and then articles, and even an occasional editorial for the local paper. The repressed spirit found its right place in Joel's life. For Joel's children as well, the bird of prey is now flying overhead, not as a threat, but as an esteemed part of the family's destiny.

LOVE RELATIONSHIPS: THE INVISIBLE LOVERS

Let's turn our attention to the most meaningful and challenging of all human activities, the love relationship. In my many decades as a therapist, I have seen hundreds of couples struggle to keep relationships alive and healthy in the face of great pain, hurt, betrayal, and despair. One of the most effective ways to re-unite with the enchantment at the heart of our love relationships is to follow the path of our dreams. I have seen couples who have reached the worst levels of dysfunction possible in relationship—the place where there seems to be no love left, only recriminations, disdain, rage, and pain—still find a way to open up to each other through dreams. Insight, good advice, and coaching are helpful, yet these fixes are often not enough. Tending to the vitality of god Eros, as he presents himself through dream images, can really make the difference.

Over the years I have created a six-step process of Dream Tending for couples that is quite helpful in working with many of the relationship difficulties people experience. This process involves partners working with their dreams, both individually and as a couple. The six steps are:

Step 1) Getting "Buy-in" for Sharing Dreams

Step 2) Creating Safety and a Responsive Attitude

Step 3) Witnessing Dreams Without Judgment

Step 4) Finding Eros

Step 5) Tending the Sacred Marriage

Step 6) Honoring the Third Body

Step 1—Getting "Buy-in" for Sharing Dreams

Before partners can start working with their dreams together, they must first agree that it is at least worth doing. Getting this "buy-in" on the value of sharing dreams is not as hard as it may sound. Relationships are born out of intrigue. It may have been long ago, but there was a time when we saw some special quality in our partner, got fascinated, and wanted to know more about the other person.

This early time in a relationship is filled with passionate curiosity and the thrill of new discovery. As time passes, our initial curiosity gives way to more functional ways of being together. Most of the time we get up, offer a hug, say good morning, and get pulled into the day. There is work to be done, things to be taken care of, children to be attended to, money to be made, and countless other activities that make up daily life. Yet when we simply accomplish tasks all day without sharing our dreams, a precious opportunity to relate with one another is gone. The very thing that we found so fulfilling at the beginning of our relationship, the juicy stories that we could not get enough of, are right there in our dreams, waiting to be shared.

Just below the surface of our functional yet often stale interactions, there remain vast resources of exciting activity in the dream world. In the dreamtime we are bold, adventurous, and always doing something out of the ordinary. In dreams we explore new worlds, have new experiences, and meet fascinating people. There is so much to share with each other, yet how often do we take the time to tell each other our dreams?

Getting buy-in to share dreams with our partner is not difficult when we see dreams as interesting stories. As tales from the other realm, we can enjoy them, play with them, and seriously consider them. Dreams are for the telling.

One thing that stops us from sharing our dreams with our partner is the fear that he or she will get too psychological too quickly. When our partner does an instant analysis on our dreams, then likely he or she is using dreams as objects for power and leverage. Neither partner will find this satisfying. By contrast, when we take the time to experience the wonder of dreams, just the opposite happens. We become curious and actively interested in our partner's inner life. Dreams can renew our connections with each other, keeping our love life fresh and strong.

In this first exercise, we take the time to agree that sharing dreams is something of value to include in a love relationship.

EXERCISE: *Getting "Buy-in" for Sharing Dreams*

This exercise is to be done together with your partner. Take time to remember the first months of your relationship. What did you find fascinating about each other? What about your partner caught your eye and ear? Recall what it was like back then to have a long talk. Do you remember any particular dreams or dream images from that early formative period? Invite these images to come into your mind.

Now explore together what it would be like to share some of your dreams with each other. Talk about how sharing these images might be of interest to both of you now, particularly if you both agree to not get overly "psychological."

Talk about what it was like for you to listen to stories when you were a child. What did you enjoy about story time in school, or when your parents read you a story? Did you find yourself captivated? What mood or state of mind opened for you? How was your imagination activated?

Discuss what it would be to tell dreams to each other as if they were stories. Explore what it would be like for one person to be the teller of dreams and the other person the listener. What would it be like to simply listen to the dream as story for the sake of curiosity and interest in the dream, rather than for ideas about the dreamer? Can you do this without the listener interrupting or judging the teller? Share your reflections about this way of telling and listening between you. Notice how this seemingly simple conversation opens a new way of being in conversation and relationship.

Pause here. Do not tell an actual story or dream, only talk about the process of listening in a new and responsive way.

Step 2—Creating Safety and a Responsive Attitude

Dreams are revealing, and it is hard not to get interested in psychological interpretation. Dreams strip away our personas and leave us naked and visible to our partners. However, the searing analysis of our partner's X-ray eyes is not just what the doctor ordered! Sometimes, a lead overcoat is just the right thing. Dreams picture bizarre desires, long buried secrets, the darker side of our psyche, and sexual activities sometimes with people other than our partner. Who wants to risk letting our partners know about affairs with dream lovers? It can also be really uncomfortable to talk about how terrified we are when the dream monsters in nightmares show up. When the intruders threaten or the floodwaters are on the rise, many people feel it is best to keep quiet. Even when holy persons or sacred objects appear, we often prefer to keep these revelations to ourselves. Often, neither person feels it is emotionally safe to share these dreams and to risk being exposed to the judgments, criticisms, or crass comments of the other.

To reap the benefits of couple's Dream Tending, both partners need to feel that it is safe to reveal themselves to the other, particularly as we invite the images to join us in the room. We need to know that what we share will not be used later against us in hurtful ways. The images themselves also need to feel that the area is secure, or they will stay hidden underground.

So before sharing dreams with a partner, it is best to acknowledge the issues of blame, shame, power struggles, and judgments that may come up. If we can create a safe zone for sharing around dreams, the dreams themselves will help to defuse these difficult interactions. Our dreams are not necessarily about our relationship or the other person. By becoming fascinated with what the dream images are doing on their own behalf in our dream life, we create the curiosity and responsive attitude required to tend dreams as a couple. Listening to the dreams of our partner without judgment opens a receptive field in which living dream images become active. The good news is that this orientation immediately generates relief, a time out from the "couple's wars." In its place we create a safe harbor to explore the imaginative stirrings of the dreaming psyche, now alive between the two of you.

EXERCISE: *Creating Safety and a Responsive Attitude*

Continuing from where you left off with exercise one, agree now to check all judgments at the door. Commit to moving your attention from the daily concerns of your relationship to an open consideration of the figures alive in the dream-time. Do this now aloud with each other.

Talk about any previous experiences of dream sharing that you have had with your partner. Talk about what went well and what did not. What are your concerns in sharing your dreams now? What are your partner's hesitations?

Discuss this. Take a few moments to talk about what each of you needs in order to feel safe in sharing dreams.

Once you feel secure, place a candle in the area in which you will be sharing dreams. Light it and acknowledge that this time is not ordinary time. Agree that when the candle is lit you are both in dreamtime, a kind of ritual time that requires mutual respect. What is said in ritual time stays in ritual time. It is not to be used later as ammunition against each other.

Now find an object to represent a "talking stick." The talking stick indicates that the person holding it "has the floor." The holder of the stick has the permission to speak openly and *without interruption.*

Before you listen to your partner share a dream, anchor yourself in your center. Open your heart and remember that you are here to witness the dreams of your partner, not to interpret them. This is not about you or your marriage, even if you are pictured in the dream. This is about sharing dreams in a safe way. The *process* is important here, not the subject matter. Breathe and trust the process.

Step 3—Witnessing Dreams without Judgment

Step three is the hardest part of couple's Dream Tending. Here both partners must listen to the dreams of the other without interrupting or interpreting. This may sound easy, but actually mindful listening is hard to sustain. We have sudden flashes of insight and want to help our partner by sharing these pearls of wisdom. Heartfelt as this may be, it takes us away from mindful listening.

We know our partner so well, we feel compelled to make sure that he or she does not miss the obvious. We feel that this is the loving thing to do. Often however there is a hidden agenda.

Control and manipulation want to be part of this "party" and often crash in without an invitation. We find ourselves gently nudging our partner into conforming to our idea of who we want him or her to be. I call this the "nudge strategy."

Our work is to be quiet and present, helping to further hold a safe space in which the living images of dreams will appear. We need to be still, actively witnessing. This is a practice of deep observation. It is not passive. Rather, it is being as present as possible without interjecting our opinion.

We must listen closely, sensitively, and with unconditional regard, attempting to let go of all our judgments. This witnessing presence is crucial. Even if unspoken, judgments will be felt in the room. We must try to give our partner the same compassionate listening that we expect in return. We are building a new way of being together that will serve the relationship through the years.

EXERCISE: *Witnessing Dreams without Judgment*

Listen now as your partner shares his or her dream images. As he or she does this, keep coming back to your body and breath. Each time a thought comes, notice it, then let it go and return to your breath. Do not get judgmental when thoughts come up, just the opposite. Give yourself an imaginary pat on the back for noticing thoughts, even the most angry and hurtful ones. Then let the thoughts move on. This will bring you back to your center. You are doing your job, by being present and non-intrusive.

Pay attention to your partner's dreams. You do not need to be "useful." Simply be your deep quiet self, responsive rather than reactive. Just witness.

When your partner is done, say aloud, "Thank you for sharing your dream with me." *Do not comment in any way on the content.*

Next, switch roles and share your dreams, as your partner listens in a responsive, nonjudgmental way. You may wish to take some time between sharing dreams to "clear the field."

Sharing dreams with your partner takes practice. Give yourself credit for taking the time to even try, and don't get discouraged. Like anything we care deeply about, it takes perseverance. Keep at it, and both of you will find it easier.

Step 4—Finding Eros

As we have learned, living images can represent archetypes, such as the Wise Teacher, Animal Companion, Warrior, Demon, Ocean, and so on. In this step we focus on the dream archetype of Lover. She or he comes in many forms, sometimes as a beloved person or animal, other times as a luminous image like the moon or a star. Surprisingly, the Lover image may sometimes appear as a distasteful figure like an old witch or an unkempt troll. It is different for everybody, and often different every time even for the same person.

The presence of the Lover affects us emotionally. It opens something effervescent inside of us. It is filled with life force and attraction. Sometimes the experience is so vital that we even get afraid. Yet no matter what, we continue to feel its invitation into the unknown. Our body reacts with instinctive energy and attraction.

Eros, the Greek god of love, is a classic manifestation of the Lover. Eros brings us into relationship with that special other in remarkable ways. Without his assistance, we would be hard-pressed to find an intimate partner. Even in the age of internet dating, when two people finally come together over dinner, it is the presence or absence of Eros that determines the outcome. This is a good thing. With the help of Eros, people find each other.

The problem comes when we do not recognize Eros as an inner dream figure. Often we may believe that Eros is a real flesh and blood person, and attribute the power of the archetype to a human being. This gives a human the power of the divine over us. If he or she were to threaten to leave the relationship, we would feel tremendously threatened—as if the God of Love himself were in danger of leaving too. If we mistake a human lover for our Inner Lover, we can experience even the slightest of criticisms as rejection by Eros. The loss of this divine Love is devastating.

Even if there is no overt crisis, the passing of time in love relationships results in the flight of Eros. Three months or three years later, when the touch of the Love God's magic is no longer apparent in our partner, we feel empty. We feel that the archetype of Love has left the relationship, and its sparkle has left our life. Our partner no longer seems the same as when he or she was the incarnation of Eros. His or her humanity with all its flaws, is suddenly apparent. These are the times we are tempted to search for love in all the wrong places.

In Dream Tending with partners, we turn back to our dreams. Our work is to rediscover where Eros is still active in our interior realm. As we animate Eros' presence and return to this inner relationship, we will again feel the pulse of libido surge through our veins.

Eros, in his true form as an inner dream figure, is a difficult figure to get to know. Just as in the Greek depiction of him, Eros is mischievous and elusive. Often we are clueless about his ways.

Our task is to find the invisible God of Love in hiding and learn about him. The Eros figure needs to be named and tended. Without engaging this central figure at the heart of the loving relationship, other interventions are just attempts at behavioral adjustment, which result only in grudging tolerance and some semblance of cooperation. Without developing relationship to this living image within, the return of authentic love, compassion, and intimacy is rarely achieved. To rekindle the flames of desire requires taking the time to bring visibility to the invisible lover. This next exercise is designed to evoke Eros and to befriend him.

EXERCISE: *Finding Eros*

This first part of this exercise each partner does individually.

Locate an Eros-like image in your dreams. Begin by looking for whatever image naturally conforms to your idea of a god or a goddess, an angelic figure, or a prince or princess. Or you may use a dream image of someone you know who is very appealing to you. This is a fine path to take, however, you will often discover that the Eros figure is instead some kind of distasteful figure. Paradoxically, your inner Lover may first appear as an old hag, a rundown workhorse, a toad, or something equally repugnant. Do not run from this revelation. Turn and encounter whoever shows up. As fairy tales remind us, the Lover is often in hiding, wearing the cloak of the repugnant, waiting for the kiss that will release him or her from exile.

In whatever way the Eros figure appears to you, work with it now. Draw it in your journal at least three times. Let it emerge more fully in each successive sketch. Or mold the image in clay with your eyes closed. Let your fingers spontaneously work the clay, with no concern for artistic prowess. Do this several times.

Prepare yourself for a journey. The Lover is an image with the power to transform. Like love itself, Eros is complicated, contradictory, and paradoxical. Often as you tend to the Eros image, you will notice changes in its shape and form. This is a natural phenomenon. Allow for the Eros figure to shape-shift. As you depict the image, make sure to stop every ten minutes or so to witness the image as it goes through its changes. Do not get thrown off if the image changes in some way. Stay with it and keep focused. Sometimes the strangest or most difficult image conceals the Lover within it. Eros may live just inside the Beast.

Be patient in tending this image. Do not get seduced into idealizing it, or making it into one of your long-lost lovers. This is not a matter of wish fulfillment or lover's remorse. It's the process of letting the revelation of the image come forward. Look for the first hints of the image revealing itself.

Once you have a sense of the figure coming into visibility, allow a good deal of time to attend to it. This is extremely important. Do not rush to the next activities of the day or turn to your partner to share the news. Take a day, even two, to be with yourself and deepen your newfound relationship to the inner figure before you talk about it with your partner. Feel your heart open, and notice what opens further in the figure itself.

You may want to continue with your sketches or sculpture, or you may read—or even write—a poem that captures the feeling of what is occurring. It is good to write your own poem to the figure. This is an age-old romantic tradition, and the dream figure of Love will respond to your offering.

As in any new love relationship, bringing yourself fully to the process makes all the difference. When the Lover visits, open yourself to it, offering back what has been bottled up inside of you for so many years: your yearning to express love.

After you have expressed yourself to the figure and experienced its response to you, wait a few more days. Then you can share what is happening with it in the safety of your Dream Tending session with your partner. You do not need to tell your partner all the details of your contact with your Inner Lover. It's a new, very personal, intimate relationship that is yours alone. Discern what is to be shared and what is still to be kept private. The important thing is to share the process in which you are engaged. Your willingness to discuss the process of discovery with your partner is what is he or she will appreciate.

Janet and Richard, an Interlude:

Before moving on to step five, let's use the example of an actual couple to elaborate each of the first four steps of couple's Dream Tending.

Janet and Richard had been married for fifteen years and had two children. Their life together consisted of fighting over just about everything: a lack of common interests, the little affection they shared, and the constant blaming and shaming of the other. The circumstances of life together drained them of excitement and interest in each other. They wondered where the love had gone, when had they stopped respecting each other, and whether they were together only for the children. Each had sexual fantasies about other people and yearned to be in a more loving relationship. Sound familiar? There are probably elements of this situation that ring true for all of us.

For Janet and Richard, the touch of Eros had long ago departed. They had fallen in love, had two children, and then Eros had gradually left the scene. Other than their love for the kids, the intimacy between them was gone. Disappointment, hurt, rage, and blame filled the void. They had experienced the death of love and feared a life sentence in the prison of a loveless relationship. They yearned for what they had lost and looked to friends, experts, and self-help magazines for a way back to love. When these attempts did not work, they felt hopeless and estranged.

Eventually Richard and Janet did rediscover their essential love for each other, but not by analyzing the dynamics of their relationship. Turning away from each other and losing themselves in hobbies and careers didn't work either. Finally, in desperation they turned to their dream life. In couple's Dream Tending, they engaged the vitality of the living images of Eros. Each tended the figures that gave spark to their life. It was this that brought them back into relationship.

A significant moment occurred when Janet felt safe to share a dream with Richard. In the dream, a small anemic man was hiding in the corner of a room. The building was run down, dark, and musty. There was no other life present. The anemic figure was emaciated. Janet told this dream aloud to Richard. As difficult as it was for him, Richard did not express his opinions about it. This act of witnessing was important for them.

Then Janet recounted the dream again. This time the dream became more present in the room. Janet used tools that she had learned for working with dream images. She told the story of the dream in the present tense, she did not rush in to interpret, and she hosted the actuality of the living images. Janet centered herself, watching the activity of the dream figure. As she did, the Man in the Corner image began to move a hand and nod his head. She noticed that the dreary room filled with a hint of sunlight. The dream was coming to life. Richard continued to simply witness.

Janet looked at the Man in the Corner with more particularity. She noticed that his skin was getting less pale, and he seemed not as withered. His flesh was more human-like. He was growing some meat on his bones. Then suddenly he moved out of his embryonic posture, into the center of the room. She recognized this dream man! He was not a friend from her awake world, but someone even more special, who had been with her when she was a little girl.

At age four she had met this man in her imaginary play world and took great comfort in his presence. Through her childhood, Janet often saw him in dreams. She woke up in the morning feeling less alone. Around puberty his visits stopped, and Janet had forgotten all about him, until now. Now in the corner of a dark, musky dream room, she had recognized her long forgotten dear friend. He had been her male guardian, and she loved him with all her heart. Janet was beside herself with deep feeling. She also noticed he was different now. He had grown up into an adult man.

As the dreamwork continued, the Man in the Corner became more present. Janet was experiencing a new kind of love, and she was awakening to feelings inside of herself that had long been dormant. Richard watched this unfolding with awe. For once he did not say a word. His breath had been taken away, he was vulnerable, his heart open. He witnessed his partner as soft, open, and in love. He saw her not as a worker, mother, or a homemaker—as much as he admired those qualities in her— but as a lover. Richard was also touched by nostalgia, remembering what he found so alluring and beautiful about Janet when they first met. Now Richard was hooked, invested in the process. He, too, wanted to explore his dreams.

When it was his turn, Richard remembered a dream fragment in which a white fox with crystal blue eyes visited him in a forest. Richard was very pleased with himself. He was now able to join the conversation with Janet by having a dream of his own. White Fox, whom he described as beautiful, sleek, and intriguing, fascinated Richard.

As Richard tended the dream, he got to know White Fox. He felt her presence in the room. Eventually, White Fox gave him permission to touch her fur coat. He closed his eyes, stroking her soft back. As he did this, Richard softened. His body armor dissolved, and his gestures became graceful and sensual.

Witnessing this, Janet was on cloud nine. She did not need to say a word. Her radiance said it all. She remembered at that moment what she loved so about Richard, her partner, a man who once lit up her world.

After Richard interacted with the image of White Fox, Janet talked about her experience of what had just happened. She did not interpret the image, or talk about the content of Richard's experience. She said that she felt honored to be present and to know White Fox. Richard felt deeply affirmed. To feel this level of vulnerability, and to be valued by a woman with whom he was intimate, was revolutionary for Richard.

The living images of Eros had made an appearance for both Richard and Janet. They were able to witness their partner come into relationship with these invisible Lovers. In turn, Richard and Janet's relationship now began to reignite. By first turning to the dream figure of Eros, then to each other, something they thought was impossible became real. They recovered their deep love for themselves and then for each other. Richard and Janet established a firm foundation from which they could meet the challenges and opportunities of their future years together.

All relationships require ongoing attention. There are bound to be peaks and valleys. The hard times, when tended to, are as rewarding as the good times. Besides giving us a way to reconnect to our partner, Dream Tending also presents techniques to go much more deeply into our relationship than we have ever gone before. The next two steps of the couple's Dream Tending process open the way for an entirely new phase of relationship, one that leads to the revelation of the "sacred marriage." To discover this new ground of relationship is, in my experience, to find the alchemist's gold of marriage. Like gold, the sacred marriage is both elemental and of the highest value. For over seventy-six years, my great-grandfather's marriage to his wife Goldie glowed with the radiance of this gold. That is because they shared with one another in very simple yet profoundly intimate ways.

In these last two steps of couple's Dream Tending, you will learn how to tend dreams in a way that opens the sacred marriage inside each partner and cultivates the ground for the transcendent "third body"—the sacred marriage that lives *between* partners. The first step is to attend to the sacred marriage within each of us.

Step 5—Tending the Sacred Marriage

There are living images in our dreams that represent the essence of true partnership. Some call these the masculine and feminine principles, the energies of Yin and Yang, or the play of a Sun god and a Moon goddess, or a Sky god and an Earth goddess. In talking about the importance of these figures, Jungian analyst and author Marion Woodman suggests that they are images of the authentic masculine and feminine in each of us (regardless of our gender) that come together in an inner relationship to form a divine union. She calls the relationship between these images inside us the "sacred marriage." Attending to this sacred marriage is the essence of this stage.

As we develop contact with these inner lovers, we discover that the condition of the sacred marriage affects our own wellbeing, as well as the quality of life with our partner. In my work, I have seen that this inner relationship greatly influences our capacity for self-acceptance and thus our ability to be in a nurturing relationship. Becoming aware of these figures and learning how to tend them is the heart of the sacred marriage.

Our relationship to these figures replaces dysfunctional or missing connections to our parents, heals historical love relationships gone bad, and supersedes unworthy friendships in which we anchor our sense of worth. As we attend to the conjunction of these inner masculine and feminine figures, we experience the love that exists between them. To be loved deeply by this inner couple opens our heart further. We become available to love our life partner at new depths. Even if we're not currently in a relationship, our contact with these immortals of inner life makes a big difference in the quality of our experience.

This process could take months or even years, and the timing can be different for each partner.

EXERCISE: *Tending the Sacred Marriage*

This exercise each partner can do individually.

Identify one of your paintings, sculptures, or writings about the Eros image from step four. Put this in front of you and begin to tune in to the image. Do this at an emotional as well as imaginative level. As you do so, allow the image to animate.

Allow the Inner Lover to attract another dream image that feels like its inner partner. What image is drawn to it in some way? Which dream image does this primary Eros figure call into appearance? Who comes alive to meet Eros?

Once a complementary dream image presents itself, take the time to express it in art or writing, as you did the Eros figure. Repeat this several times. Let this new image grow into its vitality, just as the original Eros figure did.

Once this partner figure has come fully to life, notice the interaction between the two figures. Notice how one figure evokes the other. It will help to spontaneously draw, sculpt, or write what you notice. Let this expression come through your hands into form without any contrivance. Let the dream enactment take on a life of its own.

You will notice that as you repeat this exercise several times, the interaction gets more detailed. Do not make meaning out of this now. Appreciate that there is a dance between these two figures that has a rhythm, cadence, and an intelligence of its own. Just observe. You are witnessing the sacred marriage revealing itself through the expression of the images.

After repeating the above three times, wait a day, then return to the images. Put your expressive works in front of you. Watch how they again come to life and interact. Notice how things continue to move, transmute, and evolve. Similar to relationships between actual people, the interactions between invisible lovers are dynamic and complex. Write down what you are observing.

Take some time each day for the next five days to watch the activity unfolding between this inner couple of the dreamtime. As you come increasingly into relationship with their activity, notice what opens in your emotional life. How has this sacred marriage affected you both personally and in your life with your partner?

Step 6—Honoring the Third Body

As we deepen relationship with personal inner Eros figures, yet another Invisible makes an appearance. This dream figure represents the embodiment of the relationship itself and is different from the sacred marriage within each partner. It is, rather, the dream representation of the sacred marriage between partners. Some call this living image of the relationship the "Third Body," "Relationship Body," or "Marriage Body." The Third Body of a relationship has a life of its own, beyond the two partners.

When I work with couples, I tell them that in tending the Third Body, we are tending the soul body of their couple bond. The image of the Third Body profoundly shapes our feelings for one another. The mood of the relationship is deeply affected by the presence of this overarching entity. I have seen that when the image of the Third Body is dim, the relationship suffers, and when the image is vital there is a sense of belonging to something greater. I also have noticed that the fire of this transcendent image can spark the return of lovemaking. The best sex therapist I know already lives in the heart of the relationship, and once visible, it's amazing how inventive, spontaneous, enjoyable, and passionate erotic contact becomes.

In their fourth month of couple's Dream Tending, Richard and Janet experienced a visitation. It was as if there were another presence in the room, almost a third person. The quality of light changed and the atmosphere seemed to hum. A sweet nostalgia touched Janet deeply, and then Richard. As they looked at one another, they felt the love that had originally brought them together. The image of the Third Body had shown up, and it filled them both with deep emotion.

This image, whom they named "Holder of Love," had an eternal quality. Its presence changed how Richard and Janet related to one another. Richard noticed that the routine activities of life, such as Janet making dinner, became beautiful to watch in Holder of Love's presence. When Holder of Love was in the room, Janet's heart opened and her appreciation of Richard shimmered. She even enjoyed watching Richard read the newspaper, which he did with such intent. They both felt in loving service to Holder. When situations became stressful, they remembered that their relationship included a third figure, an invisible presence who supported them as a couple.

To tend the Third Body effectively we need to sharpen our hosting skills. In the following exercise, we learn the ways of seeing an image originating in the Third Body itself.

EXERCISE: *Honoring the Third Body*

This exercise is to be done as a couple

Identify the dream image or sensation that embodies the transcendent Third Body of your relationship. Look for an image from the dreams of either partner that seems to have a quality of timelessness about it. If you have children, do not mistake one of them for the Third Body. Do not literalize the image to any concrete, external thing. The root image of your relationship exists independent of mortal persons. When you recognize the Third Body and acknowledge it for itself, it will thrive.

Give a name to the image of the Third Body. This is a process of openness and intuitive listening. There is no one right answer, just something that seems to come forward naturally from the figure.

Develop joint activities in order to tend the image with your partner. For example, when you go on a walk in the woods, you might bring an offering of some sort—a piece of fruit, a flower, or a handmade weaving, or anything that feels appropriate can be used to honor the image. Offer it to the Third Body now.

As Dream Tending continues between you, notice how your care for the transcendent image ignites moments of love between you. Take the time to talk about this with your partner. Set aside the business of life to have this conversation. Appreciate that you are feeding the Third Body of your relationship. Become tenders of your relationship's soul by attending to dreams that respond to your work together.

DREAM TENDING: CRISES AND DREAMS

I have worked for over thirty years at the same place, a place that today is called Pacifica Graduate Institute. I started as a paid work-study intern when it was still associated with the University of California. For a while I was on the clinical staff and faculty, and eventually I became the founding president of Pacifica as its own organization. As an independent graduate school, Pacifica is now a thriving center of teaching, learning, and research. As a business it has become quite successful over the years. We started out with just four employees in a one-bedroom apartment. Now we employ over two hundred and fifty people on two campuses overlooking the ocean just south of Santa Barbara.

My formal training is in psychology, not business. I have had to learn the "business of doing business" from the bottom up. I believe that listening to dreams is integral to a quality workplace and a fulfilling work life, yet I know of no career counseling methods or organizational development approaches that include dreamwork. In this section on workplace and vocation, I will show how dreams assist us in staying on mission, supporting work-related interpersonal relationships, making constructive contributions in times of crisis, and even helping guide our vocational aspirations.

The Workplace as Dream

The vision of bringing a dreamlike consciousness to the demands of business presents us right away with a challenge. This idea is usually met with skepticism. Most people think that work life and dream life seem contradictory, even counterproductive. This reaction is typical of the black and white thinking in the fields of business administration and management. Dreams, an expression of inner psychological life, and work, an application of outer world commerce, do not mix. This split in thinking is unfortunate and, ironically, quite costly. Rather than viewing dreams and work as separate, Dream Tending sees the practicalities of work and the insights of dream as expressions of one single, unified, psychic reality, not to be severed or ripped asunder. From this perspective, we see the workplace itself as a dream.

As we keep our dreams alive, we keep our workplaces vital. We discover that the business itself is always dreaming and thus is an extraordinary source of innovation, creativity, and regeneration. Dreams keep a company prosperous and contribute to its fundamental vitality. The workplace is more alive and fun when everyone tends to the inspiration of the company as expressed through the dreams of its employees. Even in times of an organization's worst nightmare, we can use dreams to inform the company's direction.

When people in the workplace can express dreams about the company, they feel connected to its heart and soul. When our colleagues listen to our dreams, we feel like a valuable member of the community, an asset to the group. When we as employees contribute to the company from the dreamtime, company morale soars. Employees who otherwise feel outcast, but who have particular access to their dreams, come forward. They may bring remarkable insight gleaned from dream images, and their participation and newfound sense of worth adds to a dynamic, enriched, and inclusive community spirit. When the dream is valued, good things happen, people are happy, and the future is bright. When the dream is forgotten, then stagnation occurs, market share is lost, and the future dims.

Most everyone has been a part of companies where the guiding dream, the mission, has been lost and a depressive atmosphere has taken hold. In my mind, the source of this despair is that the death of the company's dream spells the end of its psychic health.

The true mission of a company is located in the subjective field of dreams, rather than in the words written on the corporate brochure. This means that when the dreams of a company are forgotten, its mission is not far behind. Prosperity at all levels, including the all-important bottom line, is also sure to go south.

I tend to the mission of Pacifica in the same way that I tend to a dream, by connecting with its deepest expression. When I stay on the surface and try to manage the complexities of the business through structural interventions alone, I miss the hidden dream-based dynamics that underlie the system. On the other hand, when I attend to the business, keeping sight of the dreams, vision, and imaginings of the employees (as well as the extended network of community supporters, vendors, clientele, and elders), I gain access to the deeper wells of insight and wisdom that nourish the mission of Pacifica. Listening mindfully, I am able to hear and feel into its institutional dream body.

What we have learned thus far about tending the living images of dreams can now be applied to the matters of commerce. Using Dream Tending skills, we look now at some of the most pressing concerns in the work setting: money, disruptive employees, rapid change, and organizational crisis. After we have considered these four areas, we will focus on what perhaps underpins them all: aligning ourselves with our true vocation.

Money and the Workplace

I think that dreams of money are some of the most intriguing dreams we have. It is common, however, for us to treat our dreams about money in a different way than other dreams. When we tend to dream images of a turbulent ocean crashing on the shore, a sleek lion on the prowl, a lover embracing us, or an adrenaline-filled chase, we recognize immediately the unmistakable presence of the life force. On the other hand, our tendency is to interpret dreams of money as an unfulfilled wish (winning the jackpot) or the fear of not having enough (going broke). The terror of "boom or bust" dominates our thinking, and we almost never take the time to open the image to its more expansive possibilities.

Dream images of money can represent the life force that is circulating or stagnating in our workplace. When images of money show up in our dreams, I look to the vitality of the work setting as well as to the issues of personal worth. The name we give to our personal life energy is "libido." It is our psychic, instinctual, emotional force and is the motor that powers our behavior. It is easy to see libido in dreams of sex, power, joy, and expansiveness. In a business however, libido comes naturally in the form of money. Money is the motor of business. Currency is the motive juice required to make transactions, buy and sell products, and sustain commerce.

Dream Tending sees dream images of money as related to the flow of a company's vital energy. When the circulation of money in a dream is blocked, we fear bankruptcy. When it is freely moving, we sense prosperity. Money as a dream image tells us a lot about the relative health of a business and our relationship to it.

Money dreams tell us a lot about what is transpiring at the business. For example, when an employee dreams of finding a treasure chest full of money in the basement at work, it suggests more than something about his or her personal circumstances. It can also represent a vibrant work setting. On the contrary, when people have dreams of a robber on the loose at work, or of the paychecks being worthless, they may be revealing the impoverished nature of the business. This poverty can range from financial dysfunction to creative stagnation. In either instance these dreams signal that the pulse of the workplace is weak.

Sometimes we do not look forward to going to the office. This becomes acute when there are tensions as result of scarcity. Under these conditions, I find sharing dreams of money helps relieve these feelings before the condition gets worse. Better still, by sharing our dream images of money, we discover ways to get things back on track.

EXERCISE: *Money and the Workplace*

Start by exploring your own personal relationship to money. Make a brief list of what your wages buy for you. List major items such as rent or mortgage payments, food, clothing, utilities, and so on. After each item on the list, name the essential quality of each item, like Home, Health, Self-Image, and Warmth. You will notice that these characterizations give these things an archetypal sensibility.

Notice any money images from your dreams that correlate to these characterizations. Choose one of them. Tend the dream figure with an eye to exploring its "energy source," or libido. Where does the image get its vitality? Again, notice correlations. What connection exists between the vitality of the image and the energy you feel when receiving or spending money?

As you feel this psychic libido, personify money itself. See it as a living being. What image comes to you, either from a dream or in your active imagination? If Money were a figure what would it look like? Is it wounded in some way? If so, how so?

Observe the activity of this Money figure. What is it up to at the moment? As you watch, notice its relationship to you and yours to it. What opens further in you? Is there a corresponding wound that you feel in your experience?

Now shift your focus to money in the workplace. How does the image you are tending relate to any distress or success at your place of work? How does the image personify what is happening at work in relation to money? What is the image expressing that is going unsaid at work?

Now write a dialogue between the dream image and the psyche of the workplace. Listen to what both sides have to say about themselves and to one another. What do you discover? If you were to act as a counselor to this relationship, what might you suggest to each party? What needs to be said, heard, attended to, and acted upon? Do you notice anything new emerge from this conversation? What seeds for the future can you identify? Write these down.

Disruptive Colleagues

Why is it so difficult to work with disruptive colleagues? Because they create unnecessary stress and make it harder to do our job. I have found Dream Tending to be very helpful in creating constructive outcomes with those colleagues that are the most difficult to work with.

Some of the most effective skills in these situations are those we learned for coping with nightmares. In Dream Tending, we view the person acting out like a nightmarish dream image begging for attention. Tending this figure takes patience, tolerance, and a lot of practice. When we mentally picture a colleague as a living image instead of just a source of aggravation, our tolerance for disruptions increases and we take the time to listen more carefully. The person takes on emotional depth for us, and his or her behavior becomes relevant to us in a new way.

When we see with an imaginal eye, we view such symptoms as a mask for information that has not yet become conscious. From this point of view, at the center of the disruptive colleague's behavior is there a hint of something operating at an unconscious level? Disruptive behavior often represents a goldmine of valuable information lying right below the surface.

EXERCISE: *Disruptive Colleagues*

Write out the ways in which a difficult colleague is being disruptive. Be specific about his or her actual behavior. Then look at your dreams over the past months. Identify a dream image that has similar characteristics to the disruptive colleague. Tend this dream figure as you would a nightmare image.

Once you have worked with the dream image of the colleague, imagine that this employee is an image in the company's dream. Using your Dream Tending skills, ask the questions "What wish or intention lives beneath the bad behavior of the dream figure? Is there the germ of a new idea struggling to come forward? What is this figure calling attention to in the workplace that may be going unnoticed?"

Watch your own dreams for the next week. Notice who shows up. How has your dreaming psyche responded to your Dream Tending with the disruptive colleague?

When you are in the work setting, see how your reactions and responses have changed in relation to the actual employee. Are there ways that you now find value in his behavior? How so?

What information have you garnered about the company's dream, and how might you offer it back to the company?

Rapid Turnover

Tending to living dream images can help us effectively deal with the challenges posed by quick turnover. For instance we may have just been informed that our company needs to retool, downsize, and create a new approach to keep up with a competitor. Management asserts that new talent and new organizational structures are needed to meet the challenge. Of course we immediately feel threatened. Fear rules the day, and dream figures of threat appear.

In these moments, Dream Tending tells us to look more closely at these dreams. This will reveal a curious thing. We may discover that one of the figures in the dream is not terrified, but instead is getting quite excited by the prospect of change and innovation. This figure is not paralyzed or paranoid about the threatened layoff. Instead this figure actually welcomes the opportunity to move in a new direction. It thrives on change.

Dream images, can also point the way forward through the crisis. In an atmosphere of manic makeover, living images in dreams offer pictures of what is out of control, and also what is possible. For example, when the old ways of product marketing are no longer effective, a dream may picture a new design or promotional slogan.

When confronted with the inevitable transitions at work, I find it constructive to realize that change is an organic process, part of being alive. Dreams tap into the ever-changing creative intelligence of the deep psyche. Living images bring resources beyond what the conscious mind can generate or even perceive when events are changing at what feels like warp speed.

EXERCISE: *Rapid Turnover*

> Watch your dreams in times of rapid turnover at work. Often there will be dreams that evoke fear in you. Some of these dream images will bring up familiar themes, perhaps ones from childhood. Insecurity and threat of change have ancient roots within us.
>
> In a dream that shows rapid turnover at the workplace, look for whatever element is new. It may be only a hint, like

a seemingly insignificant gesture or something slightly different in an otherwise familiar dream landscape. Pay attention to whatever is different from what you have experienced in the past. Upon first observation this may be difficult or disturbing. Hang in there with it. Animate the figure by focusing on particularity. The new dream aspect will present itself with more force in the room. Make a sketch of what has emerged.

Notice the other dream images that this figure is drawn to. Who supports this figure? Spend time deepening your relationship to this second, supportive dream image. Sketch this figure on a separate piece of paper. You now have both the new aspect and the supportive figure in front of you on paper.

Now look for the threatening image or circumstance in the dream. This will not be hard because most likely it is the most dominant in the dream. Make a sketch of this threatening image, too.

Place all three sketches in front of you. Move them around and put them into varying relationships with one another until you find the placement that feels right. Now view the sketches from multiple directions. What new perspectives do you see? Notice how your curiosity creates comfort in you, not agitation and fear. You are centered in the resources of the dreamtime. Breathe in the confidence of being anchored in multiplicity all the way down to your feet.

Write a paragraph to yourself about how you will navigate and even thrive in the workplace as it goes through its changes. Be alert for the opportunities that open to you. As you experience one door shutting, get fascinated by the many others that open. Watch for these open doors in the dreams that come over the weeks and months. Pay attention to the figures who walk through them.

Crisis in the Workplace

All workplaces experience times of crisis. Sometimes these upheavals are external, like a stock market crash, natural disaster, or loss of customers to a competitor. Other times, the crisis may be internal and manifest as a power struggle between employees, illegal activity like embezzlement, harassment, or conflict in management style. Crisis happens. How we approach the challenge separates successful companies from those that go down.

Dream Tending helps us deal with conflict, chaos, and disruption. The key is to become responsive, not reactive, to the situation at hand. It is crucial not to get caught up in the firestorm of the moment. As we have learned, when a dream image is "hot" and acting out, a generative idea is perhaps being indirectly expressed. Our task is to see into the crisis and observe what new life is struggling to become free. Even in the circumstances of external threat it is important to remember that when a wildfire burns through the dry forest, fresh seeds will germinate with the next rains.

When we pay attention to dreams during times of turmoil, we discover that images bring knowledge of how to navigate the crisis. We can access this information by amplifying our dream images to their archetypal counterparts. These stories tell of how to engage, conquer, or solicit help in times of upheaval and chaos.

For example, imagine we have a typical anxiety dream, in which everything is collapsing all around us. We are trapped in a catastrophe, terrified and helpless. We could imagine that such a dream relates to the organizational chaos we're experiencing at work. By amplifying this image to the corresponding story of Chicken Little, we are alerted to the futility of responding to the crisis in a reactive way. Chicken Little teaches us to let go of our panic and deal directly and concretely with the situation at hand.

EXERCISE: *Crisis in the Workplace*

Look at the images arising in your dreams. Bring your attention to aggressive images such as a bully, or a predatory animal. These are examples of images that represent threat from the outside. Also look for images of tidal waves, earthquakes, forest fires, or houses with crumbling foundations. These are images that suggest there is something out of control happening.

When these images present themselves, get anchored, get curious, and explore through your skills of amplification the archetypal stories they connect to. Notice how these universal stories reveal something of the complexity of the situation at work. Often they depict both the crisis and the resources needed to navigate a constructive course through the upheaval. Identify the lessons in the story that are applicable to your work situation. If you identify a particularly important image, give it a name. This image holds the keys to understanding the restoration of the workplace.

Now reverse the process. Tend to the crisis situation at work as you would a nightmare. Look for how certain dream images of the crisis at the workplace transform and evolve as you bring your attention to them. How do images of crisis at work reveal new possibilities?

Approach your Dream Tending at the workplace with confidence and in a responsive way. Observe the emergency at work, remain objective, and view this cycle in time as if it were a dream. Write down the lessons that you have learned from your dreams in relation to the crisis at work.

Vocation: Answering the Call

"I am not my job." At times this declaration rings loudly in our lives. Beneath our job responsibilities, work tasks, and career identity lives our true and authentic vocation. True vocation is not a job, per se, but a deeper sense of calling. It is a fate that lives inside of us and may be greater than our current career. When we are in alignment with our vocation we feel productive and fulfilled. However, when work is out of alignment with our aspirations, we burn out, feel depleted, and work life becomes an ordeal.

When we feel that life is "just not working any longer," we experience a crisis of identity. We know that a new direction is required, but change is very difficult. It threatens our self worth, our economic security, and the expectations that others have of us. This is because our identity is linked to our sense of vocation. With family, life, and fortune threatened, we find ourselves on the edge of despair.

In this dark night of the soul, it is extraordinarily valuable to turn to our dreams. Dreams tell us what is happening. They depict the difference between vocation and obligatory employment. They offer ideas about unrealized aptitude and point to inherent gifts. They point the way forward to the authentic impulse at the root of our true vocation.

As we have discovered in working with living dream images, their appearance usually precedes behavioral change. First comes the image, then the response, therefore it is hardly ever a good idea to make a grand career change overnight. To do so misses the intelligence of the dreaming psyche.

What we must face first is the stark truth that the current path is no longer giving us real satisfaction. Then we follow the dream images that point us along the trail toward our true vocation. Dream Tending here becomes a process of uncovering the way back to our destiny, inner calling, and life purpose. Dreams point the way homeward.

Homecoming is a return to our essential nature and true temperament. This may be related to a more creative and intuitive self-expression. But this does not mean that we are all meant to be poets or artists. Many following the Dream Tending process find their vocations in the sciences, engineering, accounting, or psychotherapy. Vocation gives expression to the life force moving through us, whatever that may be.

EXERCISE: *Finding Vocation*

When you feel the call of your vocation, your first task is to go into business for yourself. This does not mean a literal job change. It means that you must open your own imaginal company, by yourself, on behalf of yourself. Do this now. In active imagination, form a new corporation and give it your first and last name followed by Inc. For example, I would form a new corporation called Steve Aizenstat, Inc.

Now create a personal mission statement. This statement expresses your sense of calling. Write this down.

Next, gather information from your dreams. Watch the dream images as they point you in directions that are different from what you are familiar with. This is quite different than a job assessment exercise. You are observing the generative psyche as it maps the way back to your innate desire. Write down what you are noticing.

Each figure of the dreaming psyche will have something to say regarding the questions "What is being asked of me now?" and "What is my true calling?". Begin an active dialogue between you and these dream figures. Look for the majority stockholder in this enterprise and the emerging

CEO. This may be a figure other than you. Your job is to bring all of who you are into conversation with the living images, particularly the new CEO in making.

When working with these dream images, think about your parents and their vocations. Were they happy at work? Were they fulfilled? Or did they have unexpressed desires? Name some of your parents' unfulfilled vocational hopes.

Now turn your attention back toward your own dreams. What recurring dream images from childhood come into your awareness? Find an image that seems to have as much relevance for one of your parents as it does for you, and let this image come forward. Look for the desire, the yearning, at the root of the dream figure. Does this desire match the unmet vocational wishes of your parents in some way? Now consider your grandparents and other members of your family. Continue to tend the figure.

Stay with the process. As you tend to this living image, notice what gets pushed inside of you. What clarity and certainty arises? What dream landscape do you see? Consider this as the ground of your convictions. Watch the figure standing firmly on this ground.

Now with the companionship of the dream image, you are ready to reconsider your direction in life and to realize your emerging vocational interests. Together, you are able to take steps with confidence and care. Notice how wonderful it is to begin to come home to your true vocation.

Chapter Four

THE WORLD'S DREAM

When my great-grandfather left Belarus for America, he was
dreaming of finding a better life. He was escaping persecution,
but also hoping to enjoy prosperity impossible for him in his
own country. Family legend had it that his cousin Benny, who
had emigrated to America years earlier, had become a rich and
powerful businessman in the wondrous city of New York. It was
said that all you had to do was get yourself to his doorstep and
cousin Benny would shower you with gold. For a nineteen-year-
old that story was all it took. He wanted to follow in Benny's
footsteps; he too wanted his share of America's gold. And so
he boarded a ship that crossed the ocean, and with many other
hopefuls, arrived at Ellis Island.

My great-grandfather spent a few hungry weeks knocking
about the streets of New York City, looking for cousin Benny.
When he finally found him, Benny turned out to be broke.
Disappointed but not discouraged, Zadie tried his luck in New
York for a few more years before eventually making his way
west to warm and sunny California, the Golden State. The Los
Angeles area around 1910 was covered with groves of orange
trees, their flowers blossoming, their scent sweetening the air.

With dream eyes, he saw in the landscape of California the very gold that had lured him from so far away.

With everything that he had experienced, Zadie had learned to see the world as a living dream, full of meaning. For him even the city streets, buildings, and motorcars of Pasadena were living things with interior lives, dreaming their own dreams. This aspect of the living dream—what I call the "World's Dreaming"—forms the basis of Dream Tending's most unique teaching. In this chapter we will follow this idea down the rabbit hole and discover even more powerful ways of working with dreams.

A New Way of Viewing the World

"The world is *alive!*" great-grandfather always said. As he put it in his lyrical style, "You can find life even in a shoe cobbler's knife." For a modern person to say that the world is alive is unusual, because for a long time our culture has believed that the world is anything but alive. The modern, science-based worldview has no room for a statement as seemingly irrational as "the world is alive," yet this idea is the core of Dream Tending. It is the heart of our work.

Thus far we have experienced dream images as alive. They affect how we experience our lives and influence virtually everything that we do. We now have the requisite background and experience to go to the next level of Dream Tending. Like crossing the ocean to a new world and arriving at Ellis Island, this next step is more than a leap of faith; it is a departure from the outdated and an arrival in the possible. Just as great-grandfather needed a new way of seeing to understand the richness of his surroundings, this next level of Dream Tending will ask us to experiment with a worldview that playfully and soulfully sees the world as alive and always dreaming.

In order for us to take this next step in our Dream Tending journey, it is helpful to examine the scientific worldview and its relationship to dreaming. So now I'll don my professor's robes, get out my chalk, and start scribbling on the blackboard! Hang in there with me, because understanding this background and context is essential.

For many people, the idea that the world is alive and always dreaming is quite easy and natural to accept. They may have an experience of this reality on a walk along a forest trail or down an old, winding street. For others, though, it seems to fly in the face of everything they have learned about the world. But the idea itself is actually quite natural to human beings. In ancient times, virtually every person would have agreed with such a viewpoint. As Richard Tarnas puts it in his book, *Cosmos and Psyche*:

> *The primal human being perceives the surrounding natural world as permeated with meaning, meaning whose significance is at once human and cosmic. Spirits are seen in the forest, presences are felt in the wind and the ocean, the river, the mountain. Meaning is recognized in the flight of two eagles across the horizon, in the conjunction of two planets in the heavens, in the unfolding cycles of Sun and Moon. The primal world is ensouled. It communicates and has purposes.*

Primal humans experienced a strong, meaningful, and continuous connection to the world around them. The world was like a person: it had its dreams, and it would often share those dreams with passersby. It is only in the last five hundred years with the rise of empirical science and the gradual transition to urban living that we have lost our primal relationship to nature. I often notice how people today have little awareness of the changes in seasons, the phases of the moon, the ebb and flow of the tides, and other natural cycles. We experience animals either as alien, dangerous, invading killers, or as sterilized, domesticated pets that have had the wildness systematically bred out of them. How often have we walked in a wilderness area and experienced ourselves as just another creature among many, neither more nor less important than the others? How often have we slept in a place without walls, doors, and a ceiling? Where and when do we see the stars, hear the songs of the animals, smell the loam beneath our feet? As science has progressed, we have mostly been thrown out of our Eden, forgotten our place in the world, and been severed from the wisdom of its dreamlike consciousness.

Of course it is all too easy to elevate the experience of early humans to a paradisiacal fantasy. We must not forget that their lives were short and rife with disease, pain, ignorance, fear, and oppression. The coming of modern science is one of the most positive things that has ever happened to humanity. Science has empowered us in ways that were previously inconceivable. In the course of a few short centuries, it has allowed us to substantially improve the health, socio-political circumstances, and material wellbeing of millions of people. The scientific worldview is here to stay, and that's a very good thing.

However, the rise of modern science was a dramatic transformation that revolutionized the philosophical underpinnings of our society. It changed the way we think about the world and our place in it. Many people came to see themselves not as part of the world, but as masters of it. Science lifted up and nearly deified the supremacy of the human mind—not the mind in its totality, but only its narrow, logical, rational, linear aspects. All other expressions of the mind—intuition, dreams, emotions, play, and so forth—have been for the most part devalued and marginalized. The scientific worldview sees these parts of our minds as childish, backward, fuzzy, naïve, and even dangerous.

At this late date, few people can be unaware of the drastic problems that lurk in the shadow of this philosophy. For all we have gained from our logical, rational view of the world, we have forsaken a fundamental part of ourselves. While giving us dominion over nature, the achievements of science have also allowed us to despoil the planet, eradicate countless species, and threaten the survival of life itself. People today live in such an extreme state of alienation from the natural world and one another that it can only be seen as a kind of pathology.

The fundamental cause of this problem is that we conceive of the world as a dead, unconscious, meaningless machine—an object of *quantities*, not *qualities*, that can be measured, categorized, and manipulated with mathematical and mechanical operations. The point here is not that this idea is wrong, but, simply, that *it is not the complete picture.*

SOLAR VERSUS LUNAR CONSCIOUSNESS

During the Enlightenment, in which science became the dominant philosophy of the western world, the sun was metaphorically seen as the light of reason. The rational, logical, linear, analytical mind was the source of this light, what we might call "solar" consciousness (to borrow a metaphor from Plato). In the brilliant glare of this solar consciousness, all other forms of consciousness were seen as the shadow of this one light. Human instincts, emotions, imagination, intuition, and so forth were relegated to the realm of darkness, the night of the human mind, and have come to be seen as representing everything backward and regressive.

When the world is seen from the viewpoint of solar consciousness, as Richard Tarnas has often said, there is only one right answer, only one right way of viewing the world. Yet when the world is seen as a place where everything is alive and in communication—that is, as an interactive dance of multiple subjects possessing their own interiority—then metaphorically we are no longer oppressed by the unitary, solar viewpoint. For when the sun goes down, the night sky reveals an entire universe of stars, each one of them a sun in its own right, each one of them with its own knowledge, its own viewpoint, its own truth, its own interiority. This type of consciousness, which by contrast we might call "lunar," sees all things as alive and meaningful. Lunar consciousness includes all the marginalized parts of ourselves that are so necessary to our health and to the health of the world: the emotional, the non-rational, the intuitive, the beautiful.

In the natural cycle of things, day is followed by night, which is in turn followed again by day. In the same way, Dream Tending does not suggest that the scientific mind is somehow wrong—in fact, Dream Tending celebrates this vital aspect of ourselves— but simply that there is time enough for all the various aspects of our consciousness to shine their own kind of light. To be stuck in one mode of consciousness all the time is a kind of pathology, just as if night were to disappear and the world was left to burn under the unending glare of the sun.

The concept of lunar consciousness includes dreams and the dreaming mind, and it is my hope that we may reclaim this crucial aspect of consciousness. In so doing we may find a way to rebalance our relationship with the world and ourselves. When my great-grandfather said that the world is alive, he hinted toward this healing. From the perspective of Dream Tending, it represents an essential truth that we must understand for our own sake and for the sake of the whole world. The motto of Pacifica Graduate Institute is the Latin phrase: *animae mundi collendae gratia*, which means, "for the sake of tending the soul of the world." When we imagine the world to be alive, we imagine it as having a soul as well. This ensouled world can dream, just as we do. The answer to the question "Who is dreaming?" may be a surprise.

THE WORLD'S DREAM

The deeper we go into the mind, the more the lunar qualities of human consciousness become prominent. In Western psychology, we understand the nature of the dreaming psyche as existing primarily in three dimensions of experience, all related to the human condition: 1) awake circumstances, or the *waking consciousness;* 2) personal development, or the *personal unconscious;* and 3) a trans-cultural sensibility, or the *collective unconscious.* We've always known the modern form of waking consciousness. Freud developed the concept of the personal unconscious, and Jung the concept of the collective unconscious. All of these dimensions of psychological reality are person-centered, and the understanding of dreams we use in these systems focuses on the personal or cultural human experience. When we consider the world to be alive and ensouled, we must expand our concept to include nature as well. We must move from being person-centered to being world-centered. This is not hard to do, if we stop for a moment, quiet down, and listen to what lives just outside the relentlessly chattering thoughts in our heads.

Reaching back to diverse and ancient traditions as well as forward to the new concepts found in archetypal and ecological psychology, we add a fourth dimension: an ecological consciousness, or what we might call the world unconscious. This fourth dimension of the psyche goes beyond human experience—even trans-cultural human experience—to appreciate that the psyche lives not only inside human beings, but also that humans can experience the greater field of the psyche. In Dream Tending, we see all the phenomena of the world (humans, creatures, trees, waves, buildings, rocks) as having inner natures. Dream images are not representations of our personal nature only, but are also informed by the subjective inner natures of the things and creatures out there in the world. When viewed from the perspective of the world unconscious, dream images do not come exclusively from within us, but also originate in and of the world "out there." In other words, it is not just you who are dreaming, the world itself is also dreaming. I prefer to call this aspect the "World's Dream."

In Dream Tending we experience each phenomenon, object, or creature as part of the *anima mundi* or "world soul." All things have an innate subjective quality that presents itself in dream images. In other words, when I work with an image I realize that it is, of course, part of the dreamer's experience. Yet in addition, it is part of the broader World's Dream. From the viewpoint of the World's Dream, the images in dreams do not refer only to us, nor are they restricted to our personal history or humanity's collective history. At this level dream images come on their own behalf, for their own reasons, as part of Nature's own dream of which we experience but a part. We have already worked with this concept quite a bit using the technique of animation. Here, however, we are encountering the idea *behind* animation in its fullness, which allows us to go much farther with it.

When we touch the World's Dream, we expand outside of the human realm altogether. Here we realize that dream images originate in the soul of the world as well, and we can have an experience of those dreams. A dream image of a rock, for example, shows something about its particular reality. Further, it expresses something on behalf of the World's Dream as a whole.

The same is true with a dream image of a bear, or a stream, or a building in a city. Individual images make an appearance and show themselves in dreams on behalf of their own subjective reality as well as that of the totality of the interrelated ecosystem of the world. Thus each of our own dream images contains the mundane, the personal, the cultural, and the world levels all at once within itself.

So according to Dream Tending, the deepest answer to the question, "Who is dreaming?" is "It is the multi-dimensional world who is dreaming." Perhaps the gold that entered my great-grandfather's dreams came not from his sense of impoverishment, but rather from the landscape of California itself. From the level of the World's Dreaming, we might see California's oranges reaching out and entering into Zadie's dreams half a world away, beckoning him with golden images. Because of his understanding that the world is alive, he was able to recognize the fulfillment of his journey when at last he came to California and walked through the orchards, their branches heavy with the sweet juice of golden oranges.

Landscape—The Forgotten Aspect

The world dreams and presents itself to us through its dream images. While this concept may be simple to grasp, I have found it is very difficult to put into practice. We are trained that dream images belong to us and relate only to us personally; they seem to be totally "ours." In dreamwork we continually come back to what dreams mean about us. However, if we want to go to the very deepest levels of experience and encounter the soul of the world, we have to remember that dream images do not belong just to us, and that sometimes they may be about things far outside personal concerns. They are the expression of Nature herself, effortlessly arising in our dreams.

Of course to see dreams as representing aspects of our personality or dimensions of our life circumstances is legitimate. Yet this narrow view traps us in our egoistic concerns and keeps us separate from the people, creatures, and flora of this world, as well as from the world itself. At this stage we need to break out of self-referential dream interpretation and into the open fields and panoramic vistas of the World's Dream. But how do we do this?

Through working with the dreams of thousands of people, I have found a fairly simple way to tap into conscious awareness of the World's Dream. The access point is actually right beneath our feet in every dream we have, and yet it is almost always overlooked. This doorway to the World's Dream is the *dream setting* itself, the *landscape* of the dream.

When people work with their dreams, they tend to ignore the landscape, and instead are drawn into the characters and action of the dream. This is only natural. We all watch the characters of a drama and tend to ignore the scenery. Yet just because we don't pay attention to the setting doesn't mean that it is not important.

Dream Tending teaches us to pay very close attention to the landscape of our dreams, which I call the "dreamscape." I have found that when we focus attention on the dreamscape first, it hooks us into the power of the World's Dream right away. Having done this, the other aspects of the dream, the characters and action in which we are so interested, will then animate much more vividly. It is as if all the dream figures are fed and enlivened by the dreamscape.

As we explore the dreamscape, we discover that the World's Dream is the fundamental ground of dreaming. It is the realm of consciousness through which all else happens in the dream. Let's experiment with this now

EXERCISE: *Landscape—The Forgotten Aspect*

Choose a dream from your journal to read or speak aloud from memory. Remember to recite it in the present tense, as if it were happening now. Pay particular attention to the setting where the dream takes place. Where is the dream located? Does it take place in the forest, the city, the mountains, the elementary school that you attended as a child, your backyard, outer space, or some other landscape that you have never seen before? Identify the setting.

Now prepare yourself to explore the setting. Do so by separating from the drama or the emotions of the dream. Let go of any intense or intriguing characters. Shift from a person-centered perspective to a world-centered perspective. Metaphorically, you are going to explore this landscape in the mode of a "naturalist." A naturalist is intensely interested in both the details of an area, and in how these details all fit together to make up the total environment. One way to do this is to use your narrowly focused "solar" vision to see the details of the dream landscape, but also to broaden your gaze and use "lunar" vision to take in the totality of what surrounds you. Listen for sounds of the environment, like birds chirping, water flowing in a stream, or waves crashing on the shore. Encounter this place in similar ways with your other senses of touch, smell, and taste.

Explore the dreamscape as if you were here for the first time. Relax, open your awareness, and become part of your surroundings. Do not make assumptions about what it might be like. Open up to your sense of curiosity and wonderment. What is going on here? What are you noticing?

Take a breath. Get a sense of the smell of the place. What scents are you picking up? Notice what awakens in your body as you smell these. Are you attracted or repulsed? Walk about the landscape following your nose rather than your reason. Let the landscape draw you further inside. Go toward whatever interests you in a sensual, embodied way. Follow your curiosity.

As you enter the dreamscape more fully, get acquainted with the land. Imagine that you are an animal and walk about in the dream with animal legs and an animal's sensibility. As you do, notice how the setting animates and comes to life. What stands out? What kind of place is this? What interests you about it?

As always, resist the desire to interpret what you see, reduce it to a psychological phenomenon, or pathologize it. You have already spent much time listening to dream images speak on their own behalf. Now do the same thing with this dream landscape. Imagine for a moment that it exists independent of you, speaks for itself, and is engaged in its own activity. You are not the center of its concern, but instead are merely a curious visitor in a new and fascinating place. The dreamscape is dreaming its own dream, in its own time, and in its own natural manner. Tune into its sensibility, its textures, and its mood, which may be very different from your own. What is going on in the landscape's dream? How does it express itself? What kinds of moods, qualities, atmospheres, climates, soils, bodies of water, rock formations, plants, animals, and skies reveal themselves as part of the landscape's dreaming? How do you feel as you wander, explore, and interact with this place?

Walking through this landscape, notice what comes your way. There are probably more living things in this dreamscape than you may have thought. Notice that the landscape brings with it a diversity of creatures and things, all interacting with each other. With such a large group of beings in dialogue, it would be absurd to imagine yourself to be the center of attention. Instead, you are merely one being among many inhabiting this dreamscape.

It is not necessary at this point to make any meaning out of what you have discovered. More important is the experience of "getting here" and becoming familiar with how the dreamscape has a life of its own. If it seems appropriate, write down your thoughts about what you have found here.

The Ensouled World

Human beings evolved to live in tightly knit tribal groups in constant contact with animals and nature. We have a deep psychological need to feel connected with the people, the animals, and the environment around us. We reach out to them from our souls and feel them responding from their own. The world is a place alive with soul.

Whether or not this is literally true, Dream Tending teaches that the idea of an ensouled world is certainly *psychologically* correct. In order to live full, rich, and meaningful lives, we must live as if the world around us is alive, has a soul, and is filled with meaning in its every nook and cranny, its every animal, rock, and tree. Because a world without soul offers us no intimacy, no possibility of belonging or connection, it denies us the very thing that we need most deeply. We are creatures of meaning and connection, and we can only thrive in a world of meaning and connection.

A natural route to this ensouled world is through the senses. When we touch the basic sensuality of nature, we immediately break through the cold, rigid confines of rationality and into the warm, embodied world around us. When we perceive beauty, our hearts come to life and our imagination awakens. The world becomes a place of enchantment. For example, when I walk in a cityscape and take the time to appreciate the architectural grace of a building or the sculpted curves of a fountain, I feel touched and inspired. Hiking in the mountains, swimming in the ocean, camping in the forest, I open my senses and nature responds with her music. An ensouled world speaks directly to the depth of my own soul and I feel intimately related to whom and what is around me. Without this quality of contact, the world feels deadened and so do I.

The world is always available to us. When I attune myself to the world around me through my senses, it is no longer an object for me to simply analyze and investigate, but a living, breathing subject with its own inner life and its own subjectivity

I remember playing on the beach one afternoon when I was about twelve years old. I walked away from my family, the crowds, parking lots, and concession stands with their huge letters on the roof announcing FOOD. On the other side of the point, I discovered a large rock in a tide pool. I ran over and sat on this irresistibly huge rock. Then I did what came quite naturally; I had a conversation with the rock. I looked into its face as it looked into mine. It seemed to say, "Hey, how are you? Good that you are here and sitting on me." I spent a long time with the rock, listening as it told its stories, not in words, but through its appearance, texture, and form.

After a while, a tall, strong-bodied surfer, who was about eighteen years old, came toward the rock and me. Given that I was not yet an adolescent, he seemed like a god to me. As he passed, he said, "Did you know that rocks can talk?" He said it quite casually and then walked off, but the effect these words had on me was not casual. I had always known this secret, but since Zadie had passed away, I had not met anybody else who could hear those kinds of voices.

Two hours later, as the tide was coming in, I wandered back to the other side of the point, as if in a dream. The ocean flashed with vibrant, churning color; people glowed with life, even the cars took on a glittering new wonder. It seemed that I only needed the affirmation that the world is alive to suddenly burst into soul connection with it.

As I have grown older, I have had many experiences of being touched by ensouled landscapes. I now wonder about the psychological concept of projection, which in these cases says that the life we seem to see in things is merely a product of our imagination projected onto them. In my opinion, this idea must be turned on its head, or at least on its side. The truth is that projection sometimes works the other way around. The things of this world are sharing their imagination, their dream life, with us. In an animated landscape we all affect one another with our presence. As James Hillman says,

> [the things of an ensouled landscape] announce themselves, 'look here we are.' They regard us beyond how we may regard them, our perspectives, what we intend with them, and how we dispose of them. This imaginative claim on attention bespeaks a world ensouled.

Besides encountering the soulfulness of the everyday, awake world, we can do the very same thing with the dreamscape. It too is alive and ensouled. We need only avail ourselves of our lunar consciousness, our ability to see with the eye of a poet or artist, to encounter this fabulously alive universe.

EXERCISE: *The Ensouled World*

Bring your focus to the dreamscape. Imagine walking through the dream landscape as if everything in it were alive and animated. Pay less attention to the main characters and their interactions. With an open mind and a broad vision, scan the landscape. Prepare for the unexpected. Allow what has been invisible or otherwise out of awareness to become visible now. What figures or things, previously neglected or unseen, now come forward?

When these newly visible aspects present themselves, see them aesthetically using multiple lenses of perception. With an artist's eye, see first with a focus for detail and then with a peripheral vision that opens up wider vistas. Look for the colors, textures, and patterns that show themselves on the surface of things or on the face or body of the creatures who occupy this place. Then, like looking at a piece of art, let the inherent beauty or particular quality that makes each entity aesthetically unique show itself. When experiencing the dreamscape in this way, notice how many of the residents of this place come forward, and say, "Hello." Take a moment and become part of this living ecology; experience how this dreamscape is expressed through the figures inhabiting it.

Check in with your own experience. How are you being affected by what is alive in the dreamscape? Do not project your experience into the figures. On the contrary, notice how the inner life of the dream figures makes itself known to you. Which dream figure seems to reach out and make a "claim" on you or seems to ask for attention? What are you feeling now? Record your experiences in your journal.

The Landscape Is the Dreamscape

A few years ago I was driving to Big Sur on Highway 1, overlooking the Pacific Ocean. It seemed like I was the only person on the road, winding my way through a soft, gray mist shrouding the verdant mountainsides that plunged into the sea. This is the road I take to Esalen, a journey that always fills me with pleasant anticipation.

As the road curved around another massive cliff, the fog suddenly thinned and rays of sunlight illuminated the foaming, crashing waves below. The mountain grasses shone like polished emeralds, and overhead a brilliant rainbow shimmered to life. Then, as if on cue, a huge buck stepped from the forest onto the road just ahead.

I slowed to a stop. The buck stopped, too, and turned to lock eyes with me. There, on a hillside by the sea, Buck and I looked into each other, one creature to another. In the electricity and warmth of that connection, I was no longer a driver in a car just putting the miles behind me. I was a part of this place, this moment, this world. The sounds of breaking waves, the color of the rainbow, and the presence of the huge buck drew me into the living immediacy of the landscape.

Although this was a magical experience, it was not magic. The world itself was manifesting a dream in which I was participating. This remote coastal cliff was hosting the fog, the sunlight, the rainbow, the waves, Buck, and me. For those moments, I was in a time out of time: the dreamtime.

After a while, Buck slipped back into the mountains, the fog descended again, and the rainbow vanished. I restarted the car and continued my drive up the coast. I did not analyze what had just happened, nor did I interpret the events as a sign of some kind. Rather, I just appreciated the deeper reality in which I had participated.

Arriving at Esalen, I spoke about dreamtime consciousness as a state of awareness rather than an experience that occurs only when our eyes are closed. The experience I had just shared with Buck demonstrated exactly that. Dreams are not a product of the unconscious mind, but rather a revelation of the living psyche, a dimension of experience that exists everywhere, at all times, and includes all phenomena.

Often it takes an extraordinary event, like my experience with the buck, to break through our habitual patterns and see behind the veil of our human-centered preoccupations. In these exceptional moments we experience the animation of the World's Dream. We realize that the dream does not originate only in us, but also originates in the world. We, along with everything else, are participants in the landscape of the dreaming world. The animated landscape is a kind of dreamscape, arising from the World's Dream. It is the world itself that is dreaming, and the landscape that hosts the action. The landscape is the place from which and in which dreams arise. From this viewpoint, we are always surrounded by a living expression of the World's Dream.

Tapping into this continuous dream is not difficult. It just takes a willingness to notice the dreamlike moments that are always occurring. The incident with the buck was an example of one such moment. Intrusions of the dreamtime into the waking world are happening all around us at every moment.

One way to tune into the World's Dream is simply to notice anything that strikes you as a little bit dreamlike. Sometimes the play of light, or the composition of the clouds and sun, or a dog riding as the passenger in a convertible is enough to draw us into awareness of the World's Dream. There are many of these doorways open to us all the time.

Once we begin to notice these dreamlike moments in everyday life, we naturally want to go further into the dreamscape in which we are living. We find ways of approaching the dreamscape that are sympathetic to the natural rhythms of the landscape itself. As always in Dream Tending, this means to let go of the need to be logical, rational, and analytical. The landscape-dreamscape exists for its own sake and has its own needs, desires, and modes of expression. Much like a person, it has its personality and appearance, and asks for relationship with us, not for more self-absorbed preoccupation about us. The dreamscape is not a narcissistic mirror in which we adore our own reflected image, our own shortcomings, or our own needs. Left to itself, the dreamscape shines in its own rhythm with its own life. I often wonder how it would be if the dreamscape put up "no-trespassing" signs to keep the ego and its pranksters out altogether.

Earlier I discussed the naturalist mode of interacting with dreams, to actively explore a dreamscape with as much curiosity and specificity as possible. When we work with the World's Dream, however, we can go even further than this, using a mode that I call "shamanic." In many indigenous cultures, the shaman is attuned to the land and all that is upon it. She or he serves as the mediator between the everyday world of human beings and the dreamtime. In Dream Tending, to work in the shamanic mode means to understand that every moment is filled with images from the World's Dream. In shamanic mode, we experience the landscape around us and ourselves as expressions of what Australian aboriginal peoples call the "dreamtime." We encounter everything from the smallest ant to the largest cloud as pregnant with meaning and soul.

Two skills can help us as we move through the World's Dream in a shamanic manner. The first is our ability to notice synchronicities. These acausal connections are the hallmark of a dream-like state of mind, so paying attention to them pulls us naturally into an awareness of the dreamtime. Synchronicities benefit greatly from selective attention, which means that once we start looking for them, we will suddenly notice them with shocking frequency. The second skill employed in the shamanic mode is our ability to notice complementarities. In the context of Dream Tending, complementarities are the way that certain things seem to have a funny sort of affinity for each other. Noticing complementarities can also plop us right into an awareness of the World's Dream.

When I went back in memory and tended my experience with Buck, I first realized that all the images (fog, ocean, rainbow, buck) were dreams of the landscape itself. They were all interacting as figures in nature's dreamscape. In this dream they came into a synchronistic relationship on a cliff by the ocean. At that moment, I became present and still, and actively noticed the complementarities, what liked to be with what. Fog likes Rainbow, Buck likes Mountain Grass, and so forth. I even started to notice how the creatures and the nonliving things each seemed to look at each other. Sun looked at Buck and Ocean, Rainbow looked at Me, Ocean, Grass. I became fascinated with the beauty that was showing itself. In this state of shamanic awareness I experienced a larger dreamtime consciousness. In turn, I experienced in myself a depth capable of sustaining contact with all who shared this moment.

At this level of the dreamtime, each figure is a visitation of a "god" in the ancient sense. Each image shows itself with a radiance that opens the heart and the soul. Buck was more than some seven-pointed trophy animal. He was a living image, a deity of the World's Dream. Dream Tending is the art of keeping curiosity alive and continuing one's involvement with the image. Engaging images in this way keeps us open and responsive to the world. When the landscape animates, the poetics of imagination activate, and we live for a time in the field of the World's Dream, in its wondrous ongoing process of imagining. The curtain is lifted, and the landscape becomes a dreamscape that invites us to experience its dream.

EXERCISE: *The Landscape Is the Dreamscape*

Take a moment and review the "awake" events of the last two weeks. Identify an experience that seemed out of the ordinary or dreamlike. Take yourself back into this memory and imagine it as a waking dream. Consider how you were inside a set of circumstances that originated from something more than your own making. Allow this montage of events, feelings, and images to become more vivid. What aspects stand out and take on an almost luminous quality? Notice how this experience is similar to being in a dream.

Tend to this waking dream as if it were a dream of the night. Bring to your work the awareness that the world itself is participating in this dreamlike experience. Also notice how in this experience time seems to slow down and your perception becomes more spatial, less linear. Look all around you rather than straight ahead. Take the time to see how the buildings, animals, people, and setting of this experience are part of the World's Dream.

Are you noticing any synchronicities? What in everyday life and what in the waking dream are connected as part of a larger pattern? In this larger matrix, what intersects with what? What seems to occur at the same time? Make special note of these intersections. What does this tell you about your own ground of being?

Also, notice complementarities. What in the waking dream and in the circumstances of your everyday conscious life likes to be with what? Rather than making sense, simply follow nature's way of organizing the entities and elements present in the waking dream experience. For example, notice what plants or trees are growing next to the river, pond, or fountain in the waking dream setting. What is propped up on the rock, or what kind of building is located next to a park in the dream? Notice as well what creatures or figures have an affinity for particular places or landscapes in the dream. How does one entity complement another? What organizing principles are at work in the dreamscape itself, separate from your personal system of making order? How does this realization that the world is always dreaming, with a dreamlike intelligence of its own, inform or complement some aspect of your own life?

The Indigenous Image

We have worked quite a bit with archetypes in this book, but there is another side of archetypes that we have not looked at yet, one that relates to the World's Dream. As an older man, when his understanding of archetypes became deeper, Jung developed the concept of this second aspect of archetypes. He said that a part of archetypes exists not only in the collective unconscious, but also *independently in nature*. He named this part, the external manifestation of an archetype, the "psychoid." So archetypes exist not only in the human brain; they also exist in the world around us. The psychoid is a profound and complex element of Jung's theories, closely related to synchronicity and the idea of the World's Dream.

When I was doing my early work with living images, I approached archetypes in strictly the first sense as forms in the human collective psyche. As I gained experience in working with dreams, however, I came to realize that certain images carried a relevance that went beyond the collective or cultural level. It seemed to me that they carried a power that came from a biological imperative, rooted in Nature. As I began to work with them over the years, I named them "indigenous" images. Indigenous images arise from our essential nature as well as in Nature itself.

In other words, indigenous images are foundational and link us to the deepest parts of who we are and where we came from. An archetypal image that arises from the World's Dream is an indigenous image that informs us about our deepest self. In this section we will look closely at this particularly significant type of living image.

Our Essential Natures

Indigenous images are powerful for personal growth and well-being. Because they are generated by the World's Dream, they are organic. Organic systems have a capacity for self-regulation, for balance, and for healing. Indigenous images share this capacity to balance and self-regulate, and in this way they are "medicinal" and can heal us on many levels. We will explore this medicinal aspect at length in the next chapter.

But it goes even further than this. An indigenous image carries the essential impulse of our life and relates directly to our being in the world. The indigenous image holds our essence, our uniqueness. Nature has her own intent for each of us, and the indigenous image reflects this intention. It is the expression of the natural world that we are a part of, that moves through us, and from which we arise.

The indigenous image shows up at various times in our lives, in various guises. Like the appearance of the Monolith in the movie *2001: A Space Odyssey*, these appearances mark important moments because they are our destiny revealing itself in image. And like other living images, indigenous images have the tendency to individuate. The individuation of an indigenous image is particularly important because it can directly shape our personal evolution. In my experience, these kinds of indigenous images are powerful and animate other dream images as well as our own lives.

To connect with an indigenous image is to connect to Nature itself, to the power of elemental forces like Sky God and Earth Mother. No matter how impaired, impoverished, or afflicted we may be, touching the indigenous image will begin our return to wellbeing. On the other hand, if we become disconnected or alienated from our indigenous images, it can be catastrophic. When this happens, we split off from our natures, become uprooted from our imaginal ground, and lose the connection to our unique, idiosyncratic way of being. So staying connected to our indigenous images is very important.

The Counterfeit Image

The original Jungian principle is to keep working with an image over days, weeks, months, and years in order to learn about our soul life. That may have been true fifty years ago, it may have been even more true 200 years ago, but in the world of the information age, there is a real danger in wholeheartedly accepting that idea. In the new millennium, dream images are not all created alike. I suspect that the challenge for the next generations of Dream Tenders will be to differentiate the authentic images from those that are counterfeit.

I began working with indigenous images several decades ago, and since that time I have noticed something interesting and disturbing taking place. Listening to hundreds of dreams of people who grew up in the information age, I noticed that some of their dream images originated not from their deep nature, but from the advertising industry. When I tracked these commercial images back to their essential qualities, they did not root back into the indigenous experience of the person I was working with. They tracked back to some commercial entity that was attempting to sell something. In other words, these images were not organic, and they did not arise from the World's Dream.

They are not the expression of Nature, and so they do not carry the inherent healing qualities of indigenous images. They do not individuate on their own, and so they do not help us to grow. They are like a genetically engineered plant with a terminator gene. They exist to sell a product and then simply disappear.

With the bombardment of images through various media and the increased sophistication of manipulating images, what lives at the level of dreams can no longer be imagined as pure. The task of tasks in today's world is to differentiate between counterfeit images and indigenous images.

Indigenous images are particularly needed now because of the domination of the commercialized, industrialized, computerized mindset over the artistic and intuitive aspects of ourselves. Our increasingly machine-like consciousness is exacerbated by the progressive loss of wilderness in the world. We have fewer opportunities to witness Nature's intelligence. Our reference point for the authentic is no longer located in Nature's fabric. It is located in the dream of commerce, urban life, and the information screen. The dreamscape is fast becoming the *screen-scape*.

To work with an indigenous image reconnects us to our sense of being, belonging, and authenticity. It also feeds the World's Dream, and helps to keep the World's Dream alive. It is crucial to learn to find and work with our indigenous images.

EXERCISE: *The Indigenous Image*

> Look through your dream journal of the last three months and identify those images that seem in some way out of the ordinary. You may work with an image from a night dream or from a waking dream. The important thing is to differentiate between images that seem to be generated by the marketplace and those that are rooted in the deep organic psyche. Images originating from these two distinct sectors may be

similar in appearance, but their essential qualities are very different. Your work is to identify the indigenous images.

To find the indigenous image, follow these guidelines: 1) look for images that are not obvious media images; 2) pay attention to the odd, deformed, aberrant, peculiar, even mutant-seeming images; 3) notice which images have a deeply "resonant" quality different from the artificial "charge" of commercial images; 4) pay particular attention to those images that originate in the natural world; 5) if the image is human-made or manufactured, look for those images that are artistic or that have a "handmade" personality, a radiant, alive quality, different from those that seem mass-produced or artificial; 6) allow your "instinctual body" to participate in the selection process. Certain images evoke a sense of connection and relationship, so bring your awareness to these figures.

Most of the time, indigenous images will feel profoundly resonant or hint at a connection to an older, generative impulse. Conversely, the image may not conform to anything recognizable at all, yet you still feel that there is something essential or elemental about the figure. Notice which image in this list seems to be originating from somewhere beyond the personal or collective human psyche. In other words, choose an image that right off seems to point toward a nature-centered, ecological origin. Make a list of six or so such images.

Once selected, write about the image in great detail in your journal. Let the image itself draw your attention to its unique qualities. Do this several times over. After you describe one feature of the image with increased precision, go on to the next characteristic. Continue this practice for at least fifteen minutes. Keep yourself in present time and in full relationship with the image. Your work here is not to associate or make meaning. The image itself will take you to its own depths.

As you continue to watch, listen, and mindfully tend to the indigenous image, become aware of what awakens in your experience. How are you being connected, through image, to a broader landscape? What about this experience feels most natural to you? Even if what you feel is unexpected, stay with it. Allow for the sensations of surprise or remembrance. These feelings or connections may be cognitive, intuitive, or somatic. Let these experiences take you back to the image itself.

Once re-engaged with the image, discover where and how it is situated in the landscape of your dream. What location in the dreamscape does the image naturally favor? How is the image elementally connected to this place in the dream setting? What about this place in the dreamscape is important to the image? How does the dream landscape feed or nurture the indigenous image? What is the organic relationship between image and dreamscape?

Now, imagine that this image is the "heart" of your being. Imagine further that it is a touchstone that connects you to your essential tendencies and instinctual wisdom. Write in your journal how you will act in the world, how you will be different in relationship to yourself and to others when connected to this primary image. How is your unique way of being supported and enhanced through your relationship with this elemental image? Return to this practice once a day for a week.

Archetypal Activism

In this chapter, we have explored several ways in which the world can speak for itself. The images of the World's Dream pour forth without end, giving shape to the dreams of nature, as well as to our personal dreams. We have seen how tuning into the World's Dream can fundamentally change our relationship to our environment, our community, our dreams, and ourselves.

But before we finish with this chapter, there is a further step we can take into the realm of the World's Dream. It is a logical consequence of everything we have already learned in this chapter, but this last step must be addressed specifically. Even though it is a thoroughly natural and even inevitable path for Dream Tenders to walk, it is also the path that flies most directly in the face of our solar consciousness.

The idea is actually quite simple, even though its ramifications are potentially enormous. It is this: if our dreams arise from the World's Dream, then we can perhaps glimpse what the world itself desires. And knowing this, we can then act in the world, on behalf of the world. This is the concept that I call "Archetypal Activism," and to me it's one of the most exciting aspects of Dream Tending.

Forging a New Relationship with the World's Dream

Archetypal Activism is not something that I created, but something that presented itself to me over time. I noticed that whenever people began to see dream images as speaking on behalf of everything in the world, often their relationship to the world transformed into something radically new. By consistently asking the fundamental Dream Tending questions ("Who is visiting now?" and "What is going on here?"), at a certain point they heard the voices of other creatures and inanimate beings around them, and having heard these dream voices, they felt compelled to make a response. They felt the need to not only interpret dreams, but also *to take action on behalf of dreams in the world*. It is as if the "world behind the world" has a voice that asks to be heard and acted upon.

I have seen this take place hundreds of times. Images will begin to speak from the viewpoint of a stand of trees in the neighborhood, or from the viewpoint of a nearby creek, or the ocean, or the mountains, or the whole earth. When a person hears such a dream communication from an external aspect of the world, it is often a startling or stunning revelation. People don't want to believe it. "It's like the rocks themselves are talking to me!" But once they feel reassured and understand that this is a typical, even normal, manifestation of the World's Dream, they naturally shift into a new relationship with the world. And often this new relationship includes wanting to do something about what they hear from these newly befriended figures of the dreamtime.

Gradually, I realized that I was witnessing the renaissance of an ancient/modern kind of activism. It is not political at its core, and therefore it is not beholden to the majority opinion of the collective or the self-interest of lobbyists. Nor is this activism like a religious movement. It is not motivated by the fundamentalist's yearning for redemption, nor is it some kind of rehashed 1960s human potential movement with the promise of personal liberation and self-fulfillment. Instead, Archetypal Activism is rooted in something deeper than political gain or enhanced self-esteem. Archetypal Activism is nothing more than our response to the call of the dream images.

When facing the challenges of today's world, we need all the help we can get. When we rely solely upon our willpower or personal judgment, we quickly feel depleted, stressed, and often powerless. On the other hand, when we take the time to listen and consult with the living figures of the dreaming mind, we experience an inner strength that is generative. In my own life I have seen how profoundly different it is to conduct business in the awake world while informed by the living images of the dream world. I experience myself in service to a way of knowing that is much bigger than myself, and I feel tremendous clarity and confidence in my actions. When I wake up in the morning raring to go, ready to meet the challenges of the day, charging ahead with eyes wide open, I am in "power mode" and am active in the ways of solar consciousness. When I take the time to first consult with my dreams, however, I begin the day by listening to the intelligence of the image and I am in "receptive mode," active in the ways of lunar consciousness. The choice is always there to make: charge forward with the power of the intellect alone or engage the challenges of the day while informed by the intuition as well.

Taking Archetypal Activism to the Streets

It is easier to get a sense of Archetypal Activism through a story. Several blocks from where I was working a number of years ago, there was a walking bridge over a creek that was in disrepair. It was a hazard and the county had accepted a bid to build a new, modern, safe bridge. A sketch of the bridge appeared in the newspaper, and it was obvious that the design had been selected for its low cost rather than its beauty. It was ugly and didn't fit the sensibilities of the neighborhood. A number of colleagues and I decided to become advocates for new possibility by employing our skills as Archetypal Activists.

The first task was to listen to the guidance of dream imagery and to translate it into effective political action. We not only wanted to hear our own dreams, but also those of other people living in the neighborhood. So we went from door to door asking people what they imagined would be a more appropriate and beautiful design.

Dream Tending takes into account the many levels of the psyche: the personal, the collective, as well as the World's Dream. Our neighbors' dreams and imaginings spoke of what kind of bridge would serve individual tastes and needs, as well as collective images of classical images of bridges. Significantly, we also listened to the landscape itself describe what kind of bridge it would like to have located on it.

We gathered this information and passed it on to the decision makers at the county. Of course, it didn't hurt that it was an election year, and the local Supervisor was locked in a tight race to keep his seat. Passing this feedback from his constituency on to the Planning Commission was darn good politics. The final design the Commission adopted for the bridge was in fact shaped by the dream images we had collected, as well as that of the land itself. The newly-designed bridge stands today, an integral part of the landscape and an aesthetically-pleasing part of the neighborhood. For me, this represents a perfect example of what Archetypal Activism can achieve at the local level. We acted on behalf of dream knowledge, we heard what the world was asking of us, and developed a new way of heeding its call.

Archetypal Activism can impact the global stage as well. For over a decade I have been working with a United Nations-sponsored initiative called the Earth Charter. The Earth Charter is a declaration of fundamental principles for building a just, sustainable, and peaceful global society in the 21st century. It seeks to inspire in all peoples a new sense of global interdependence and shared responsibility for the wellbeing of the human family and the larger living world.

In order to accomplish such a task, we needed a method to figure out the core principles that would guide the development of the document. Peoples from around the globe have gathered again and again to write a charter similar to the Universal Declaration of Human Rights that the General Assembly of the UN can consider for passage. I was asked to contribute the Depth Psychological perspective, as informed by the insights offered in dream work. I introduced the concept of the World's Dream and the idea that to hear what the planet urgently needs at this time of peril, we must first listen to the voices of the Earth, as they speak through the dreams of our species. Too often we rush in, armed with good intentions, using our rational intelligence to find immediate fixes to crisis situations. Though we mean well, we act reactively and impulsively, and tend to be predictable, human-centered, and ineffective. Meanwhile, the planet continues to be grievously injured, caught in the endless power struggles over these human-fashioned "solutions."

Something new was needed; something more was required. From the perspective of Dream Tending, I suggested that we turn the question on its head and instead ask, "What is the planet asking of us?" In this way, the voices of the earth are heard on their own behalf as they make their presence known. As with all living images, the intelligence needed to respond to the problem is located in the images themselves. Bringing the wisdom of the dream to the proceedings of the Earth Charter deliberations is an ongoing effort. This approach is an expression of Archetypal Activism on a global level. We listen to the World's Dream, and what we hear contributes to a charter that offers hope and a call to help create a global partnership with all beings at this critical juncture in history.

Of course, what we hear is both promising as well as devastating. As they present themselves in dream images, we experience the extinction of species, the deforestation of once lush continents, the toxicity of the oceans, and the spreading decay in our cities. Helen Caldicott said, "It is as if the destruction of our planet is being grieved in the dreams of our children." Feeling the pain is an inevitable consequence of being an Archetypal Activist.

Self-Neurosis Is World-Neurosis

Engaging in Archetypal Activism, we soon discover that depression, anxiety, and even our deeper pathologies can originate in the world, not only in our immediate relationships, family of origin, or biochemical predisposition. In other words, when the world is sick, we experience psychological disturbances as well. It is as if all the beings out there project these maladies through dream images into our own psyches. The pain of the world expresses itself to us through its images, and we feel and respond to its suffering.

Archetypal Activism understands that suffering is not just a human condition. The world, too, is in pain and in need of our attention. The hallmark of an archetypal response is to turn toward the source of the hurt rather than seeking to distract or medicate our personal pain away. We want to help directly.

Allow me to share an example.

A few months of each year several factors combine to pollute the ocean around Santa Barbara. "Stop! Stay out of the Water!" signs are posted up and down the beach, telling us that the sea is toxic. The ocean, always dreaming, voices its ills through its images, and these appear as images in our dreams. During those months many Santa Barbarans feel depressed. Even when we haven't visited the ocean for weeks, we feel its toxicity in our own bodies. Most of us don't recognize that our feelings of dread have nothing to do with our personal condition, but rather with the state of an ocean in distress, making its sickness known as a disturbance in our physical and emotional lives.

When we practice Archetypal Activism, we do not deny these experiences or attribute them to a "bad mood" or biological virus. Rather, we realize that the world around us is always dreaming and calling to us through our dreams and symptoms, asking for a response. When we directly confront what the World's Dream is telling us, we respond from the strength and resources found in our dreaming bodymind. A dream loves to be met in the way of a dream.

I believe that at this time in history we are being asked to act globally as well as locally. This is a time when humanity must choose to co-create with the Earth a future for us all. As the world becomes increasingly interdependent and fragile, the future at once holds great peril and great promise. We can no longer take local actions without reflecting on the global implications of those actions. We urgently require Archetypal Activism, the ability to access the wisdom of the World's Dream, when taking action in matters such as fair trade and global warming. Whether we are working with the issues of international relations or human rights policies, it is imperative that we declare our responsibility to one another, as well as to the World's Dream that unites and informs us all.

EXERCISE: *Archetypal Activism*

> Imagine yourself walking in your neighborhood or driving slowly to work on local streets. As you journey, look around the landscape and discover what places have a dreamlike quality to them or actually have appeared in your dreams. Identify what is asking for attention. It may be a littered field in need of clean-up, an abandoned building that needs repair, a creek badly wanting the cement removed from its

bank. Or, in an opposite mood, it may be a field of beautiful wild flowers gone unnoticed, or an exquisitely designed park gone unseen, or a beautiful structure unperceived amongst the clutter. Whatever seems to request your notice, go spend some actual time at that place.

Be there for a while. Notice what opens up in you emotionally. Allow this response to bring you closer to this particular location. Allow your heartfelt feeling to connect with the "heartbeat" of this place. Notice how this empathetic regard creates a sense of caring for and belonging to one another in this moment. Let yourself deepen into the emotions that get opened up inside of you. Acting on behalf of these emotions, connected originally to the intelligence of the dreaming psyche, is the essence of Archetypal Activism. Motivated by the urgings of the deep psyche, what is it that you feel "pushed" to do? What actions, informed by dreams, do you wish to take?

What is the psyche of this place asking of you? What are your dreams pushing you to do? What restoration, acknowledgement, or action does this place seek as you hear it speak through its dream? Now think of three concrete ways that you can engage this place, informed by what you have heard and your connection to your deep psyche. Take these steps of Archetypal Activism and write about them in your journal as if you were writing about tending to your dreams.

In your writing, bring your attention to how your world view has been extended and expanded. Notice the multiplicity of perspectives that have come into awareness. Also notice that the injury you were attending to originated first in the world and then in your body and emotions. Make an observation of how the suffering in the world affects your mental and emotional health. List one thing you can do each day for the next seven days that attends to the "breakdown" of a particular place or thing in the world. After seven days, write about the change in your own psychological wellbeing. Pay particular attention to how your dreams have been affected over this time period.

The Mexican Cathedral: A Story of Archetypal Activism

Before we finish with Archetypal Activism, I'd like to share a particularly poignant story that I had the good fortune to witness. Ian, a lawyer in his early forties, had a recurring nightmare. The dream always took place in a small, seemingly deserted village, practically a ghost town, haunted by dust and wind. The rundown shops were shuttered; the houses neglected and empty. In the dream, Ian wandered to the village square, which was dominated by a small cathedral that looked particularly abandoned and decrepit. Whenever he came to the part where he saw the cathedral, the silence was broken by the sound of an old woman wailing in despair. This keening filled Ian with a sense of dread, and for days after this dream, he always felt overwhelming anxiety and despondency.

Ian had made many attempts over the years to get relief from this nightmare. He had tried traditional therapy, using association to explore the desolate nature of the dream and compare that to his current life situation. Not much came of this, as he felt reasonably fulfilled at work and at home. He had also worked with the wailing sound at the end of the dream, associating this to his experiences of grief, loss, and sorrow. As he had learned to express these feelings, he had gotten some relief, but the dream kept coming back, and was actually getting worse.

He tried some Jungian approaches in which he had investigated a number of themes in the dream—such as the poverty of the town square. He had explored feeling impoverished, both inside and out. He had also considered his religious orientation, as he was stimulated by the image of the cathedral. All of these reflections had been useful and added to the range of his life experience, yet the nightmare kept repeating.

Eventually, Ian came to see me. I was interested to hear that he had already used the methods of association and amplification with the dream. It was time to give animation a try. I had him tell the dream in the present tense and bring the dream to life. He described the town and its environment in detail and brought particular attention to the cathedral, using his senses to explore the texture of the crumbling walls, the smells of the dusty court-yard, the sounds of the wind moving through the wooden rafters. As the dream unfolded, he became more engaged, observing the small shops, the manner of the townspeople, the rhythm of village life. The images of the dream filled the space between us, and the sounds and smells became vibrant. Suddenly Ian had a strong reaction. He said, "Wait! I know this place! It's a village that I visited as a child." He went on to say that his parents had taken him to a village in Mexico to visit his grandmother right before she died. "I was very young and didn't really get a chance to know her, but I do remember driving a long way in a car to get to this tiny village. It was the only time that I ever saw my grandmother." He said that although the time they had together was brief, he was touched by her warmth and felt a deep connection to her. As these memories started to come to life, his attention was drawn back to the cathedral. He was fascinated by it and its dilapidated condition.

The atmosphere in my office shifted dramatically. His anxiety and unrest was replaced by intense curiosity. Ian felt compelled by the dream images to listen more closely, to do something.

"What does this mean? Why is this happening? What is being asked of me?" The cathedral, the shops in the village, the wailing sound at the end of the dream all demanded attention.

Up until this point, Ian had felt the dream was somehow commenting on his own life. But I now had a hunch about the nature of this dream that suggested something different. Maybe this actual setting, this village in Mexico, was dreaming this dream of itself. What if the dream was commenting on the actual circumstances in the village?

Ian was immediately struck by this possibility. Over the last few years he had felt a call to visit the homeland of his grandmother, to recover a lineage that he had not really fully known, and to re-connect with his ancestral inheritance. I suggested that to tend this dream meant to actually travel to the village and discover what it was asking of him.

Ian found out the name and location of the place, which had by now grown into a small town, and made arrangements to travel there. Upon arriving, he discovered that his grandmother, long deceased, had a living sister in the town. Ian was very surprised that people recognized him there. People in the town greeted him as family, as many had heard stories about him from his grandmother. Ian was deeply touched and filled with a sense of belonging. Yet there was also a sense of impending threat in the air. As the locals explained to Ian, part of the town was scheduled to be bulldozed and replaced by a resort development. People were particularly concerned about their ancient little cathedral being destroyed, and felt powerless to do anything about it.

At that moment, Ian understood the meaning of his nightmare. It was the village itself putting out a distress call, beckoning him to come so that he might be of aid. Even the spirit of his grandmother, whom Ian now recognized as the wailing woman, had taken up the call. This realization put everything into a new and exciting context. Ian realized that he could take action on behalf of the village and became an enthusiastic archetypal activist. In the months that followed, Ian dedicated himself to putting a stop to the impending development. He used his skills as a lawyer to navigate the complex, confusing, and often corrupt land usage and planning processes in that region. He also visited the village many times to bring medical supplies to the small town hospital, athletic equipment to the kids, and building materials to repair the cathedral. Ian rediscovered his sense of generosity and caring, and reunited with his grandmother's lineage. The nightmare had turned to a dream that provided him with an inspired context for concrete action in the world on behalf of the World's Dream. The restored cathedral stands to this day. This is archetypal activism at its best.

The World as a Dream

California's Sierra Nevada Mountains are home to one of the highest peaks in the world, Mt. Whitney. The range extends 400 miles from Fredonyer Pass in the north to Tehachapi Pass in the south. It is bounded on the west by California's Central Valley, and to the East by the Great Basin. Each year I return to the eastern slopes of the Sierra Nevadas to make a wilderness retreat.

Unlike the more heavily wooded Western side, there is an almost desolate look and feel to the eastern slopes. Stark granite escarpments plunge to the desert floor below. Vivid in the clear air and bright sun, the mountains look barren and lifeless.

Yet when I walk the high mountain passes, I encounter the abundance of life that fills these mountains. Groves of pine, backcountry mountain meadows, and wild flowers of every description litter the area. Deer, bear, and marmot are plentiful. Trout swim in the waters of streams and hidden lakes. Soaring overhead are hawks and ravens, along with an occasional, wayward sea gull. In the trees jays and owls make their homes.

In this wilderness I feel captivated by a world that is bigger than I thought possible, a world that has an imagination of its own. Entering the dreamlike consciousness of this place, I experience the world as if it were a dream. Here I realize that I am just another figure in a dream that originates in the World's Dream. I, too, am one image among many being dreamed by the *anima mundi*.

This quality of awareness changes everything. At a primary level of existence, we are all part of the dreaming world, all being dreamt into existence by a larger "Dreamer." We see the entire world as nothing but a grand dream.

Several great Asian traditions hold this view of the world as a dream. Some schools of Buddhism and Hinduism make this concept a focal point of their philosophies. For example, in the Diamond Sutra, a sacred Buddhist text, the Buddha himself taught that the world is "like a dream, an illusion, a bubble, a shadow, a dewdrop, a lightning flash." In the Australian Aboriginal tradition as well, all beings, landscapes, and each one of us is a manifestation of the dreamtime, a dreaming consciousness that originates in the realm of the Dreaming.

Experiencing myself as an image in the World's Dream places me differently in the world. I am part of something larger than myself. This extends my sense of being, expands my consciousness in ways that allow me to realize all that we have been talking about in this chapter: that the world itself is animate and expresses itself in the images that occur in our dreams at night. When I am interacting with people or navigating difficult situations in life, this quality of consciousness offers a more deeply rooted, spacious perspective. Then, in a certain way, my actions and emotional responses are shaped by a dreamlike intelligence.

Understanding life and the world as a dream opens up a new way of being. As an image in the World's Dream, we let go of the narrow and the petty, and take in the wider design. We release unnecessary attachments and bring attention to the matters of the heart.

EXERCISE: *The World as a Dream*

In this exercise you will use the same dream for two sessions. Both sessions will take place outside, one in the daytime and one at night. Start by identifying a dream that pictures you in a setting with a detailed landscape and a number of figures. First, sketch the dream on a piece of paper. Make sure to sketch yourself as an image among the other figures. Now take the drawing outside and find a place that is sympathetic to hosting your work. Place it on the ground, a boulder, or in a bush.

Notice how the sun lights up your dream picture. Then take five steps back and experience the dream picture as part of the larger landscape that includes the things in the surrounding area. See how the sun lights both the images in the picture and everything in the landscape. Watch the ways the images of the dream animate and begin to interact with the things in the landscape.

Give this process a good ten minutes. It breaks the "boundaries" surrounding the dream. Small creatures may come and go, the wind may create sound, clouds may change the quality of light and shadow. The figures on the page will begin to interact more fully with the creatures and landscape around them. Allow this to continue for some time.

Get a sense that from this perspective there is no separation between the dream picture and the outside landscape. It has all become one dreamscape. It is as if the World is dreaming and the figures in the dream picture, the elements in the landscape, and even you are part of a larger dream. Write down what you are experiencing.

Repeat this same exercise at night under the open sky. Include the vast nighttime sky in your Dream Tending. As the light of the moon and the hundreds of visible stars illuminate the land, notice how the dreamscape broadens, and you feel held by a larger dreaming consciousness.

Imagine for a moment that you are standing on the moon. From this perspective notice how the sky, the landscape below, and the animated figures "coming off the page" of the dream picture are all part of a larger dream.

Ask yourself, "Who is dreaming this dream?" Take this question inside of yourself for a moment and reflect upon it. Experience how here, in the night sky, it is even more possible to experience the world's dreaming. Become aware of how every creature, every event, every interaction originates from the World's Dream. Imagine that all creation is the world dreaming itself into existence, moment by moment. Write down your reflections. Don't hold back. Be bold, and write poetically and without hesitation.

Chapter Five

MEDICINES OF THE SOUL

My great-grandfather was a very healthy man. People said his good health was due to the three good meals he had a day, as well as the snacks he enjoyed. But I remember he told us that his healthiness came from three important things. First, the twelve-egg yellow cake that my great-grandmother (whom I called "Bubba") made for him on special occasions. "What wealth in a cake with a dozen eggs!" he would exclaim. Second, it was important to have great humor, lively conversation, and good cheer while eating. He and Bubba laughed and teased each other like children around the dinner table. Third was the sweet wine Bubba made herself that they served with every meal. This was, he said, "The nectar of the Gods, a healing tonic, and my fountain of youth."

The foods and wine that were prepared each day, and the good mood with which they were enjoyed, constituted a kind of homespun ritual, an offering of sorts for their health and happiness. In these moments of living deeply in his humanity and joy, Zadie renewed the essence of his health.

Dream Tending also offers us rituals of wellbeing. Dreams make great medicine and can even heal physical illness. The psyche itself has natural healing properties. It is often hard for people to believe this assertion. The first time I ever spoke publicly about Dream Tending's relationship to physical healing, I had been asked to give a lecture to a group of adult education students. It was a Saturday morning and the place was packed as I spoke about how dreams can often predict illness. I said, "An illness will first show itself in the imagery of dreams, sometimes long before the onset of physical symptoms."

As I spoke I noticed a fellow in the back, sitting with his arms wrapped around his belly with a bored, skeptical look on his face. The woman next to him, clearly his wife, seemed receptive. I guessed that the only reason he had come was because she had dragged him there. Everything about his body language told me that he would rather be at home watching the football game than sitting there listening to this peculiar idea about dreams as medicine.

Then I asked the audience for a volunteer to offer a dream as an example for discussion. His hand shot up immediately; not in a gesture of offering, but one of aggression and challenge. If he had to be there, then at least he could have some fun by disrupting the proceedings. His wife squirmed uncomfortably, her hands over her eyes.

He stood up, glared at me, and said, "Dr. Aizenstat, I had a dream last night. It was a dream of a piano leg. So what do you make of that?" It was an insolent question, challenging me to make something of such a pointless, empty dream. "Well," I said, welcoming the challenge, "can you give me a little more detail about the image? What did you notice about the piano leg?"

He said, "Yeah, certainly I can. You know, this piano leg was the kind from one of those pianos from years ago. It had the classical lines, kind of rounded and carved, and it came down in such a way that showed it was part of a very expensive piano." Probing a little further, I asked, "Sir, is there anything that's been occurring in the last twenty-four to forty-eight hours that would bring such an image to your attention?"

Despite himself, he started getting drawn into the discussion. He said, "Interesting you should ask. I move furniture for a living. And just the other day, in fact, we needed to move a piano. Of course the piano that we moved wasn't anything like the one in my dream, and the leg didn't look anything like this one, but the piano that we moved was really heavy." "That's interesting," I continued, "Now could you go on with your description? Tell me in more detail exactly what you noticed about this particular piano leg in the dream."

Intrigued, he described a piano leg that was ornately carved in four rounded sections. Looking more carefully at the image in his memory, he also recalled that between the third and the fourth section there was a crack in the leg, in which a wooden wedge was stuck.

I asked him to come up in front of the class and draw this image on the chalkboard. Curiosity overcame his reluctance as he drew the image on the board. I looked at him and said, "Sir, I'm wondering if you have recently been feeling any pain in your back." Instantly all the blood rushed from his face. "How could you tell that?" he asked. I continued, "I'm wondering, sir, if there is some kind of discomfort that you might have been experiencing over the last few days?" He said, "I don't know how you would know that, but the truth is that over the last twenty-four hours I've been feeling a lot of pain in the middle of my back."

Glancing over, I saw that his wife was obviously enjoying the fact that her husband was now fully engaged in the process. I then asked, "Have you received any medical attention or have you taken the opportunity to investigate this feeling that you're having?" "No sir, I work from eight to six every day and, quite frankly, I do not have time for doctors."

I said, "You know, noticing where this particular wedge is, I'm wondering if you take any time in life to play, to enjoy activities with your wife and family?" His wife was grinning from ear to ear. He said, "Frankly, that's a personal question. But to answer you directly—not really. I simply don't have time for that either."

Not wanting to venture further into what would surely become "family counseling," I ended the conversation that morning by encouraging him to have a physician fully explore his back condition and also to add something of play into his life. That seemed to be the end of it.

Two days later I got a phone message at my clinical office. Hearing the voicemail, I realized it was the same fellow. I called him right back, and he said that he wanted to thank me. "I took your advice and I went to a physician. The doctor took an x-ray of my back and discovered there was a ruptured disc right where you said. He said that if I would have continued to move furniture, I could have permanently damaged myself and might have created a real health problem. As skeptical as I was, Doc, I gotta thank you." Then he asked how it was that I could have possibly known all this about his back.

I told him that the images in dreams often point directly to an affliction in the body. They almost serve as psychic X-rays. They will tell us specifically what is injured, what is out of sorts, where a problem is located, and sometimes they will even suggest a cure. This was the case in his dream, because the spine contains "chakras," according to its mythological amplification. Having a wedge between the third and fourth chakra – between the place that symbolizes hard work and the place that symbolizes the heart—indicated to me that he needed to play more, to live more from his heart. Furthermore the dream image pointed toward his actual physical injury and suggested to me that he should see a doctor. This is an example of how dream images can be used as a kind of medicine.

DREAM IMAGES AS MEDICINES

As Dream Tenders we work with dream images as "medicines of the soul." Jungian therapists, drawing on the classical Greek healers of the Asklepian tradition, as well as practitioners of modern integrative medicine, have found maintaining a healthy relationship with our dream life to be integral to physical health. Over the past forty years I have seen that to be true many times over. I have also discovered something further that I continue be amazed by: dream images have inherent healing properties. They function as imaginal medicines that can be used in the treatment of physical disease symptoms. Based on this principle I have developed methods to activate these healing properties of living images. A number of these methods are similar in orientation to traditional homeopathic practices, but with one significant difference: in Dream Tending we discover, prescribe, and administer the medicinal properties of living images as if they were tangible organic substances. We become like alchemists, learning the craft of transmuting dream images into medicines that can heal physical afflictions. I have found that working with dream images in this way is effective in preventing and treating illness and is useful as an adjunct to regular medical treatment.

I am in no way saying that dream medicines are meant to replace regular medical treatment by a physician. In my clinical practice, if a client has a physical issue, I always refer them to a competent medical professional for an evaluation. Dream medicines are intended solely as a complement to standard medical treatment.

Using dream images as medicines works because the body is always dreaming. When we have an upset stomach, a headache, or sense the onset of a cold, for example, the body feels some distress. Our subconscious mind notices these distress signals and represents them as images in our dreams. In the story above we saw that the man with a sore back dreamed of a broken piano leg. As we learn to read dreams in a somatic way—that is, as messages from our physical body—we view the figures, actions, and feelings in dreams as commentary about our physical condition. In this way dreams sometimes tell of disease formation long before the occurrence of tangible physical symptoms, particularly in severe afflictions that take a long time to develop such as cancer or heart disease. Dreams become a kind of early warning system, telling of the problem long before we are faced with actual symptoms. Images pointing to our physical condition will appear again and again, clamoring for us to notice something that we may be too busy or afraid to consider.

Dreams also speak to us about our capacity to heal. The same bodily intelligence that knows how to fight off an infection or generate new cells can also use dream imagery to give us clues about how to cure whatever ails us. In fact, dreams will often prescribe a means of complementary treatment even before we go to a conventional physician.

I have witnessed the connection of dreams to our state of health so often that I have learned to scan every dream I work with for imagery containing concrete associations to physical conditions.

HEALING THE WOUNDED IMAGE

The dream images linked to our bodily disorders are themselves often out of order, broken, malignant, or damaged in some way. For example, an image of a rusted gate creaking in the wind may symbolize my hurting elbow. A dream of a foul, stagnant pond might represent my upset stomach. A vision of torn tree roots may be an image sent by my hurting feet. This same idea holds true for more extreme bodily disorders. When cancer strikes, the infected area may send up dream images of an infestation of parasites teeming inside a large melon that is growing inappropriately in our living room. A dream of the family dog, emaciated and suffering, may be sent by an ailing body to announce the condition of anorexia. I call these kinds of images "wounded" dream images.

In Dream Tending we treat the physical disorder by treating the wounded image. When we heal the dream image, this begins the process of healing the physical disorder from which the image arises. This is the essence of the practice. *To heal the wounded dream image is to heal ourselves.* When the image returns to vitality, so do we.

When we consider healing the wounded dream image there is a central idea that underpins our "doctoring." When we meet the wounded image, we do so in the way of our own experience of woundedness. The attitude necessary to activate the flow of healing energy in the wounded image is a result of bringing our own vulnerability into contact with the afflicted image. We do not rush in with the intention to bring an immediate fix. Rather we meet the wounded image from the depths of our own woundedness—developing a relationship of compassion and empathetic caring for the image.

This attitude of healing is informed by our relationship to our own mortality. In virtually all healing traditions, a conscious relationship to death informs the life cycle at every turn. We realize that the wounded dream image and we, as persons who are afflicted, are both wounded healers. We are both carrying the illness, as well as the medicines necessary for healing. It is important to keep this idea in mind as we explore the Dream Tending Healing System.

Two concepts common to alternative healing modalities help guide our dream doctoring, although we will here be using them in an imaginal, metaphoric context. The first is the idea that healing comes from removing blockages to the life force (call it chi, ki, or prana) and restoring its free flow. In the example of the creaking gate, we might discover what is restricting the gate from opening and closing freely. Once we remove this restriction, the dream gate opens smoothly, and this allows the elbow to do so as well. To heal dream images does not always mean that they "get better forever," but instead refers to the restoration of life force in them.

The second concept is the homeopathic principle, the idea that "like cures like." Just as we give a small dose of polio to vaccinate against polio, a very small dose of the acute fear that is causing the dream dog to stop eating may be exactly what is required to attend to the anorexia that is devastating the physical body of the dreamer. Both of these practices, removing the obstacle to the life force and working homeopathically, long established in alternative healing practices, are very useful in benefiting wounded dream images. I will elaborate further and give several further examples of their use as the chapter progresses.

Healing with dreams is a powerful practice. I have developed a systematic approach consisting of three steps: Naming, Offering, and Ritual. The application of each step is a subtle and complex art. Each operation requires completion before moving on to the next. I will first describe the operation, then offer the methods, and also give examples from my own work.

It is important to remember that most of us do not have medical training. Our work as Dream Tenders in relation to physical illness is meant as an adjunct to proper medical treatment, not a replacement for it. The key to success is to keep the approach to healing straightforward, while at the same time attending to the depth and subtlety of our dream life.

THE DREAM TENDING HEALING SYSTEM

Step 1—Naming

The first step in the Dream Tending healing system is called Naming. In its simplest form, this means finding a wounded image and learning its name. We have already learned to name images in the Living Image and Nightmare chapters. For example, in the dream of the piano leg at the beginning of this chapter, I simply named the image Piano Leg. But to do healing work with images we must take this Naming skill and really go forward with it. By making an extended search, we will come to find a deeper name of the image, what I call the "medicinal name," or the "true name." This is not the first or the most obvious name, and discovering it is something that takes a little while to master. The work we have done so far with animating living images will help a great deal in this. Once we find the medicinal name of an image, the true healing work can begin.

The idea of the true name is a venerable one that exists in many cultures. For example, there is an East African tribe in which the birthday of a child is not based on the day of its physical birth nor even from the day of conception. For these people, the birthday is the first time the child was a thought in its mother's mind.

Aware of her intention to conceive a child with a particular father, the mother goes off to sit alone under a tree. There she sits and listens until she can hear the song of the child she hopes to conceive. Once she has heard it, she returns to her village and teaches it to the father so that they can sing it together as they make love, inviting the child to join them.

After the child is conceived, she sings to the baby in her womb. Then she teaches the song to the old women and mid-wives of the village so that, throughout the labor and at the birth itself, the child is greeted with its song.

After the birth, all the villagers learn the song of their new member and later sing it to the child when it falls or hurts itself. It is sung at times of triumph, as well as during rituals and initiations. This song eventually becomes a part of the marriage ceremony when the child is grown. And at the end of life, his or her loved ones will gather around the deathbed and sing this song for the last time.

This story of naming is both beautiful and instructive. It reminds us of the value of knowing our authentic name, which precedes our conception and extends beyond our death. The essential curative properties of an image are found in the heart of its medicinal name. In the process of naming, it is crucial to identify the essential quality in the living image that gives birth to its name. This activates the healing process and allows us to make an Offering, which is the next step in healing.

Remember from Chapter One that taking out the modifying article(s) gets us closer to the actual name. The dream image of "a bear" becomes simply Bear, or even more essentially Black Bear. But most people do not have just one name. Over a lifetime, we acquire many names, nicknames, and handles of various sorts. Some of these names are more formal or informal than others, and some seem to refer to us in a deeper way. For example, I'm called Steve, Doctor Aizenstat, Dad, and many other names, but the name that touches me most deeply is Stephen.

Dream images also come with a name that is elemental and directly connected to the World's Dream. It is this name that we are looking for. Calling an image Black Bear gets us close, but it still may not represent the medicinal name of this image.

By properly naming a wounded dream image we will reveal its essential identity. This is where the medicine is located. But how do we go about actually doing this? We first connect with the dream figure in its outer form, as we have been doing throughout this book. Next we must go further and engage a process of mindful interaction and deep listening to slowly invite the figure to open its innermost levels to us. When asking an image to reveal its medicinal core, we must open our own innermost self to the image. As we open to the image, the image opens to us. Black Bear reveals it true name, "Bear of the Mountain," or "Mountain Bear." This is how friendships, loves, and all true relationships work. Our friend Mountain Bear reveals his medicinal name.

Often the image whose name we seek will present itself as injured, crippled, blocked, unhappy, or broken in some way. In classical Greek mythology, for example, we encounter the wounded centaur Chiron who taught Asklepios the art of healing. We often refer to Chiron as representing the wounded healer archetype. In many cultures, this figure is common in the guise of the medicine person or animal. The wounded healer image is both the cause of the problem as well as the cure. Outwardly it is sick in some way, but when we look deep inside the wound, we find the cure, and this dream image reveals itself to be a divine physician. Let's look at an example of this process.

Naming Example: Jamie

Jamie, a woman in her fifties, was experiencing pain in her legs and was being treated for arteriosclerosis, or hardening of the arteries. She said she loved listening to classical music, but that she had not actually played her violin or piano for some time. Recently she had been working overtime at her job. She was tired and yearned to have more fun.

One night she dreamed of a severely crippled older man stuck in a wheelchair. He had a glint of happiness in his eyes and he loved music. He entered a concert hall with only a broken wooden flute. Attached to his ear was a peculiar oversized hearing aid that looked like an old time "ear horn."

Using Dream Tending techniques, Jamie gave a name to the man in the wheelchair. He first appeared as Master Musician, who loved his art but had not played for some time. His life force was still vital, but his bad hearing and difficulty getting around limited him. The name Master Musician was right for this figure, but Jamie knew that she needed to look more deeply into his wound to find the most essential name for this figure. She engaged Master Musician for some time before he revealed his medicinal name, Old Composer. Old Composer was indeed a wounded healer, a mentor of music who was suffering from neglect. As a once great composer who knew the elemental ways of music, he could communicate with the muses, yet his faculties were deteriorating through lack of use. As Old Composer, the wounded healer image became a medicine with healing properties capable of treating Jamie's hardened arteries. Through the process of Naming, the crippled musician image became alive, his music once again flowing freely. Old Composer was revitalized and the song that Jamie was born into could be heard.

EXERCISE: *Naming*

> Before identifying a particular dream image to work with, connect to a sense of your archetypal ego. This is essential in the Naming process. Often as a defense or out of fear you will resist this move into authentic self. This is because in coping with illness you may have identified with some of the symptoms. Now it is time to become conscious of this. Out of self-protection are you acting in ways that somehow resemble the illness itself? You must look beyond these responses.

Listen for expressions of your authentic self in word, gesture, or feeling. Cultivate this awareness. Again, this state of mind is essential in discovering and evoking the medicinal name of the healing image. It may help to remember that behind your fear of the illness is the desire for something more. Amplify this positive intention. It will take you into the attitude required to engage the process of Naming.

Once you feel connected to your archetypal ego, observe what dream images come forward. Note any image that may be connected to your illness. If you are not certain, start with the dream figure that is most visible and persistent. Do not worry if the image does not conform to your preconceived notion of the "wounded healer." The image may appear as something familiar, like a person, a plant, or a thing. The medicines are found in the Names of all beings. The simplest thing is to look for is a figure that is broken or hurt. There is no right or wrong image, so don't get stuck at this point. Choose the figure that seems most appropriate and move on.

Animate the figure and allow it to come to life. Become present, use your senses, get particular, follow its activity, and activate the field so the image becomes a living presence in the room along with you. Tend to the image in the ways you have learned. Part of the process of Naming is bringing life to the dream image.

Ask the questions, "Who is visiting now?" and "Who are you?" Do this several times. Who or what do you see?

In the chapter on the living image we stopped at this stage, but now you need to go further. The medicine is in the essential name of the figure, in its core. I find that it helps to tip your head a little to the right. This simple gesture will change your mode of perception. Be subtle. Pause and listen. Do you hear a sound? Imagine a song coming through the figure that began long, long ago. In imagination, follow the song to its source. Again ask, "Who is visiting now? Who are you?" You may notice the image begin to change. Let this unfold naturally.

Stay connected to your deeper sense of self. Guard against falling into familiar styles of coping or sliding back into a reactive state. It is critical that this does not happen. In the activated field that exists between your archetypal ego and the essential image, listen for a name.

This may take some time. Naming requires patience. Let the image reveal itself from the inside out. You cannot force it. Relax, stay aware, and listen.

Once a name is revealed, you need to go yet further and discover the name behind the name. Listen carefully and locate, even feel, if possible, the pulse of the image. Do not make this process esoteric or hard. Use your empathy. Let go and trust the life force. Feel the natural rhythms moving through the image.

Now the image is fully present in the room. It is as real in its own way as you are. Look again at the image. Use your eyes of intuition and empathy. Who greets you here? Is there a name behind the name?

Naming is a joint process between you and the living image. Imagine it as an eternal figure of the psyche, an old soul, rooted in the generative dream of Nature. This attitude helps you hear the medicinal name, the true name, the medicine of the soul. If you believe you have heard the true name, speak it back to the image and see if the image affirms it. The healing image knows its name.

Step 2—Offering

The second step in the Dream Tending system of healing is to make an Offering. Making an Offering to the ancestors, to the shaman, or to the priest is an age-old healing practice that continues to this day in many forms. Special food, a particular animal, precious jewels, or a personal vow are examples of Offerings used by peoples worldwide. Offerings are used to seek favor, express appreciation, or set in motion the medicinal powers of the healer. Sometimes Offerings are made with the hope that an affliction will be transformed into something new and helpful. Other times, the desire is for the disease to be cured altogether. The gift of Offering is intended to activate the healing process in very specific ways.

Offerings vary in shape, size, and stature. The man in the story of Piano Leg, for example, could have offered to the image some kind of play activity. Yet whatever kind of Offering we are making, Offerings are meant to enliven the wounded figure. Making an Offering is essential to acknowledge the healing dream image, to deepen the relationship with it, and, most importantly, to activate its healing energy.

Making an Offering is quite simple. We are going to give the image what it needs to get better. The resuscitated image can then participate in our healing process. I have created a three-step process of Offering that is a good way to get started. The three steps are:

    a) Determining What Kind of Offering Is Needed

    b) Formulating the Offering

    c) Administering the Offering

I've found that the best way to teach the three steps of Offering is through example, so let's take a look at two examples to see how this works.

Offering Example: Jeff

A client of mine, Jeff, was suffering from a severe case of anemia. He had a dream of a dog that was badly wounded and bleeding from its hip. The dog's life energy was draining away. Jeff recognized the dog in the dream as Burt, a familiar pet that had been energetic and playful all his life. In awake-life Burt had not only been Jeff's best friend, but also a healing influence in the home. In the dream he was bleeding to death, losing his will to live. He licked at the wound, but could not staunch the blood. Jeff understood how this related to his own illness. He saw that Burt carried both the wound and the capacity for healing. In order to access the medicinal properties of the image, Jeff needed to connect with Burt more deeply.

Jeff looked deeply into the eyes of the dream figure of Burt. But Jeff saw something more than just his pet looking back at him. An immortal figure emerged and revealed its elemental name, which was "Burton." He was an ancient dog with a grizzled muzzle, deep brown eyes, and a noble demeanor. Burton had an eternal wound that seeped blood.

Now that the image had revealed its essence, Jeff was ready to create an Offering that would heal both Burton and himself. Creating this Offering is the second step in the Offering process.

Jeff *determined* that the Offering required was something to stop the flow of blood from the hip wound, and so he identified an Offering that originated in the friendly, energetic, curious nature of the dog. Jeff had always admired how Burt would just dive in and make contact. He recognized that the dream Burton needed direct contact now. Jeff *formulated* an Offering of a commitment to be in dialogue with the wounded dream animal in written form once a day for five days. This ritual vow was Jeff's way of doing step three of the Offering process, which is to *administer* the Offering. By administering the imaginal dialogue to the wounded dream figure, Jeff knew that the image of Burton would be healed. His dialogue with the image of his wounded pet would bring Burton back to life, which would, in turn, help Jeff to heal. This is how healing works in Dream Tending: healing the wounded image heals us.

As the days went by he saw that Burton's imaginal wound was healing. The bleeding stopped, and the dream animal got his vitality back. As Burton returned to health, Jeff also found himself feeling energetic, eating more, and yearning for physical activity. When there is a shift in health of the image, there is a change in the health in the physical body. There is a direct relationship between the image body and the physical body. Jeff had, of course, continued regular medical treatment, and reported two months later that his red blood cell count was significantly up. He felt more robust than he had in a long time. Jeff continued his journal work with the dream dog. Burton became an inner companion and a healing presence that Jeff brought with him to all his medical treatments.

Offering Example: Gloria

Gloria was in her thirties and suffered from irritable bowel syndrome. She had become emaciated because of her difficulty retaining food in her system long enough to absorb its nutrients. As she grew weak and lost body mass, she also became vulnerable to infections of every sort, particularly strep throat and influenza. Gloria was under a doctor's care and worked with a naturopath, yet she continued to suffer with intense lower bowel cramping and illness. Once a confident and powerful woman, her illness had reduced her to a tepid shadow of herself.

Then Gloria dreamed of an earthquake in which a seven year-old boy was caught in a landslide that buried him under rock and dirt. His head was above ground, but the rest of his body was crushed by the weight of the earth. In the dream his lower body consisted of wood pieces held together by a string, like a stick puppet. Though badly injured, he radiated vitality. His face was filled with childhood innocence, trust, and helplessness. She returned his gaze and touched the boy with the "eyes" of her heart. She awakened from the dream feeling helpless herself.

Gloria knew at once that she must help the dream boy. His pain reminded her of her own physical ailments. Her first thoughts concerned what Offering would allow him to recover his body. In the first step of Offering, Gloria *determined* that the boy needed to regain life in his legs. Gloria, as well, needed the strength to stand on her own two feet and regain the healthy functioning of her body. In the second step of *formulating* the Offering, the necessary Offering had something to do with certitude and inner authority. Gloria had plenty of willpower and drive, but these attributes were not the inner authority that was needed for the image. Instead she felt that the boy's inner authority came from his sense of wonder and trust. As always the Offering came from the image itself. Further, the boy was buried by the power of the Earth, his lower body cut off by the land. Gloria felt that this signified her ancestors, who trusted in the ways of nature. Gloria's Offering was composed of her natural, earth-based certainty.

The third step was to *administer* the Offering. She did this through active imagination, in which she spoke aloud to the boy, saying, "I am here. I belong to and trust this land." This began to open up the boy's sense of independence and confidence. Then Gloria told him, "I'm here for you. I understand the pain you're in, and I won't leave you."

This set in motion the boy's healing process. As his relationship with Gloria deepened, the dream figure filled with the life force and continued to animate. The boy's legs grew back and he regained independence. The gaze between Gloria and him intensified, and both became more self-assured. The pain in Gloria's intestines relaxed. As Gloria continued to administer the Offering over the following weeks and months, the boy developed a healthy image body. The health implications for Gloria were correspondingly positive. Gradually food stayed down, she regained strength, her immune system recovered, and she did not get sick as often. The cycle of recurring strep throat was broken, and over time, under doctor's care, she went off of antibiotics altogether.

EXERCISE: *Offering*

Determining What Kind of Offering Is Needed—Identify a wounded image in your dreams, or use the image you have already identified. Choose an image that seems particularly vivid or appropriate. Next, go through the process of Naming that you are familiar with. This will animate and give body to the image. Now that the image is in the room with you, look at it with increased specificity. How is the dream figure wounded?

What is the exact nature of the wound? Is there an obstruction blocking the life force of the image? Is there a missing body part or organ? Do you see what bodily function is crippled, impaired, or dysfunctional? It is important to be precise about the nature of the wound. Take your time here. As you make this assessment, remember that the Offering you will formulate is intended to free up the life force of the dream figure.

Formulating the Offering—Now that you see the wound clearly, determine what the wounded dream figure needs to set its healing process in motion. The quality that you are looking for already exists both in you and in the wounded image, so take into account both of you as you develop your Offering.

Once you have an Offering in mind, check it out with the wounded dream figure. In active imagination ask, "Would this Offering be of value to you?" In this first attempt you may not get the affirmation you seek. If you sense a tentative or ambiguous response from the figure, look for a more appropriate Offering. You may have made an Offering of something that is too easy for you to give.

If this is the case, try again, this time engaging the figure more deeply. Determine what qualities or traits distinguish it. Ask yourself if these very same traits or qualities live in you at some level. Include any such qualities in your Offering.

Be sure to make your Offering something concrete. Create something tangible like journal writing, a montage, a painting, or a sculpture to represent your Offering as a way of incarnating your activity. Writing a song, lighting a candle, offering food or natural objects are also ways of giving physical form to your Offering. Remember the Offering must always contain what the wounded image needs to heal.

Administering the Offering—Once you have put your Offering together, administer it to the wounded dream image in whatever way seems appropriate. Stay very close and aware of the image as you do this, just as you would with a person you were caring for. Notice how the image reacts to the Offering, how it changes. Look for indications of what part of the Offering is most effective and concentrate on that. You want to sustain a connection with the wounded dream image as it returns to health. You should notice an immediate response and even an energetic reaction, as if the healing has been jump-started.

If this is the case, you have found and administered the Offering needed to heal the wounded dream figure. You have created and given what is needed to restore the well-being of both the image and yourself.

Step 3—Ritual

Ritual is the third step in the Dream Tending healing system. It functions like a follow-up visit to the doctor or aftercare, helping to sustain the healing process over time. This aftercare is crucial because healing is not instantaneous. The body needs time to restore and regenerate. In the case of Piano Leg, our furniture mover could have gone on over the next several months to create a Ritual of play and rest on Sundays in order to help heal his aching back. This is one simple example, but many types of Ritual are possible.

Ritual is not a new construct. In many cultures, ancient and modern, the practice of Ritual is used to connect the living world with the realm of the ancestors or the angels. These cultures access deities through Ritual, often to assist in ceremonies of healing. Ritual allows us to maintain relationships with the figures on the other side. In modern life, outside of the church, synagogue, or mosque our society is virtually devoid of the practice of community Ritual. The Dream Tending system of healing reintroduces Ritual into our lives as a necessary part of treating physical illness.

The procedure of Ritual is easy. Ritual, like Offering, consists of three parts:

a) Creating the Appropriate Environment for Ritual
b) Enacting the Ceremony of Ritual
c) Repeating the Ritual over Time

To *create the appropriate environment for Ritual,* we must set time aside from our regular routine. It is also essential that we choose the right place. The best guide in helping us choose a location is the dream setting itself. It does not need to be an exact match of the dream, but finding a place that is sympathetic to the dream setting is important. Including elements from nature is also significant. If we cannot conduct the Ritual outside, then integrating objects from nature into the ceremony inside our home is key.

The next part is *to enact the ceremony of Ritual.* It is like participating in a special ceremony, such as a wedding or a funeral. In Ritual we are in direct contact with dream figures, and the form of the ceremony varies widely, depending on the guidance of the dream and the activities of its figures.

The third part of Ritual is to *repeat the Ritual over time.* This is the crucial component. As we will see in the examples in this chapter, repetition is important to regularly re-activate the flow of curative energy essential in the process of healing. Without the follow-through of Ritual, the dream medicines will not be effective.

Although doing Ritual is straightforward, the very openness of the possibilities here is sometimes daunting or confusing. There are virtually limitless ways to do a Ritual. In order to better illustrate this process, I have included three examples of Rituals that were created by people working with Dream Tending. Included in each example is a brief description of Naming and Offering which places Ritual in the context of the entire practice.

Remember that the enactment of Ritual includes aftercare. It is designed to provide the means to administer the medicine over time. Notice that in each example the dream itself helps to shape the design of the Ritual. Furthermore, each of the three Ritual examples demonstrates working with a different type of image: an animal, an invisible force, and a plant. Also, notice that elements from the natural world are integrated into each of the Rituals.

Ritual Example: Margaret

For many years Margaret, in her fifties, suffered from intense anxiety. This condition manifested as migraine headaches, high blood pressure, insomnia, and an assortment of other physical aliments. She felt "explosions of energy" surge through her body without any way to release the tension. When sleep finally came, horrific nightmares would torment her. Various physical symptoms would then follow, one after the other.

After decades of this debilitating syndrome, clinging to the thinnest thread of sanity, one day she did something new. She started to paint. The terrors of her dream life, the white-hot electric energy streaming through her body, found expression in her art. As she opened up to the activity, one canvas led to another. In a few years her new paintings were being shown all around Los Angeles. Her physical health improved and her anxiety subsided. She started working with cancer patients, and felt helpful and productive.

Then one night, just as suddenly as it had begun, everything stopped cold. Her hands would no longer pick up the brush. Immediately, the anxiety was back, and she became consumed by agitation and fear. The severe headaches returned, followed now by joint pain and a stomach disorder. For over two years she suffered terribly in this condition.

Then a dream came. It was an image of a large crab caught in a net. The crab had a very unusual anatomy, with a small elephant's trunk protruding from one side of its body. Seemingly dead, the crab lay at the bottom of the ocean. Surrounding this crab were smaller crabs with similar elephant trunks. The dream image seemed bizarre and repugnant to Margaret. The creatures themselves seemed "deformed, misplaced, unnatural, and weird." From the perspective of the dreaming psyche, on the other hand, there was great intelligence and healing potential in the image.

Using Dream Tending, Margaret first discovered through the process of Naming that there was another vital living image trapped inside the crab's shell. The elephant's trunk seemed to "reach out and trumpet" this figure's presence. Instead of being trapped and inert, he was vibrantly alive, a "very old, primal, and confident leader of the rest of the crabs." Margaret discovered his medicinal name, which was King Crab.

Next, Margaret made the Offering of her aesthetic curiosity (not her psychological sophistication), and tried to see King Crab through the eyes of artistic appreciation. As she did this, he crawled about and lifted his trunk skyward. As his body came to life, so did Margaret's animal body. Her hands energized and heated up. She experienced an inner push to paint King Crab, weird trunk and all. Her hands shook with desire, tears rolled down her cheeks. She felt creative again.

For her Ritual, Margaret used paints made of natural materials, like crushed stone, distilled flowers, and seeds. She watched how King Crab manifested, moved about, related to the other crabs, as well as how he used his trunk. She painted King Crab as if the aqua blue light of the sea illuminated him, and she repeated the process over time, creating five paintings.

As a result, King Crab activated, enlivened, and became healthy. Over the following months Margaret kept painting and felt the life force return to her body. Her headaches, her stomach afflictions, and her hypertension began to fade away. Furthermore she remembered that in the past her paintings were considered to have a healing effect and had in fact been displayed in treatment centers. Margaret hung her paintings of King Crab at a cancer treatment center where she worked. One patient in particular reported that, "the paintings had a healing presence. I looked at them every day and felt supported in my recovery."

Ritual Example: Ron

Ron, a man in his forties, suffered from severe stomach disorder and bouts of colitis. He said that it felt like his "stomach was eating itself up." He suspected some kind of immune system weakness was playing a part in the illness and was taking a variety of medications to control the disorder. Nonetheless his condition would flare up time and again.

One morning Ron bolted out of bed to the sound of a booming voice that came from "somewhere else." He clearly heard the words "Eat your dreams." Ron's whole body shook at the sound of this voice. He had no idea what to make of it and felt apprehensive. Because he was "hearing voices," he naturally wondered if he was losing his mind. "It's like the voice of God is out to get me," he said

In the Dream Tending system of healing, we are concerned with both the content of the images and the energetic force of the figures. Dream images have both imaginal substance and energetic qualities. In the case of Ron's dream, the voice seemed to have no substance. Yet its energetic presence was as powerful as if it were visible.

Reflecting on the phrase "Eat your dreams," Ron discovered very little. He wondered how he could eat his dreams, and what possible difference it would make if he managed to do so. He thought that perhaps the process of eating might have had something to do with his stomach disorder and his health problems. But he had no idea how. The dream voice did not offer enough concrete information on first review.

Using the process of Naming, Offering, and Ritual, on the other hand, produced significant revelations. In Naming the image of the voice, Ron moved beyond considering, "What does this mean?" and instead asked, "Who is visiting now?" Tending an invisible image may be challenging, but Ron listened carefully to the deep guttural tone of the voice for thirty minutes. Doing this, he came back to his first intuition, which was that it was the voice of God, and so he named it God's Voice. This Naming had a powerful effect on the dream image. At first it had been very loud, but its tone and definition had been shaky. As Ron tended to God's Voice, the figure gradually developed a strong, clear sound, and became a clear energetic presence in the room. God's Voice never took on a visual body, but its sound energy was now full-bodied.

Ron then made an Offering to the dream image of God's Voice, which was intended to revitalize its sound. Ron did not like the idea that the voice had something to do with God. The sacred was an aspect in him that he greatly esteemed but of which he also felt afraid. As he worked with it more, however, Ron transcended his fear of God's Voice and stopped his need to make rational sense of it. He realized that God's Voice was not a religious god, but a dream god with a spirituality particular to Ron. Ron's Offering was composed of his acceptance, his willingness to listen, and his open heart. He felt that one more ingredient was necessary, the most precious Offering he could make, what he called his "birthright," his right to exist, to be here. For Ron, this was a transcendent conviction that he had denied himself since childhood. When he made his Offering, God's Voice energized, animated, and surged with life force.

The Ritual Ron created was designed to enable him and God's Voice to make direct contact with one another and to be responsive, not reactive. Ron followed the ways of the old traditions, elements we find in virtually all spiritual practices. He went into the wilderness and engaged in mindful listening. Deep in the forest Ron listened with his whole body to God's Voice, whose sound now arose with a fully embodied richness and depth. He went back into the wilderness and repeated this Ritual once a day for seven days. It is often helpful to use well-known forms like this to give structure and value to the practice of Ritual. As the Ritual unfolded day after day, the dream image of God's Voice became stronger, yet not louder. Ron listened from "inside his bones." In his "talks with God" Ron found that as God's Voice became more assured, so did he. His body relaxed, and his lower intestines started to unwind. God's Voice fed and comforted him.

For Ron, listening to God's Voice was not some kind of religious conversion as much as a coming home to his authentic life energy. By becoming more embodied, Ron felt less anxious. He experienced a focus to his actions, guided by the dream figure. Instead of running around scattered and defensive, Ron felt increasingly grounded and relaxed. His digestion improved, the colitis subsided, and his medications worked more effectively. Listening to the dream image of God's Voice became a daily healing practice for him. I find it fascinating that something as seemingly anonymous and random as a dream voice saying, "Eat your dreams" could end up becoming a source of tremendous healing.

Ritual Example: Judith

Judith was the high-powered CEO of a very successful company. She developed painful, chronic arthritis, and was losing motion in her arms, her shoulders, and her neck. She had gone to various doctors, and yet the condition grew worse.

Then she had a dream in which she was wandering through a jungle. As she walked, she got entangled in a monstrous, vine-like rubber plant. The plant was not like an actual rubber plant, but rather it was mutated in some way that caused it to grow wildly out of control. In the dream, Judith could see more of these mutant plants bursting from the ground. One of the vines wound up her arm and began to strangle her. She felt threatened and helpless. As she reached for her machete and tried to hack her way out of the vines, she felt paralyzed. Just before the dream ended she realized that if she breathed deeply, she might be able to use her intuition and slither out of the plant's grip.

Judith began to work with this nightmare, trying to find its medicinal name. She dialogued with the plant in her journal, writing spontaneously without punctuation, capitalization, or paragraphs. Using her intuition Judith gave voice to the image, and as she was doing this, she became aware of the dreamscape. She noticed that the surrounding area had been clear-cut, and the landscape out of which this plant was growing uncontrollably was barren. This gave her a hint about the essence of the plant.

Naming is more than observing. For Judith, the most interesting aspect of the plant was its tenacity and relentless drive. Upon closer inspection, she could see the plant was "sweating with sap as it strained to grow at an ever-increasing, feverish pace." She realized that what was important was the out of control, mutant aspect of the plant. As the plant further animated, the name of the plant began to present itself. Judith continued to ask, "Who's visiting now? What spirit of the plant presents itself now, here, in this room?" Finally Judith heard the essential name of the plant, which was Potency.

Judith next formulated an Offering. As a CEO, she had ambition to spare, an abundance of motivation, rigorous discipline, and sheer tenacity. Though all were of considerable value for Judith, none of these qualities was important to the health of the rubber plant. In fact, for this wildly advancing vine, growing uncontrollably in a barren landscape, intensity of any sort was counterproductive. No. Potency had enough of these qualities and needed something else.

Using her intuition, Judith found a clue in the arid dreamscape. What was missing was water. Without water the ecosystem was sterile. There were no other plants or creatures necessary for a balanced, sustainable biosphere. Judith realized that it wasn't just any water that was needed, but the water of her tears. She rarely cried, but when she did she felt refreshed and grounded. Judith offered her tears, and the ground became fertile again. Potency began to grow in a balanced way in this rich, new soil, and Judith's healing process also began to take hold. She stretched her arthritic body, first gently, then with more confidence and range. Like putting the juice of the aloe plant on the skin to relieve a burn, the liquid of Potency eased muscle tension, relieved pain, and promoted healing.

In Ritual, Judith warmed the juice of the plant between her hands, then massaged this medicine into her neck and shoulder muscles. When she felt the warmth open her range of motion and the pain begin to dissipate, she cried. She collected this liquid, her "water," and continued the massage. Next Judith did something homeopathic. With her fingertips she imaginally formed a concentrated bit of the juice from the dream image, dissolved this dream material in a vial of tear-water, and in active imagination drank it. She allowed the green, radiant quality of the healing herb to work from the inside.

What was inside Judith—her tears—watered the imaginal plant, and what was inside the plant—its sap—nourished Judith. She repeated these activities twice a day for one month. In combining this Ritual (and the rest and stretching it allowed) with the medicines her doctor prescribed for her, Judith experienced great relief from her afflictions.

Hopefully these examples have given you a strong perspective of how the practice of Ritual is enacted, as well as an overall sense of Dream Tending's healing system. Each dreamer identified and Named a dream image that was integral to their healing process, formulated an Offering based on the embodied reality of the image, and then created a Ritual. When followed through with consistency, these practices substantially contribute to health and well-being.

While all three steps—Naming, Offering, and Ritual—are important, the centerpiece of the practice is the Offering. Determining the correct Offering to give the wounded image is the crucial step and one that takes both practice and intuition. We saw in these examples how each person spent some time to formulate an Offering that was specifically attuned to both their wounded dream image and themselves. If we were to stop here, we would already have a powerful way to work with our dream images for well-being. However, we can venture much further into the mystery of healing through a more complete understanding of Offering. In the next section, I will illustrate a method for creating what I call a "Full-Strength Offering," which results in a more potent image-based medicine.

THE FULL-STRENGTH OFFERING

So far we have learned the basics of the Dream Tending healing system. This allows us to work with physical problems using our dreams in a general way. Many people will find this basic system sufficient for augmenting their everyday healing needs. It is possible, however, to go much further with this practice, and there are several reasons to do so. If an illness has taken a central role in our lives, or if we wish to work as "dream healers," or even if we just want to learn some of the advanced healing methods of Dream Tending, then this section will be helpful.

The key to empowering our healing work is to concentrate on the Offering. By learning to create a more specific, granular, and multileveled Offering, our Offerings will become more effective. This will give us more powerful medicines, because in essence the Offering is the medicine. This section focuses on a technique that I call a "Full-Strength Offering." A Full-Strength Offering is not different from the Offering we have already looked at, but represents a more complete encounter with the concept.

The body and the dreaming mind have a close, intimate connection. When I describe it as a connection, it often sounds like it is a one-dimensional relationship, and that is how we have treated it so far. However *the relationship between psyche and soma has many dimensions.* By looking at the dimensions of this relationship individually, we will greatly enhance our Offering.

Using a tried and true approach from depth psychology we can divide these dimensions into four categories: the physical dimension, the personal dimension, the archetypal dimension, and the elemental dimension. Each of these dimensions is found inside the other, like peeling away the layers of an onion. Like boxes within boxes, as we open the first, the second is revealed. Each level provides its own insights and curative properties. Of course, the box analogy is just intended to help visualize how these levels are stacked inside one another. In reality, there are no sharp divisions between them. They interpenetrate and interact in a fluid, non-hierarchical way. The deeper layers of the physical and personal are expressed in the archetypal and are rooted in nature.

From each of these dimensions we will gather the ingredients to formulate an imaginal medicine, which will become one-quarter of the final healing elixir. The alchemy of such a four-fold image-substance is the most potent Offering, and therefore the most potent dream medicine that I know.

The Physical Dimension

Dream images relating to the body's condition exist in the outermost layer, the physical dimension. Sores, blisters, fever, cough, and deformity manifest as symptoms of the body as well as in images in dreams. In this dimension, dreams will often picture the body's affliction, either literally or metaphorically. For example, a dripping faucet may suggest a runny nose; a broken or dim car headlight may imply trouble with the eyes. Like the dream image of Piano Leg, physical images are useful in diagnosing the onset of illness and initiating preventative care.

The first quarter of the healing elixir we are going to create comes from this physical dimension of the affliction. For example, think of a dysfunctional electrical system in a house, which (as a dream image) is a psychological expression of an actual physical problem or affliction. This image may indicate some nervous-system disorder like burning dermatitis, something similar to extreme heat rash. The Offering we will make comes from an aspect of the affliction itself or the emotional state it creates in us. In this example, the first ingredient of the Full Strength Offering might be the "shame" that the dermatitis creates because of its visibility and social stigma.

The Personal Dimension

The content of the second level of the psyche is the personal dimension, and includes our personal history. Each of us comes with our particular, sometimes dysfunctional, set of developmental circumstances. These influences from our early life shape our patterns of behavior. Psychologists of all stripes name these organizing structures the "complexes." Personality complexes underpin our physical afflictions, and dream images help us see them. The personal dimension is the source of the second quarter of the Full-Strength Offering. It lives within the physical dimension, like a doll within a doll.

Imagine again the wounded image of the dysfunctional electrical system. Picturing it in detail, we might see a wire sparking in the basement of the home we grew up in. Let's say these sparks ignite a fire. Furthermore it might be that the dream of fire in the basement has recurred many times over the years. This dream imagery symbolizes something of the psychological complex inside the physical affliction. The constant fear of the "house on fire" may have created a condition of intense anxiety. This ongoing state may be what underlies the physical ailment. The neurological disorder can be seen as a physical manifestation of the personal complex. Dreams use imagery to depict the nature of our illness and also to comment on the personality complex fueling it. The second ingredient of the Full-Strength Offering comes from the complex itself. In this case the Offering might be the "intensity" or "tenacity" at the core of the personal complex.

Both levels, physical and personal, structural and symbolic, offer enormous insight to the healing process, each contributing their twenty-five percent of the Offering to set the healing process in motion.

The Archetypal Dimension

The third box contains the archetypal aspect of the dream image. As we have touched on previously, an archetype is an inherited memory represented in dreams by a universal symbol. It is a basic image that can be found repeatedly in art, literature, and personal expression. The archetypal image is the third quarter of the four-part Offering. We can see the archetypal image as the force responsible for the creation of both our bodily afflictions and our personal complexes. Archetypes are the nuclei around which our behavior, moods, and afflictions revolve.

In order to bring out this archetypal dimension, it helps to contact our archetypal ego. In the Living Image chapter, we learned that touching our archetypal ego invites the animated spark alive within dream figures to emerge. Through this deep encounter, dream figures come to life and reveal themselves as embodied entities. Engaging our core ignites the medicinal core of an image. The Offering required in both instances, to our deep self and to the wounded/healer image, is one and the same. The essential medicine of an image mirrors back our path to health.

Let's return to our example of the fire burning through the basement of the childhood home. From an archetypal perspective, we amplify the mythic figure in the fire. In this case it may be Prometheus, the mythological Greek Titan who stole fire from the gods and gave it to the people, thus becoming a great hero. In this dream Prometheus would represent the archetypal image in the disease, and as such, he would also be a figure to set the healing process in motion.

Imagine for a moment how we could work with the archetype of Prometheus to understand its healing properties in this example. The Prometheus myth is a story of theft. We would then ask about the "theft" that took place in our early life. What was stolen from us? Was it self-worth, esteem, joy, or love? Who, or what god (parents, grandparents, or earlier ancestors), took the archetypal fire of life that now must be returned? This exploration of the early "crime" may reveal the archetypal roots contributing to our physical disorder. Further, the theft of fire long ago may have created defensive or defiant patterns of behavior (the personality complex) that now manifest as illness.

By exploring the archetype of Prometheus as a wounded healer, we gain understanding of illnesses of a "fiery" nature such as neurological disorders, fevers, rashes, and so forth. The Promethean qualities of creativity and imagination, when excessive, can result in imbalance and disease. However, Prometheus also offers hints of the cure.

To begin with, it is next to impossible to be curious and anxious at the same time. Getting creative puts a stop to anxiety. Prometheus' role in stealing from the gods was to give fire to humanity. Without fire, all is dark. Developing a relationship with he who knows how to get the fire back is key to the healing process in this example. Learning what Prometheus knows, reconnecting to his knowledge of fire and theft, is to experience him as a healer. When we relate to Prometheus as an archetypal figure at the center of the illness, he becomes a wounded healer, reconnecting us to a life-giving fire. As with other archetypal figures, he gives us access to the storehouse of wisdom found in the healing stories of the collective human psyche. The medicinal name of this wounded healer, which might be "Promethean Knowledge," is the third quarter of the Full Strength Offering in this example.

The Elemental Dimension

The last quarter of the Offering originates in the essential nature of the image itself. Here the Dream Tending system of healing goes beyond contact with the archetypal image and makes what I believe is its most important contribution to the healing arts. The essential medicinal quality of an image is contained within the metaphorical fourth box. It is this aspect of the medicine that is rooted in the elemental matrix of the World's Dream.

For example, recall the image of the broken electrical system in the basement with Prometheus as its medicinal name. Here we go beyond our physical, personal, and mythic references. We now view the image as an elemental expression of Nature herself. Fire and electricity (as in lightning) are powerful forces of Nature's creation or destruction that point directly to the life force. As such they are primary to the wounding/healing processes active in our disease syndromes.

Dream Tending teaches that the inner physician comes not only with information, advice, and wise counsel, but also with medicines. The image is the medicine; its medicinal property is the elemental vitality at the core of the image itself. The healing impulse of an image is the same life-affirming drive that is embedded in all creatures of the World's Dream. The organic nature of the image is key. A bit of the imaginal flesh or a drop of the blood of Prometheus is more than an informed perspective about a neurological disorder; it is also the psychic substance needed for physiological healing to take place.

All living things carry inside of them the biological capacity to grow, fight disease, regenerate, and die. I have found the same to be true for the images in dreams. When dream images are experienced as embodied, the life force with all of its medicinal properties is present in each image.

Going back to the example of Prometheus, we can see that once we name the figure inside the illness, it becomes possible to tend to it not only as a mythological figure, but also as an embodied image. The living image possesses instinctual, organic, biological knowledge of what is required to get well. In this case it was how to properly host the fire of life. This elemental dimension to the psyche is the final box and the one that will give us the pure drop of the healing elixir, the final twenty-five percent.

Now let's look at how to combine the four aspects of the affliction—the physical, the psychological, the archetypal, and the elemental—into the Full-Strength Offering. From the physical affliction we get "shame," from the personal complexes we add "intensity and tenacity," from the archetypal figure we contribute "Promethean knowledge," and to complete the Offering we mix in the element of "fire."

The following example illustrates how each of the four aspects contributes to create medicine to help cure illness.

Example: Mary and Wise Earth

Mary was a organizational development consultant who was highly driven and overworked. She had suffered serious neurological damage to her neck from a brain injury years before. When she came to my office, she broke into tears, saying how her neck throbbed in pain around the clock. She confessed that she had not had a medical check-up for over a year and a half and was experiencing occasional dizziness. She said, "After the initial ordeal of my brain injury, things hurt, but then started to get better. Only recently has my condition again become intolerable. I just do not want to go to the doctor and risk getting bad news and feeling crippled again." Common sense told Mary that she must overcome her catastrophic fears and go for a checkup.

Mary had a recurring dream of an old woman, who reminded her of her grandmother. Her grandmother had been a stern woman, but also had the capacity to be strong and wise. The old woman had arthritis and tried to walk with the support of a broken cane. The wood of the shattered, splintered cane was held together by duct tape.

Mary saw the Grandmother with Cane image as wounded, much like the condition of her neck. Grandmother with Cane's arthritic joints and the broken cane represented the *physical dimension* of Mary's affliction.

She also saw how Grandmother with Cane symbolized her own long-standing personality complex of being too controlling. Her controlling patterns had become a source of stress. The stress, and the muscle tension it created, had contributed to her neurological disorder. Thus the Grandmother with Cane image personified the *personal dimension* of Mary's condition.

Mary saw how all this related to her condition, but she was not sure how the image spoke to her terror of going to the doctor for a checkup. As Mary connected to her deep self, her archetypal ego, she felt more centered. This allowed the Grandmother with Cane image to begin showing its archetypal qualities. Then she realized Grandmother with Cane, as a wounded healer, represented the *archetypal dimension* of Mary's situation. This figure had the strength and balanced outlook necessary to follow through on things. Mary remembered her real-life grandmother as dependable and self-assured. In the dream Grandmother with Cane began looking at Mary in a new way, and though frail and feeble, she carried both the wound and the cure. As Grandmother with Cane animated and became more vivid, Mary saw her in her archetypal amplification as Wise Grandmother with Cane.

Then Mary remembered how amazed she used to be at her grandmother's love and care for things of the land. Grandmother with Cane knew the healing powers of being connected to the rhythms of nature and knew of the elemental healing properties of the land. Mary named this *elemental dimension* of Grandmother with Cane "Wise Earth."

Now Mary proceeded to formulate the Full-Strength Offering. From the affliction in her neck (the physical dimension) she recovered "humility," from her complex (the personal dimension) she pulled "perseverance." From the wound in the archetypal figure, Grandmother with Cane, she found "know how." From Wise Earth, she added elements she called "salt of the earth" and "nature's way." Mixing these ingredients together in active imagination, she distilled the Full-Strength Offering, a medicine she called "Earth Knowledge." She saw Earth Knowledge as a concentrate that would help her slow down and be more present. She offered this Earth Knowledge to the wounded Grandmother with Cane image in the dream. This mixture helped Mary find the resources to return to the doctor and get the proper, professional care for her condition. The elixir also gave strength to Grandma with Cane. Once the wounded dream image began to heal, so did Mary.

To make her Offering, Mary turned to Wise Earth, which nudged her outside. Walking around in a natural area, Mary discovered a beautiful willow tree, beneath which was a fallen branch in the shape of a body, with curves, outstretched limbs, unopened buds, and a covering of thin bark. These kinds of synchronicities are common when we are in touch with the World's Dream. Mary felt the branch represented her own physical body, and she saw the spot on it where her neck injury would be located. That same section of the branch also resembled the broken Cane in the dream. She whimsically tied some long, thin, dried grasses in a bow around this fracture in the branch.

As she watched the wind set the grasses in motion, she knew just what to do. She planted the branch firmly in the soil. With the grasses dancing in the breeze and companioned by Wise Earth (the elemental aspect), Mary administered the Offering to the Grandmother with Cane image (the archetypal aspect). Using the voice of her conviction and connecting to the energy of Wise Earth, Mary said aloud to Grandmother with Cane, "Use this Earth Knowledge to be sturdy and find your natural balance."

The only way to know if an Offering is correct is to observe the image's response to it. In this case, Grandmother with Cane turned toward Mary. In her eyes Mary noticed a kind of clearing and focus take place. Mary realized that she was making contact. The figure was gaining strength and looking at Mary in a centered, attentive way. As Grandmother with Cane became stronger and more self-reliant, Mary felt her own life energy circulating in a healthy way. Her shoulders and neck muscles relaxed, and she felt warmth return to her body. She said, "As Grandmother with Cane gets more sure-footed and capable, so do I." She said that she felt secure and unafraid of what the doctor might tell her. "I will handle what comes my way. I am ready to make an appointment for a full physical examination."

Mary's Offering was the creation of the symbolic art piece that she planted outside. Through this "talking stick" Mary offered an energetic statement to the wounded image. The potency and correctness of the Offering stopped her frenetic pace of overwork. Over time, the image of trying to support all her activities with stiff joints and a broken cane transformed into one of strength, ease, and suppleness. Like a calming herbal tea, the medicinal quality of the Offering re-established balance and allowed Mary to reconnect to a more present, related, and authentic way of being.

After Offering comes Ritual. Mary created a Ritual of going outside once a day for thirty days to make an Offering to Grandmother with Cane and to act in the world on behalf of her newfound life rhythm. She finally visited her physician and resumed physical therapy. Each day she filled her neck and shoulders with the radiance she experienced in her on-going Ritual called, "Slow Down, Be Present."

EXERCISE: *The Full-Strength Offering*

This exercise assumes that you have already found a wounded dream image and have gone through the Naming step, as you did in the first section of this chapter.

Determining the Full-Strength Offering—Start by determining the nature of the wound in a dream image. What kind of wound is it? How is the wound causing the image to be dysfunctional or ill? What is preventing the free flow of energy in the image?

Now, ask yourself the same series of questions. What is the nature of your illness? What is stopping your return to health? How is the disease taking a toll on your body?

Once these questions have been answered, you are ready to begin the formulation of the Full-Strength Offering.

Formulating the Full-Strength Offering—Remember that the actual object, gesture, or behavior that you will offer is made up of equal parts taken from the physical aspect, the psychological complex, the archetypal figure, and the elemental quality of the wounded image.

Identify the central quality of the *physical dimension.* Particular qualities might be humility, limitation, aging, or even the prospect of death. In this quality you will discover the positive, constructive intention of the affliction. For example, from humility you may find the capacity to be in service. From the fear of death, you may find the possibility of being present. Go through a similar process with whatever quality is at the center of the affliction that you are working with. Now write or draw something you have learned from this physical aspect of the affliction and put it aside for a moment.

From the *personal dimension,* find the psychological complex that is fueling the disease. For example, syndromes like addiction, depression, or compulsion may contribute to illness. Personality tendencies like victimization, aggression, or obsessive rescuing, when taken to the extreme, may tend to cause or perpetuate disease.

Once identified, discover the aspect of the complex that has constructive properties. Inside a pathological provider you may find heartfelt compassion. In the addictive personality you may find the quality of tenacity. Inside aggression you may find decisiveness, focus, purpose, clarity, or an unfulfilled wish. Write or draw what you have found. Place this to one side. You now have two parts of the Full-Strength Offering.

At the core of the complex lives an *archetypal dimension.* Evoke the presence of this wounded healer figure now. Discover what the wounded image needs in order to heal. What emotion, behavior, quality, or attribute would restore the flow of vitality in the figure? The medicine is found in your archetypal ego and is also found in the most indispensable quality of the figure. Find what connects you in a direct way to your deepest sense of self.

This third component of the Offering is very important. Spend whatever time you need finding the attribute that is of your most essential nature. Recall that this essential nature is neither your learned nor your adaptive character. Ambition, structure, and sensitivity, for example, are not necessarily the "gold" of your most essential Self.

Once you have recognized it, determine if this characteristic is what will heal the wounded nature of the archetype. You may also do this the other way around by starting with the archetypal figure and looking for correspondences to your archetypal ego. When you have found the correct quality, write or draw a description of it. You now have three quarters of the Offering.

The last quarter of the Full-Strength Offering is the most tangible yet the most elusive. This *elemental dimension* is found in the natural world and is the imaginal substance from which the image body is made. Think of this aspect of the Offering as being elemental. Start with the four elements: earth, water, air, and fire. Choose the one of these qualities that most closely bears resemblance to the natural environment of the wounded archetypal figure. For example, if it is a bird image, choose air; if a snake, select earth; if fish, pick water. If it is a person, go for the spark of life, fire. Make a picture of this element. Draw it with its particular qualities, form, and intensity. For example, if the element is water: is it cold salt water or warm mineral water? Is the dirt fertile and moist, or sandy and dry? Continue to distill the element until you have a good sense of specificity. This is the last twenty-five percent of the Offering.

To complete the act of concocting an Offering, bring each of the four written descriptions or drawn expressions together in one place. The medicine is the composite of these four parts. Imagine that you are mixing them together into a solution or healing elixir. This elixir is the Full-Strength Offering.

Administering the Full-Strength Offering—Determine how you are going to apply your Full-Strength Offering and do so now. Carefully observe how the dream figure responds to this application. Readjust and respond to its feedback, just as you would with another person. Be kind, compassionate, and loving in your application. Let the figure know that you have its best interests at heart.

If the wounded image is in a depleting process, such as bleeding from an injury, then apply the Offering to the wound itself. If the dream figure is losing life force or pulse, then apply the Offering like a salve to the exterior of the figure and rub the energy of the Offering into its skin. Also imaginally apply the Offering to your own body. If a disease is taking hold inside the figure, eating it away from within, then allow the image to swallow the Offering.

To complete your application of the Offering, repeat it often. Use your common sense to determine how many times a day it needs to be administered. Similar to taking medication, this may require between two and four applications a day. To support this follow-through, use the structure of Ritual.

Chapter Six

DREAM COUNCIL
–A LIFE PRACTICE

"This is my bank book," my great-grandfather said to me once when we were alone in his shop. He held up a small, worn-looking book and gestured for me to come closer. "Since I'm turning ninety-five soon, I've been thinking I should add up all my possessions. Then when I finally go to that place where everyone must, I'll take this little book with me and show them the fortune which I've saved here on earth." I was all ears.

With a large, callused finger, he pointed at the first page while he explained what was there: an account number, his name, some dates, and deposits up to the sum of two hundred dollars. Then he turned to the second page, again, a number, name, and some dates but on this page, no more deposits, only withdrawals that continued until the account was closed. Entries written in his hand lined the next pages. There were dates and figures, but he explained that they had nothing to do with money. "In the world to come, when they ask me, 'Zalman, what did you accomplish on the earth?' I'll say to them, 'Here, take a look for yourselves. It's all recorded here, so many thousands of shoes made in my life. Shoes to protect people from wetness and cold. Thousands of shoes repaired for those who could not buy new ones. And hundreds of good friends made during the course of my years in America, not to mention my children, grandchildren, and great-grandchildren.'"

On the last page there was just one number: 2,000. He pointed to it and smiled, his face turning pink with pleasure. "This is the greatest capital that I have, capital that you can touch." With that, he took a box out of a drawer and placed it on my lap. Inside there were two thousand picture postcards from places his customers had traveled on vacation, the Grand Canyon, Niagara Falls, Paris, Rome, Switzerland, and so on. Friends had written a personal message to him on every one of them. He had collected these cards over forty years, and some dated as early as 1912.

Pointing toward the ceiling, he said, "I'll tell them up there that other people saved up money, bought houses, and kept other earthly riches. But I saved up friends and the memories of everyone I talked to. Anyone who told me a story or sang me a song, filling my shop with love. *They* are the riches I will have collected while I was here, and the riches I will take with me to the next world."

THE DREAM COUNCIL PRACTICE

My great-grandfather had made a life practice out of working on people's shoes. It was his way of bringing soul into everything he did. The most significant life practice Dream Tending offers is the Dream Council. It is a systematic way to bring the power of the Dream Tending teachings into the center of daily life. I developed Dream Council over many years of working with my own dreams. It is at the center of my life's journey and my professional work. It is the life practice that unites the many other exercises you have learned in this book into one practice.

In its most basic form, Dream Council is simple to do. We take a few dream images, create physical objects to represent them, and interact with these objects. These embodied figures meet with us and with each other in a Council setting, where we all can have our say. And in my experience, once these figures start speaking, there is no holding back the conversations.

Council is a kind of ritual. It is a forum to gain and maintain relationship with dream images. It grows in complexity, depth, and meaning the more we engage in it. Dream Council forms a container for ongoing Dream Tending; it is the bridge between dream world and daily life, the path between worlds. I find it as fun and uplifting as it is profound and meaningful.

While it may take years for the practice to have its full effect, even the first encounter with Dream Council offers tangible rewards.

DREAM COUNCIL BASICS

Dream Council is a seven-step process. The seven steps are:

1) Choose Images

2) Make Figures

3) Select Location

4) Place Figures

5) Listen Deeply

6) Engage Council

7) Close Council

I will explain and explore each of these steps in detail as we move through Part I of this chapter. We will experience the full Dream Council in a series of seven exercises. By the time we do all seven steps, we will be fully initiated into the Dream Council practice. This is a wonderfully fulfilling new way of interacting with our dreams, and I am very pleased to present it here.

In Part II of this chapter I will take you through a series of exercises designed to deepen your experience of each step of Council practice.

PART I: LEARNING DREAM COUNCIL STEP-BY-STEP

Step 1—Choose Images

Perhaps one of the most important choices we make in this lifetime is our choice of friends. Good friends are more valuable than gold, diamonds, and technology stocks. They can help us through any difficulty in the world, including loss of livelihood, loss of relationship, and even loss of life. Aristotle said long ago, "Without friends no one would choose to live, though he had all other goods." I can't help but notice how similar this is to what Zadie told me as a boy.

It is interesting that the process of choosing friends is not completely under our control. There is the mix of chance and kismet that determines who we will meet and whether we will take to them or not. Jung suggests that "The meeting of two personalities is like the contact of two chemical substances: if there is any reaction, both are transformed." Yet it is up to us to decide with whom we will make friends.

Choosing images for Dream Council is like picking our friends. Our Dream Council friends will be very valuable to us. We want to choose our dream friends for Council very carefully. And as with our waking world friends, we must recognize that a strange and beautiful paradox underlies the process. For while we choose which images to take to Council, in a way the images have already chosen us by appearing in our dreams.

But first, let's remember that in real life we sometimes make friends for only a short while. Time and circumstance separate us from many good people. Others seem to stick with us for a lifetime, no matter what happens. The same is true in Dream Council. We may choose some images who work well on Council, but that stay only for a short while. Others may become permanent members on our Dream Council and provide us with guidance and companionship for our entire lives. We can only find out by going through the living of it.

Furthermore, some of our dearest, most important friends can be the most difficult to get along with. We do not want to include only those images that are pretty or make us feel good, but also those who may make us uncomfortable with their clear view of our situation and their sage advice.

So let's begin our first Dream Council by choosing which dream images we wish to get to know more deeply.

EXERCISE: *Choose Images*

For this first Council, identify six to eight important dream images. Read over your dream journal and see which images stand out. Some images may seem unimportant at first but somehow grow more intriguing as you consider them. Use your intuition in the selection process. Suspend your judgment and see which figures you want to include just because you want to. Follow your desire.

Do not include human images only. Broaden your view to include images of dream entities, animals, elements, machines, or whatever catches your attention and curiosity. Do not choose exclusively beautiful or happy images, either. Be sure to include those images that are repulsive, horrifying, or terrifying. As you learned in the Nightmares chapter, these intolerable images are often the most transformative.

It helps if you give each image a formal name for Dream Council. For example if you choose the image of a house-cat, refer to it as Gray Cat, or whatever name is appropriate, in Council. You learned to do this in earlier chapters, so continue this practice here.

Once you have gathered enough images for Council, notice how you feel. Has your state of awareness changed? How do you feel about each of the images? Which ones are you happy to include on the Council? Which ones are you unsure or anxious about including? Note your experience before moving on to step two.

Step 2—Make Figures

In Dream Council we express our dream images in *physical form*. This is what makes Dream Council different from all other dream practices. I have also found that this is the one necessary step for Dream Council to function. When I give dream images physical form, I can relate to them directly. This is very different from engaging them in the imagination alone. When we just imagine the figures, they can remain abstract concepts, fully relegated to the realm of fantasy. As incarnate figures, I see them in three dimensions, feel their texture, and enjoy their beauty. I can walk around them, gain different perspectives, and feel my relationship to them and theirs to each other. Manifesting dream images physically transports both them and us into the immediacy of the present moment. I can now gain insight through my encounter with the physical figures.

In Jung's autobiography, *Memories, Dreams, and Reflections,* he describes how he moved beyond writing down narrations of his dreams and began to actually draw and paint his dream images. He found this useful because it allowed the figures to break out of the confines of language and expand into vibrant, colorful, visual forms. This led directly to his breakthrough psychology and remained a lifelong personal practice for him. He ended up crafting figures from clay and stone to embody the physical form of his dream images and to surround himself with their presence.

Making figures is the step that is usually the most uncomfortable. It is the one we are likely to try to skip or shortchange. This is because many of us have been told that we are not artists, and that we have no business creating anything representational. There is also the sense that as long as something is locked in our mind it is safe, other people cannot find it, and we will be spared embarrassment. I tell people in my workshops to let go of their adult inhibitions and remember what it was like as a child to make designs in the sand or make objects out of mud, just for the joy of making something.

Really, creating these figures is a very simple idea. Giving shape to the characters of vision, story, and dream is a natural impulse. Human beings have always painted on the walls, carved shapes into wood, or even embedded them in our flesh. Making dreams visible is one of our deepest fascinations. Returning to this primal creative urge can be fulfilling and pleasurable.

So even though there is some possible discomfort with this step, it is clear that it is a powerful, natural, and necessary move to make. It is the way it has always been done, although modern culture has forgotten this. This is not only the next step in Dream Council, but a vital step in rediscovering our creativity.

EXERCISE: *Make Figures*

> Now it is time to create the physical forms for your Council members. Choose one figure to begin with. Picture as clearly as possible in your mind's eye how you want this figure to look. Sometimes writing a verbal description of the image can enhance the details. Use animation to help bring the figure to life. Once you see the image in bright, sharp focus, you can give it concrete form.

You sketch, draw, or paint the image. You can also sculpt it from clay or even Play-Doh. Your skill level as an artist is not important. Let your hands naturally give shape and body to the image. Some people close their eyes and allow their hands to take over completely.

You may want to experiment with collage, using cut-outs from magazines and newspapers. You might find items around the house that in some way represent the entities, like buttons, a piece of fabric, or matchsticks. A photograph of a family member or friend who has appeared in your dreams is another way for you to create a tangible figure. You may also find that a stuffed animal or figurine sometimes does the trick. There are countless ways of giving form to the figures. Use your imagination, your ingenuity, even your chutzpah.

As in all creative work, this is only partly rational. It also depends on your curiosity, your spontaneity, and your imagination. It is important to allow the figures to help create themselves. Just like making art when you were a child, let the flow of the process take over.

Now create the rest of the images on your Dream Council. One by one, bring them into being. Many people find this step to be powerful because of how the creative process can lead directly into the dreaming mind. Once the dreaming mind is engaged, the practice of Council comes to life. As each figure animates, it will influence the creation of the next.

When you have finished, notice your feelings. How has your awareness changed? Your breathing? How do you feel about the figures you have created? Be sure to note your experience before moving on to step three.

Step 3—Select Location

Now that you have a cast of characters, it is time to locate a proper setting for them. In many cultures, a house includes a special area designated for statues of deities, guardian figures, ancestral elders, and the like. Often it is a corner of a room, an alcove, or a shelf devoted to sacred items. Most of us have not made such a place of reverence in our homes. We have areas for family pictures, even ornate boxes for jewelry, complete with lock and key. But many of our homes lack a designated area for sacred items, a seat for the divine. To practice Dream Council in a sustained way, we need to create a place in our homes for the physical objects that represent our dream images.

I often call this special spot by its Greek name, *temenos.* Originally temenos meant the protected grounds of a temple. The temenos was the property of the gods and offered people a safe haven from the secular world. It was also the place where seekers could prepare themselves emotionally and physically for the initiatory rites of the temple. So temenos means a sacred space or ritual container, and this is the way we use the term in Dream Council. The temenos is the space where your Dream Council will take place. When I work indoors, an end table covered by a weaving that I got in Ecuador serves as the temenos where I host my dream figures.

EXERCISE: *Select Location*

Locate a place in your home that will serve as the temenos, or sacred space, for your Dream Council. This area can be a tabletop, a section of the floor, a shelf, the bottom of a window casing, or part of a counter. It could be the top of a chest or some kind of tray or box.

The temenos need not be big, nor any particular shape or form. Choosing this spot is a playful, intuitive, yet intentional process. Follow your gut feelings about where you might like to work with Council.

There are some caveats, however. The area should not be a heavy traffic zone, or cluttered with household stuff like bills, photographs, or mail. You want to choose a spot that is protected from outside disturbance, because you may want to leave your Council in place over time. You will spend time alone here, and you want to be free from distractions. So a secure and private area is best for Dream Council practice.

Once you have found a spot, you may want to decorate it in some way. Many cultures do this using candles and incense, and this is perfectly acceptable for Dream Council. You might want to paint the surface or cover it with tiles. There are many ways to set it apart as a ritual container. Allow your creativity to guide you.

Now that you have located and decorated the temenos for your Dream Council, how do you feel? How has your awareness changed? Do you find yourself pleasantly anticipating the next steps of Dream Council or are you feeling subtly anxious about it? How does your body feel? Note your experience.

Step 4—Place Figures

Now it is time to convene our first Dream Council. Although not a formal, ceremonial ritual in the traditional sense, this practice does take on some of the attitude of ritual. As such, it is important to create a time and space that is separate from the everyday interruptions of the telephone, conversations with others, and the noise of the television. This is time out of ordinary time. It is an opportunity to re-enter the dream world in a mindful way.

We can think of Dream Council as a kind of connection to the dream world. When we practice Council we are learning to live in two worlds: the regular world and the dreamtime. Living in two worlds allows us to permeate our lives with the wisdom of our archetypal egos. Although it's not always an easy thing to do, there is a mythic figure that serves as a perfect example for us: Hermes, the messenger of the gods. In Greek myth, Hermes carries the wishes of the gods to the realm of mortals and returns on high with news of earth. He also can travel to Hades, the underworld, the realm of the deep unconscious. He is the archetypal image of a being that can move with speed, grace, and ease between realms. Hermes has special wings on his feet that allow him to travel so easily. In order to facilitate our own movement between the realms, we need a practice that will develop metaphoric wings for us and exercise them until they are strong enough to carry us. In one way, we are simply physically placing figures in the temenos. In another way, there is a palpable sense that something else is helping us here. Our deep intuition is engaged. Our hands seem to be guided by a dreamlike knowing. It is as if the figures themselves have a clear idea of just how and where they should be placed, both in relation to us and in relation to each other. Perhaps Hermes has a hand in the process as well.

This intuitive knowing has always consorted with imagery and metaphoric figures. Myriad traditions from around the world express their relationship to synchronicities, complementarities, and non-casual correspondences through the throwing of the bones, the yarrow stalks of the I Ching, the tarot cards, the coffee grains, the tea leaves, the runes, and so on. There is something in the ritual of finding meaning in these images that sparks our intuition to flame. Yet unlike these culturally based systems, Dream Council uses images indigenous to our own minds. The emphasis here is not based on an external oracular system, but on intuiting the contours of our own inner landscapes.

I feel that this step is perhaps the most extraordinary phase of the practice. Placing the figures provides a portal through which we enter the realm of the living dream. How we place each figure is critical, because the layout reflects the story that is moving through the Council. Five figures in a line express something very different than five figures in a circle, for example. It is here that we get our initial taste of what the Council is expressing, what the meeting is about. And it is here that we feel the transition that happens when we move between worlds.

EXERCISE: *Place Figures*

Take the figures you have created to the temenos. Look at each of them carefully. Notice which seem to grab your attention. Choose about six and place them in a semi-circle in the temenos. This is the default beginning position for the figures.

Now rearrange the figures. Set them in new positions over and over again. You will notice that there are certain arrangements that feel better than others. Once you discover a placement that feels right, allow the figures to stand there for a while.

Next just sit back and listen. Give yourself time to observe the Council from different perspectives. Open your awareness and see if any of the figures come to life. Notice where the figures themselves want to be placed. Often they will tell you their feelings, show you their preferences toward other figures on the Council and where they want to be situated in relation to these figures. This is where the Council really activates and the "agenda" of this meeting comes into focus.

Make a final placement of the figures based on the input you have gathered so far. Once the figures are in place, step back and observe them once again. What are you now noticing from the Council? How are you feeling emotionally? Physically? How has your awareness changed? How has your attitude toward the Council figures changed? Which Council members seem to be coming to life? Note your experience.

Step 5—Listen Deeply

I have been interacting with dream figures in Council for over thirty years. The tradition of council is not a new invention, although it has usually been practiced between humans, rather than dream images. References to Council can be found in Homer's *Iliad,* where it is used in an attempt to resolve a bitter dispute between Achilles and Agamemnon. Native peoples of the Plains and Southwestern Pueblos practiced a form of Council to govern themselves, and its contemporary application can be found in the practices of the Native American Church. The Quaker meeting is a form of Council, and modern groups like the Ojai Institute have extensively developed council for use in virtually all environments from large corporations to personal relationships. From the mythologies of ancient Greece to the storytelling circle found in modern preschools, people have always met and engaged in Council.

What distinguishes Council as a practice from a simple get-together is that in Council we bring a sense of deep listening, mindful regard, and responsive speech to the circle. Listening openly without having a pre-formulated response is not the way we have been trained in our society. We feel obligated to have an immediate answer for anything anybody says.

In Council practice, however, this tendency is the opposite of what is required. Dream Council is respect-centered, not reaction-centered. When we listen to a Council member, we are not expected to have a quick or intelligent comeback, but simply to listen and witness. We want the figures to speak on their own behalf, not on ours.

We must slow down, get quiet, and listen deeply. This will help to activate the figures. As we listen more fully, the dream images will feel the space that we are making for them. Given this respectful attention, they will feel freer to speak authentically. As they do, we fully enter the realm of the dreaming mind.

Although we call this step "Listening Deeply," it actually involves all the senses. When we look at the figures without judgment or labels, we see them with the eye of artist. "Listening" in this way may involve vision, touch, smell, and taste, if any of these senses seems appropriate.

EXERCISE: *Listen Deeply*

Take your place on the perimeter of the temenos and watch the figures with an imaginative eye. Allow your curiosity and sense of play to arise. Remember Hermes, who feels comfortable and confident between worlds. Listen in a relaxed, attentive manner.

The essence is to listen with great attention and relaxation. It helps to remember when you took the time to hear a child's telling of her day, or the moments you spent listening to the birds singing in the backyard. Bring this way of listening to the Dream Council.

Deep listening transforms the space in front of you into a living dream space. Figures will animate and grow in complexity. When this happens, do nothing. Be patient. Breathe. Slow down and let the figures speak of their own accord.

Now engage your visual sense as well. Notice which figure grabs your attention. Who is visiting now? What is happening here? Open your curiosity and follow the activity. Pay attention to the details of who or what is revealed.

Experiment with being in the temenos yourself. Try seeing through the eyes of a figure, hearing through its ears. You will experience the dream figure's point of view.

Notice what new perspectives come forward. What are you learning from this figure? What does it have to say? What does it know? What does it want?

How does deep listening make you feel? How has your awareness changed? What thoughts, memories, or ideas come to you now? Pay close attention to everything you are experiencing and note it on paper.

Step 6—Engage Council

Over the years, I have come to profoundly value the impact Dream Council has on my life. I can bring my concerns, problems, bad feelings, and questions before the Council and afterward I always feel a lightening. I see things from a new perspective. I gain confidence, guidance, and comfort. When I feel frightened, out of control, or out of balance, I go to Council and seek the support of the figures. It is only in small part about finding answers. Mostly it is an experience of deep belonging with the multiple figures of my dream life. In the presence of these embodied images, I feel reconnected to my tribe.

In step six of the Dream Council practice, we engage our dream figures in exactly this way. Here we bring our needs, problems, questions, and desires before the Council. We feel the comfort of their presence, and allow them to work with our concerns. This step can vary widely from session to session, because this is where we interact with the figures and conduct the business of Council.

This step works best when we are deep into the dreamtime. In a way all the other steps of Council function to take us as far into this realm as possible for this step. It is here that we are most fully in the other world, and here that we may access the power, insight, presence, and wisdom of the dreaming psyche.

EXERCISE: *Engage Council*

Identify a particular life issue or emotional state that is bothering you. Take the time to get specific about the real concern. What is hurting you the most? Where and how do you feel the pain? What is pressing on you at the moment? Get as clear as you can about the problem and if possible find the essential question or challenge that this issue confronts you with. For example, if I feel overly pressured at work, I might frame the challenge this way: "What is really being asked of me beyond the mundane details of the work itself?".

In order to bring this question before the Council, state it out loud. Then simply wait. Notice which figure comes forward with a response and watch how that figure may implicate other figures on the Council. Notice the interaction between the figures and listen for what comes your way. You may not hear an answer per se, but be patient and feel into the response that comes forward.

Let the Dream Council hold the question or concern for a while. Give this process time to gestate. Stay in a receptive state. What are the Council members saying about your question? What perspectives do they offer?

Do you notice some distance now between you and your concerns? While the Dream Council figures are working with your problem, it is likely that you will feel a little distance from it. The figures are now holding the problem for you. This is a great service. We all need others to help us hold our pain and challenges at times.

What are you learning from the figures that is new or different? How does your body feel? Do you feel as alone in this struggle as you did before consulting Dream Council? How will you now confront the problem, given the new aid that Council has brought you?

Step 7—Close Council

In Dream Council we move like Hermes between worlds. In step one, we ritually open the door to the dream realm, and then move further into that realm with each step. As Dream Council comes to an end, it is vital that we bring this connection between the worlds to a close in a ritual manner, and mark our return to the everyday world.

In all ritual the process of a closing ceremony is vital. Think of a marriage ceremony, for example. When the officiant says, "You may kiss the bride," we all know that the marriage has occurred and the ritual has finished. There is the need to clearly mark the closing, to acknowledge the shutting of one door and the opening of another.

When we fail to adequately close Council we are left in a state of suspended ambiguity. We feel caught between two worlds. Proper closing of the Dream Council is as important as setting up Council to begin with. Mindfully closing Dream Council allows us to bring back into our everyday life the gifts we have gained, and allows the figures of the dreamtime to return to their realm of being. We each have home ground to stand on in order to continue our activities.

EXERCISE: *Close Council*

The ritual of closing Dream Council stems from a feeling of gratitude. The idea is to acknowledge the interaction you have just had and then offer your gratitude to the figures for taking part. You can do this in a number of ways.

The most basic form of closing is to bring your attention to each figure, one at a time. Simply look at the figure, thank he/she/it, and offer a silent tribute of your choosing. When you are done, look at the Council as a whole and offer your appreciation to the full assembly. You can get much more elaborate with your offering of gratitude if you wish. Take a moment to reflect on how you will bring your Council experience back into your day. At this point, the Council is closed.

Yet there is still a little more to do. The Dream Council has finished, but the figures are still there, scattered around the temenos. You have several choices here. One choice is to leave the figures the way they are. If you choose this route, offer one last look of gratitude, separate mindfully, and return to your day.

Another possibility is to pick up the figures and set them to one side. Some of them you may want to use again in future Dream Councils. Others can be respectfully disassembled, returned to their boxes, jars, or discarded in an appropriate way. As you set the figures aside, separate mindfully and return to your day.

Notice how you feel. How has your awareness changed? What do you experience differently after this Dream Council session? Note your experience.

You have now ended the ritual of Dream Council, yet you carry the experience with you throughout the day and into the night. Notice in the hours and days that follow how you are visited by the echoes of what happened for you in Council. How are the decisions that you make during the day informed by the insights gained at Dream Council? How has the Council affected your dreams?

Counting on Council

We have now completed our first Dream Council. It is a fascinating practice, but it is also natural to wonder what good is all this fantasy play? At this stage you may be asking, "How does Dream Council have any useful application in the everyday responsibilities of my life? Is it relevant to the demands and crises of the real world?". Let me answer these questions by sharing a story.

The figures of dreams have been some of my best friends since I was a child. Even when I was very young, I would play with them, entertain them, go on adventures with them, challenge them to duels, and get scared by the monstrous ones. Through the ups and downs of childhood, and on into adulthood, these figures were my constant companions, essential to my wellbeing. Eventually they became the basis of my career path and my life's work. The most important thing in my life was my connection to my dream figures, to whom I always turned for support, guidance, and care when things got rough.

But just a few years ago, things got rougher than I had experienced before. The graduate school which I had spent my entire adult life building was attacked by wealthy developers. Through some complicated legal shenanigans they were trying to get us kicked off our property, where we had been for so many years. Given their deep pockets and aggressive attitude, I had no choice but to begin consulting full time with lawyers, developers, county officials, my staff, and many other people in order to craft a strategy to save the school from this threat.

My life had been going full-bore for several years in the relentless struggle to protect the institution. The heavy load of my administrative work had drained dry my emotional reserves and left me vulnerable. Things had been so hectic for so long that I had, little by little, cut back on my dreamwork, the very thing that grounded me and gave me balance and peace in life. So often when we need an inner life the most is when we have the least time and inclination to work at it. This disconnected state can be described as a kind of "soul loss." To lose our inner connection is to lose all purpose and meaning. Neither sick nor crazy, such a person is nevertheless in danger of total collapse.

As the crisis with the school deepened, my personal situation grew worse. I isolated myself from family and friends. I had not done Dream Council practice for over a year. I was as alienated from the figures of Council as I felt from everyone else in my life. Every day I felt more and more helpless and alone. I felt anxiety spiraling out of control. I felt numb and spiritually bankrupt.

The developers kept raising the stakes with new and innovative attacks. They slandered me in the local papers with articles depicting the school as a plague on the community. I began to wonder if it was possible to beat them, or if I really was going to lose my life's work. What could I possibly count on to save myself in this crisis?

I decided to try Dream Council. In a way, I had no other choice. I had used Council to help so many other people in their time of need; people whose condition was far worse even than my current one. If my life's work had any meaning at all, then Council should be of some assistance to me now. It was time to find out the hard way just how real, how valid, and how useful Dream Council actually was, if at all. It was time to put it to the test.

I arranged to take a retreat at a cottage, cut off from communication or interruption. For five days and four nights, I would follow the path of my dreams. I had no idea what would happen. I was, in a sense, in search of myself and prayed that I would be found. More than anything I hoped that the figures of dream, who had always been there for me in the past, would reappear.

Once at the cottage I set about structuring the retreat for myself. It was hard to do because I had no energy or belief left in me, but gradually I put together a program. I would eat as well as possible. I would take long walks. I would swim in the ocean nearby. Most of all I would pay attention to my dreams, do my best to remember them, tend to them as thoroughly as possible, and engage them in the Dream Council practice.

It was a struggle even to begin. I knew that I would have to write my dreams in my journal. Although I had kept dream records for many years, I had abandoned this practice in the past months. To restart took an enormous effort of will, of pushing myself back into the practice. After so many years, I knew some surefire tricks to make it a little bit easier. One was to bestow the dream journal with personal value. I covered mine with beautiful leaves and shells I found on my walks, and kept it beneath my pillow. I also stated aloud my intention of remembering my dreams each night and made sure to allow myself time in the morning to do this. Finally I wrote a letter to my dreaming psyche in an effort to open a dialogue with her. Dreams like to be befriended, require attention, and respond positively to this gesture of greeting. Having emptied my bag of tricks, I went to bed on the first night of my retreat wondering if anything would happen at all. That night a dream appeared:

I am in the wilderness with a friend. We are fishing in a big lake. All around us a wildfire is burning out of control. Our campsite is destroyed. Everything is ruined but the fishing pole. All around me is devastation from the fire. I need to call home to tell people that I am OK. Then I get back to fishing and catch a big fish. It struggles, but I am able to bring him back to shore. As he's flopping around on the ground, I notice he's no ordinary fish. It's some species I've never seen before. It's bigger than the trout I am used to, multi-colored, shimmering, and very much alive.

Needless to say, I was grateful for this beautiful dream. Out of a natural disaster emerges a shimmering Fish. Not a normal fish, but something all together new, different, separate, alive, and other, filled with a vitality all its own. That was as far as I took the analysis of the dream. Anything more would have led to an explanation, and the last thing I needed was another explanation. I required something life-affirming and grounding, something real that could touch me to my depths. It was time to set up my Dream Council.

It was time to give material form to the wondrous dream Fish. It was hard to do. I dragged out some watercolors and large sheets of paper and began making simple paintings of Fish. I paid special attention to its bright colors and the details of its shape. Once that was done, I decided to continue this process with some sculpture, for which I used the only material suited to my artistic talents, Play-Doh. I began molding Fish with my eyes closed, just trying to get a basic shape without judging my work.

Once I had a simple figure, I sat and watched it for quite a while. I just observed it, making room within myself for the reality of Fish, for an imaginal presence with a life and intelligence of its own. I had no clue where this would lead, so I kept myself oriented around the two crucial questions "Who is visiting now?" and "What is happening here?" Also I steered myself clear of the kind of intellectual, analytical questions that would throw me back into my anxiety and obsession, such as "What does this mean? What am I doing? Why is this happening?". It took a lot of work to overcome the voices of panic, derision, and blame inside me, but I doggedly kept focused on developing my relationship with Fish.

After doing this for a while, I remembered a few other figures from past dreams of mine. The Woman with the Crystal Blue Eyes (a very common member of my Dream Council from past years), and Harpy (a demonic figure) showed up. Again I used paints and clay to give form to these images. As I was shaping them, I noticed that they were also working on me. I no longer felt like a lone hero and instead had plenty of help. The cottage had begun to fill up with the beings of my dreaming consciousness.

Right away this made me feel less alone, which had been one of my worst fears going into this retreat. At first I was surprised. I had felt completely alone for so long. Then I wept with relief at the feeling of homecoming. For the first time in many months I was not completely absorbed in my external trials or the internal whirlwind of my mind. I experienced a moment of presence, a brief contact with my inner self.

Now it was time to actually set up the Council. I hunted around for an appropriate temenos. There was a window facing a stand of sycamores in the back yard. Their leaves were changing color with exquisite beauty. I decided that the floor just beneath this window was the right place. At first I put them in a semicircle, the default Council position. Then I started moving them around, listening to the figures themselves to help find the best arrangement.

Once they were all in position, the Council could properly begin. Right off I was met with a big surprise. The beautiful Fish was actually in acute distress. He was freaking out because he felt threatened by Harpy and defenseless against her. I was shocked that Fish was so worried, and I felt a strong desire to help him. But then Woman with the Crystal Blue Eyes spoke up. She helped me to realize that there was no need to do anything, no need to save Fish. Her way was to simply observe the activity of the Council. In her blue eyes I saw my proper role here, which was as a witness. I was not the center of the Council, just one of its members.

I surrendered and let go. Feeling the terror of Fish was very painful, and yet I also began to feel something I had not felt in a long time. It was a sense of being part of a story that was much larger than myself, a story bigger than my current identity of being helpless, lost, and desperate. I was getting some perspective on my problems. I knew from my personal experience that out of *pathos* (great suffering) we come to know *pothos* (our sense of emerging self). Through the portal of the intolerable, we deepen into soul.

I felt some hope and relief at last. The practice of Council was already having some effect. The problems waiting for me already felt less threatening. I was even able to take a nap for the first time in months and re-acquainted myself with my appetite. I treated myself to a full lunch, complete with strawberry short-cake for dessert.

Then I was struck by a sudden jolt of fear. I remembered that lurking right outside the cottage was the judge who in three days' time would rule on the order to cease and desist all operations at the school. I was shaken by a terrible angst that came crashing in like a tidal wave. In surges of complete panic, a voice inside my head screamed, "What the hell are you doing? Your world is falling apart and you're hiding in this cabin playing with imaginary fish!" I utterly collapsed. I lay on the floor, among my paintings and clay figures, surrounded by journal and pens, immobile with fear. "What am I doing?" was all I could say, repeating it over and over with no answer. It seemed my little ray of hope had been nothing more than a trick to sink me even deeper into despair.

Still I knew that Dream Council work stirs up the deep unconscious. That night I wondered how my psyche would reflect this Council experience. In the morning I recorded this dream:

I am in a home and there is a fruit like a pomegranate. Each of the seeds is about to ripen into a bee. Each seed is giving birth to a beautiful bee of deep purple, red, and yellow. Over the radio I hear that when bees are born in this manner they must be fed milk with a dropper in order to survive. I try to get my son to find a dropper. I tell him over and over that he must get one quick or the bees will die. But he can't find one. Frustrated, I get a carton of milk, and spilling it everywhere, I attempt to pour it on the bees and into bowls on the floor. Some survive, but many drown in the milk. I think what a shame it is not to have a dropper. Here they all are in so many bright, beautiful colors and they're dying. Frustrated and angry, I listen as the remaining bees continue to buzz.

Writing this, I still felt upset. I didn't feel up to the task of tending this dream. Mechanically I returned to Dream Council. This time I set up the Council outside, where it is always a little more powerful for me. I left the cottage and went to the nearby beach, looking for objects to represent the dream images. I gathered ocean rocks, seashells, feathers, beach glass, whatever seemed to find me. There was a place that seemed to call to me, and so I set up the Council there. Then I settled in to watch.

Immediately a gnarled, weather-worn piece of bark that represented my great-grandfather came to life. It had been a long time since I had felt his presence. Feeling him there with me gave me a sensation of being grounded. For the first time that day I could breathe deeply. I felt present and connected to my heart. As I breathed, the array of tiny, colorful stones that represented the Bees started to awaken. With Zadie by my side the Bees were no longer frightening. I didn't need any dropper. Instead it felt like the opening of my heart, which is to be active and purposeful, was feeding the Bees. Their beauty and the genius touched me. The Bees became even more alive, coming into their essential nature right before me.

It was good that great-grandfather had shown up. Without him there I'm not sure I could have done this work at all. It was too deep, too disturbing for my limited ego alone. I was so grateful for his support. I found a rock that reminded me of him. It was heart shaped, and I brought it back to the cottage and held it close on the following days. It was good to be in the company of this compassionate Heart. It became part of the community of support that was growing in the cottage. I was feeling less detached and alone.

As the days passed, many more dream figures joined the circle. Elder Woman, Small Stray Dog, Snake of Red and Yellow. All contributed to the Council, and each of them helped me in some way. In return I felt compelled to make them an offering of gratitude, my renewed commitment to the Dream Council. In this practice, I found myself once again.

It was time to return to the world and confront the challenges there. The legal actions continued against the school. I still had a school to run, and a family with my wife and three school-age children. In fact, all of these pressures only got worse for a time after my retreat at the cottage. But something had shifted deep inside me. I was no longer a lost soul in danger of drowning. It was the Dream Council that I had turned to for strength in the worst hour of my life, and it had not let me down. Eventually we were able to defeat the developers and keep the school at its original campus.

PART II: GOING MORE DEEPLY INTO THE DREAM COUNCIL PRACTICE

I have taught Dream Council to thousands of students. Council leads practitioners right into the realm of the living dream, where their inner resources await. However we have only just begun to learn to make the most of this opportunity. Council unleashes primal, unconscious energies that contain tremendous power for change but that can also cause some psychological discomfort if this new relationship is not taken further. Once we open dialogue with dream figures, Jung asserts, we have personal responsibility to continue the interaction. I have found this to be true, but it is not as ominous as it may sound at first. It is simply that our dreams love to be in communication with us.

In this section we will learn four methods of deepening the Dream Council practice. Each of these methods encourages us to look at Council from a new angle. Each of them adds to our understanding of the practice and to our toolkit for working with dream images. Each exercise takes us through an entire Dream Council ritual so that we will grow more comfortable and familiar with the basic practice as we learn these more advanced variations. We will take it step by step, as I have found that this is the best way to internalize the Council practice.

Working with Shadow Figures

The unconscious sends all sorts of vapors, odd beings, terrors, and deluding images up into the mind—whether in dream, broad daylight, or insanity; for the human kingdom, beneath the floor of the comparatively neat little dwelling that we call our consciousness, goes down into unsuspected Aladdin caves. There not only jewels but also dangerous jinn abide: the convenient or resisted psychological powers that we have not thought

or dared to integrate into our lives. And they may remain unsus-
pected, or, on the other hand, some chance word, the smell of a
landscape, the taste of a cup of tea, or the glance of an eye may
touch a magic spring, and then dangerous messengers begin to
appear in the brain. These are dangerous because they threaten
the fabric of the security into which we have built ourselves and
our family. But they are fiendishly fascinating too, for they carry
keys that open the whole realm of the desired and feared adven-
ture of the discovery of the self. Destruction of the world that we
have built in which we live, and of ourselves within it; but then
a wonderful reconstruction, of the bolder, cleaner, more spa-
cious, and fully human life—that is the lure, the promise, and
terror, of these disturbing night visitants from the mythological
realm that we carry within.

–Joseph Campbell, *Hero with a Thousand Faces.*

Here Campbell vividly describes both the peril and potential
of horrific dream images. In the first part of this chapter I speci-
fied that we must include such images in our Dream Council
practice. When we do this, we find out right away just how compelling shadow material really is and why it has such a reputa-
tion as strong medicine. We also underscored the importance of
tending to shadow images in the earlier chapters on Nightmares
and Medicines of the Soul. Here we will specifically work with
shadow images on Council, turning them into an important
aspect of our life practice.

In my experience, including a shadow figure on Council has
several effects. As we have already seen, people can sometimes
experience extreme anxiety—such as a fear of annihilation or
of going crazy—when they work with shadow images, and this
fear initiates a fight or flight response. We either become reac-

tive or shrink into a feeling of powerlessness, either acting out or withdrawing. When we make this dynamic explicit on Dream Council, we have the opportunity to make peace with the darkest forces within us.

The secret is to engage the nightmarish figure fully. As before, this means that we bring all our awareness to the details of the image and its activity. We coax the image out of the shadows into visibility. What was once a dim, fuzzy, alien, threatening force lurking at the edges of the mind we now see with clarity and focus. Because we can see it, hear it, and feel it as a figure on Council, even the ugliest, scariest demon changes into something we can reckon with. This is a huge advantage. Better to be in continuous relationship with the horrific than to be blind to its presence.

Bringing a shadow figure to Council forces it out of the shadow. Yet there is a reason it has been marginalized, usually because it is too terrifying, too violent, too repulsive, or too depressing to bear. When we bring this energy into Council, one of the first effects is that it begins to surge out of the unconscious and into our everyday life. It is no longer safely contained and now seems to be a wild beast suddenly loose in our life. The shadow feels like it is everywhere. This is an intense period because we now experience this threatening figure both internally and externally. We feel ashamed to have such an ugly shadow figure within us. We struggle with bad feelings about ourselves and we project negativity all around us. This is a necessary step to bring the shadow material into consciousness. This is why creating actual, physical figures in Council is so important. The figure gives us a single, obvious, external object upon which to focus this energy. We do not feel the catastrophic fear of the unseen force that seems to be invading our life. The invisible is made visible. This makes us feel less overwhelmed.

In a way, the shadow material is the fire of the unconscious. That is, it can be a powerful force for creation or destruction. Handled properly, it can heal us of our deepest psychological difficulties. Its energy becomes life affirming and enhancing rather than crippling and depleting. In this exercise we will go through an entire seven-step Dream Council practice of working with a shadow figure.

EXERCISE: *Working with Shadow Figures*

Bringing shadow figures into Council can be very intense. Do not begin this exercise unless you feel up to an encounter with the darker forces within you. If at any point during this exercise you feel overwhelmed, take a break and allow yourself to find your ground again. The point here is not to be heroic while traumatizing yourself in the process. In the ongoing relationship with a shadow figure, always treat yourself with mindfulness, compassion, and firmness. It is OK to take this slowly. It is also perfectly legitimate to ask for help if needed.

Choose Images—Choose an image that you feel is negative, repugnant, horrific, repulsive, violent, depressing, or terrible in some way. A shadow figure of this kind often lurks in the corners of your consciousness. It is usually the last figure you want to admit exists at all, let alone spend time getting to know in Council. Do not work with more than one shadow image at a time.

Make sure you include a strongly positive figure on this Council as well. Sometimes shadow figures are too hot to handle alone, and you will need a strong ally on the Council to help you. You made use of such ally figures in the Nightmares chapter, now bring an ally to Council.

Make Figures—Shadow figures require more time to create than any other kind. It is important to spend time getting the details of the image as specific as possible. This allows you to see it clearly as a separate entity. Visualize the image as specifically as possible. You should make several versions, each time getting more detailed and specific. Don't worry about your artistic skills, but instead focus on clarifying and sharpening the figure.

Use materials that depict the intensity of feeling in the shadow image. Do not shy away from unpleasant colors like fecal browns, necrotic grays, blood reds, or sickly greens. If anything, exaggerate the repulsive appearance of the image in order to capture its force and intensity. Make it as ugly and awful as it really wants to be.

As you create the figure, you may experience some strong feelings. Harness these emotions to fuel the creative process. Go for a primal, raw, elemental version of the figure first. Then slowly begin to add detail. If the image is a person or animal, pay extra attention to getting the eyes just right. If it is a not a living entity, like a machine for example, render it as literally as possible. If it is some kind of invisible force or sensation, then your work is to symbolically render the energy as a physical figure, to interpret it as a shape or form.

Select Location—Remember that we consider the temenos to be a sacred container, which metaphorically is an alchemical alembic or boiling pot. When working with shadow figures, this pressure cooker aspect of the temenos becomes quite pronounced. A ritual vessel like the temenos must be strong enough to withhold the forces unleashed during Dream Council. In order to contain the energy, you need to emphasize the temenos as a place where there are no distractions or interruptions. The location you choose must be big enough to give the shadow figure room to express itself fully. You are working with a lot of energy, and there needs to be a lot of space to handle it. One of the chief intentions of working with the shadow is to give yourself separation from the figure, so the bigger the temenos, the easier it is for you to get some breathing room.

You can also encourage the figure to emerge by finding a location suited to its temperament. Not surprisingly, some shadow figures often prefer dark, hidden, or underground spaces, like a basement. Others prefer fiery, bright, sharp-edged, metallic environments like a granite boulder in a flinty desert. It all depends on the nature of the shadow figure. Hold your Council in a location the shadow image likes and it will be easier to activate it.

Place Figures—Shadow figures are fascinating. When you attempt to place them they will almost always claim center stage. Notice what other images you place nearby, as well as those you put off to the side. These incidental figures will often become your allies in working with the shadow.

The shadow image does not want to be caught or controlled by you. It has survived a long time by hiding from sight. The shadow finds being revealed in Council to be intensely threatening, and it will respond by either getting much bigger or retreating into the darkness, trying to hide again. It will move around a lot, trying to present a difficult target. Be prepared for it to come and go, or suddenly disappear. Eventually things will settle down.

Giving place to the shadow figure in Council is extremely important. It relies upon you for its existence, and yet it is terrified that if you see it clearly, you will kill it. It has a terrible fear of annihilation. But you do not want to get rid of it, because you would then lose its power. When you give it a place on Council, the figure eventually feels less threatened and calms down. You have called a truce. You have relieved its fear of extermination.

Listen Deeply—Now that neither of you is trying to kill the other, your job is to learn as much as possible about this figure. Focus on it. Begin by simply looking at it and acknowledging its presence.

You may notice right away that connecting with the shadow figure brings up strong emotions like terror, despair, revulsion, or rage. Which emotion does this figure trigger in you? Where do you feel it in your body? What kinds of body sensations accompany this emotion (muscle tension, cramps, breathing changes, etc.)? Carefully note the specific flavor of emotion you are feeling. This is part of the emotional signature of this figure. Do not try to stop, suppress, or ignore these emotions. Let them flow through you as much as possible and continue with the exercise. If the feelings are overwhelming, stop, close your eyes, and breathe. When the feelings become bearable again, continue.

Engage Council—Now take notes on the figure itself. Describe the physical features of the figure down to the smallest detail. Be as specific as possible. Then explore its habits, such as what it eats, when it eats, where it sleeps, how it moves, and its daily activities. Become fascinated with this creature or figure, whatever it may be. Remember that it may not fit the characteristics of any living thing on earth. This is a dream figure and has its own unique properties. Learn these properties to the best of your ability. Some of them may be disgusting or awful, and some of them might be quite surprising. Write everything down. Draw pictures, diagrams, and close-ups. Make the shadow figure the subject of a sort of research project.

Engagement here also means finding the inner strength to relate to the shadow figure. If taking notes on the shadow figure is too anxiety-producing, let go of that for a while and instead connect to a figure that symbolizes something of your deepest strength. Nurture your relationship with this ally figure. Feel your power grow. When you're ready, sustain contact with the helpful power figure while you bring your awareness back to the shadow figure. You have done this before in the Nightmares Chapter. Draw on your earlier experience to help you. Let the ally figure support and empower you while you take notes on the shadow figure. Do this in tiny steps that are comfortable for you. There is no point in going too far. However, if even this method produces too much anxiety, then stop your solo attempts and work in the company of a therapist.

As you spend more time learning about the shadow figure, you will notice that its difficult qualities become less intense. Because you are no longer in conflict, the shadow can afford to show you some of its positive qualities.

You will gradually become accustomed to each other, and spending time together will be more comfortable. This allows you to go even deeper with your investigation.

See if you can track the shadow to its place of origin. Where does it come from in the first place? Where was it born? Notice how your feelings change as you work with the shadow. How does your body feel? What emotions are arising? What insights are you gaining from this figure? It is possible to learn a lot from this step.

Close Council—It is important to close a Council of this type firmly and concretely. Say something aloud like, "I am now closing Council, but closing Council does not mean that I am closing you out of my life. I will see you in the next Council, but I am now ready to go out into my life of relationships with others."

Complete the closing of the Council by acknowledging all the figures present. Take the time to put them away and make a smooth transition into everyday life.

Engaging a shadow figure can take many Dream Council sessions over the course of weeks or months. Slowly the image will come into sharper and sharper focus. Notice the effect this has on the image itself. How do you feel now when you work with this image? What effect does this figure have on the rest of the Council? Do you notice this image coming more often into your daily life? How is it different now?

Finding the Essential Impulse

Dream images are like animals. They are alive and have instincts. A dream cat knows the instinctual ways of a cat. Even images that represent inanimate objects have an innate propensity to be what they are. A bridge "knows" the ways and functions of a bridge. As we explored in the indigenous image section, dream figures are elementally connected to their primal identities, their unique selves. A dream Lion contains, at center, the essence of Lion. The same is true for Ocean, House, and Mountain. Intrinsic to each dream image is its true nature.

What is most essential about dream images is their beauty, their innate aesthetic quality. Whether they are traditionally lovely, or in some way sublimely terrible, Dream Council comes alive with newfound depth when we allow the radiant beauty of the figures to show itself. Our reaction to their "shine" is immediate. Their beauty touches our soul.

When we connect with the essential impulse of a dream image, we are really experiencing an image's intrinsic beauty. When we strip away all the layers of the image, we arrive at its simplest, most primitive, and most aesthetic form. This is a powerful moment to experience. In doing so we reconnect to our sense of who we are and to our essential, natural beauty.

One way to experience the aesthetic dimension of an image is to look at it with the eye of an artist. An artist is constantly looking into an object, stripping away what is superfluous, in order to see its innate beauty. Even a careful look at the surface of an object reveals that which is lit up from the inside. Tending to images in this way on Dream Council involves a special sense of craftsmanship.

Usually we think of craftsmanship as something artificial, highly cultivated and aesthetic. But there is another sense of craftsmanship, which is the ability to construct something out of the most fundamental materials possible. Suppose we were to try and create something as complex as a computer out of the most basic materials. We could actually do this with pebbles. Ancient people did this by creating the abacus (the verb "to calculate" comes from the Latin word *calculus,* which literally means "pebble"). We can think of an abacus as a primal computer, something that cuts right to the essence of what a computer does, counts things. It is this almost "caveman" sense of craftsmanship that will take us to the essence and the elegance of an image.

An actual example from one of my Dream Tending workshops illustrates this principle well. A young man, Tom, had a dream about making a guitar. He was in his garage, affixing a wooden bridge onto the face of the instrument. He struggled to attach the strings to the bridge. In the dream he couldn't figure out how to do this. But he knew that when he finished he would have his own handmade musical instrument.

It was clear to all of us in the workshop that the image of the guitar was important to him. It was an image that he should include on his Dream Council. His task was to give form to the image and capture the essential impulse of his musicality. Following the motif of the dream, I recommended he construct the figure himself rather than finding some object to represent it. I suggested he go outside and build a primitive instrument out of natural materials. By not worrying about getting it perfect, and instead just focusing on the bare essentials, I hoped he would get to the deep impulse of the image and discover its exquisiteness.

At the beach he picked up driftwood for the frame, dried sea grass for the strings, and a piece of bark for the bridge. Then he found a quiet spot and made this primitive guitar. The energy of these raw materials infused Tom's work. The spark alive in the elemental materials converged with his creative drive to bring artistic form to the figure. Guitar, in its elemental beauty, was now ready to be placed on Council. This figure became very important to Tom. It helped guide him to the source of his musical talent.

EXERCISE: *Finding the Essential Impulse*

Select Images—In this exercise we will focus on human-made, "constructed" dream figures. Find an image in your dreams that is either under construction or that has been hand crafted or machine-made. It should have the feeling of having been assembled or put together in some way. If no such images come to mind, then choose an image that stands out, seems to glow, or catches your eye. Notice how the image operates in the dream. What is its function? What is it used for or what does it do? Watch its activity.

Make Figures—Look at the figure as a craftsperson might. What material is it made of, how is it put together, what makes it tick? Get clear on all these details. Imagine how you would give form to this image from natural materials without using any tools.

Then gather sticks, twigs, grasses, bark, pebbles, leaves, or whatever is available in the natural environment. Use these to make a simple figure of the image. Your work here is to co-create with the image itself. Together you are making a figure, allowing the essence of the figure to emerge, to shine through.

Take notice of how the life force present in the materials combines with your creative juices. Feel the confluence of energies. Attempt to represent the image in the most basic way possible. Strip it down to its essence. Make it crude and impressionistic, and full of energy and vibrancy. The radiance of the figure is inherent in the materials, waiting to be released. Let the inner beauty of the image come to the surface.

Listen to your sense of ingenuity, the age-old wisdom in your hands. Human hands have known how to craft things for millions of years. What does it feel like to make this figure? Listen the natural materials, too. What are they saying about how they want to be assembled?

Select Location—Find a natural, outdoor temenos or, conversely, an indoor place that is very modern. You may want to choose the place where you have gathered the materials to make the figure. This place has given of itself for your Council and is therefore already a participant.

Use your intuition to locate the intersection where the impulse of the figure meets just the right spot in the landscape. Here you set up Council.

Place Figures—Notice the compatibility between the handmade figure and the landscape. Place the figure in a way that is harmonious with this connection. Then put all the other Council figures around it.

Listen Deeply—Now listen to the handmade figure speak. Council practice at this level asks you to be present, outside of your busy mind and inside the World's Dream. The handmade figure reconnects you to a mode of hearing that is attuned to the rhythms of Nature. Listen to the figure with your ears, not with your mind. Take the time to touch and feel its texture and to smell its aroma. Look at its shape and details with focused eyes, then with soft eyes. Let its beauty find your own. Wait for the aesthetic moment when your breathing changes and you experience a sense of awe. Breathe in the beauty as it shows itself to you. That which can be personified and animated can be loved.

Engage Council—Now playfully interact with the figure through physical contact. For example if you made a primitive musical instrument, fiddle around with it. Can you make a sound? Can you play some kind of tune with it? What is it like to play this primal instrument? Play with the figure in whatever way is fitting.

Engagement here also means feeling what has opened in you through contact with the essential impulse of the image. How have you activated or engaged its beauty? What kind of ancient memories/echoes/instincts have you awakened in yourself? How does your body feel? How does your body want to move? What are you rediscovering about your essential nature as you get to the essence of the figure?

Close Council—Do this as before. You will probably want to add the figure you just made to your ongoing Dream

Council practice. This figure that carries the essential impulse will continue to be a useful one.

Images from the Waking Dream

Up until now we have been choosing our Council members exclusively from our nighttime dreams. Even an image of ourselves on Council comes from how we saw ourselves in last night's dream. Yet the veil between nighttime dreams and other dreamlike experiences is an artificial, albeit useful, one. The dreaming mind of the night does not hunker down all day in some basement of the unconscious, impatiently waiting for night to fall so it can escape and dance through our dreams. On the contrary, the dreaming mind is a foundation upon which all our states of awareness rest, thus it is continually present in our waking consciousness to a greater or lesser degree. We are all part of the World's Dream. All material being is shaped by the dreams of the world.

Dream images enter our consciousness throughout the day, even when our eyes are open. The most obvious example is when we slip into a daydream. The name exactly describes the nature of this phenomenon. Less obvious are small fragments of fantasy or repetitive images that arise in our thoughts during the day.

We sometimes experience certain people or places in a dreamlike way. For example an old woman we see in the grocery store may take on some aspect of a crone figure from our dream the night before, or a town we are visiting might remind us of a cityscape that has recurred in our dreams. We may be shocked to see the woman of our dreams, our beloved, walking downtown on State Street, pausing for a moment before disappearing into a department store. On many occasions we experience the circumstances, the people, and the places of our day in a dreamlike way. In Dream Council we engage these daytime dream figures just as we do the images of the night.

In many ways, we experience the world as a waking dream. The whole world and all the things in it are dreaming together. At this level of the dreaming psyche, we are participating in the World's Dream. Dream Council helps us to open up more completely to an everyday awareness of this complex, interwoven dream network. Let's try including the images from the waking dream on Council.

EXERCISE: *Images from the Waking Dream*

Choose Images—Select images for this Council from your waking dreams. Review your week and ask yourself if anything out of the ordinary happened. Was there something you experienced that was dreamlike, a situation or interaction that seemed like a waking dream? What stands out from that experience? Which waking image seems to be something otherworldly? Select that image for Council.

Make Figures—Make the figures for this Council just as you have been doing. Since you are now removing the separation between waking dreams and nighttime dreams, there should be no difference in the way you create these figures. However the physical reality of some daydream images gives you new techniques for making figures. If one of your waking dream images is an actual person, you can use an actual photograph of that person. If it is a place, you can use materials from that place; if it is a forest image, you could use leaves, pinecones, soil, or other objects from the actual forest.

Furthermore, waking dreams often use different senses than nighttime dreams. Because your eyes are open all day long, daydream images contain more sights and visual textures. Making figures of these images can be challenging. If your image is texture or touch based, then creating a figure with a similar texture is of course the way to go. If your image is sound-based, your approach can be much more impressionistic, like (if you are outdoors) using a leaf or sprig of grass that moves in the wind to represent the sound, or (if you are indoors) making use of a noise-making object, like a bell, to represent the sound. The figures are symbolic stand-ins for the real thing, so the sounds do not have to be the same. They are not meant to be literal representations.

Select Location—Physical locations also come into our awareness as waking dream images. If this happens you are lucky, because this gives you a unique opportunity to hold Dream Council in a location from your daydreams. The concept of the temenos takes on added layers of meaning here, since this actual place in the world intersects or overlaps the place in your dreams. You are donning the mantle of Hermes, standing at the crossroads between worlds.

So go to the physical location that was in your daydreams or reminds you of a dreamscape. Walk around that space in an unhurried way, feeling your way through it. This waking dreamscape will be your temenos for Council.

If no physical location presents itself from your daydreams, use your regular temenos for this step.

Place Figures—Having gotten this far, you should already be in a fairly deep state of consciousness. Making use of waking dream images opens us up to the synchronicity that is the signature of the dreamtime. In this state, placing the figures becomes charged with meaning and playfulness. The figures seem to participate in placing themselves.

Another variation here is to place the first figure and

then allow that figure to help you place the second figure. Next let those two help you place the third, and so on. Notice what happens as you do this. Placing the figures becomes a creative act in its own right.

Listen Deeply—The waking dream requires a new way of listening. Not only are you bringing your witnessing presence to the figures, as you did before. Now you are also maintaining awareness of the world around you. In a waking Dream Council, the weather, the sky, clouds, ambient sounds, intrusions, accidents, and all manner of things actually become parts of the Council itself. The entire temenos is active in the Council discussion. Your body sensations, your emotions, your reactions to the world around you, your thoughts, your associations, even your distractions, all become parts of the dialogue. This is a deep meditation and requires you to stay open, relaxed, and highly focused. You are encountering the dreamscape in the hermetic mode, watching the junction of all worlds.

Engage Council—As you continue watching and listening, you will eventually be called into the unfolding dialogue with the world. As images from both daytime and nighttime dreams flow together before you, you will become part of the story you are watching. You are drawn into the present moment in a continually fresh way. Your problems and questions become daydream images in this kaleidoscope of interconnected imagery.

Become aware of who is visiting now. What concerns do each of the figures bring with them? What are you feeling emotionally? What are you feeling in your body? Continue for as long as you wish.

Close Council—Until now, closing Council has been a formal way to shut the door between worlds. With waking dreams, you recognize that there is actually no such door and that you always have access to dreaming consciousness. Closing Council now means to skillfully differentiate from, but not to close off or separate from, the transcendental realm of the waking dreamtime. Closure means changing your state of awareness back to normal waking consciousness, but remembering that dreams are always present in the day as well as the night. So say goodbye to the figures in Council and yet recognize that they will be with you all day long, as you walk through the dream of life.

How do you feel? How is your awareness different? How do you perceive the world around you? In the following days notice the times when dream images enter your mind or when something in your environment reminds you of a dream.

The Dream Council of the Soul

Perhaps no word is as notoriously difficult to define as the word "soul," but it is certainly not through lack of trying. Many bestselling books have attempted to make matters clear, such as *The Soul's Code, Care of the Soul, Soul Mates,* and even *Chicken Soup for the Soul.* Popular culture constantly plays with this powerful word using ideas like soul mates, soul music, soul food, soul baby, and even soul train. We are either soulful or soulless. Pacifica Graduate Institute's motto is *animae mundi colendae gratia* ("for the sake of tending the soul of the world"). Yet among my students and faculty there is a lot of controversy about just what this soul is. It seems to mean something different to nearly every person.

Yet despite all these divergent views on the subject, I am willing to offer a definition of soul here. This definition is operational not conceptual, which makes it particularly easy to work with. In the practice of Dream Tending, soul is defined as the *ongoing activity of the dream images.* The living experience of the dreaming mind is our experience of soul.

As we have seen in these exercises, images become alive and embodied when we tend to them in Dream Council. They are much more than just static images representing fixed ideas linked to our personal memory and life circumstances. In ongoing Council practice, we experience these images as part of an unfolding inner story with a reality of its own. These are the imaginal representations of the fundamental energies of our soul life. We can literally see the soul in action when we are watching the activity of the images in Council.

These images of the soul are responsible for making our dreams to begin with. As the characters in a story give meaning to the narrative, it is our dream images that give meaning to our life's story, the journey of who we are and who we are becoming. In Dream Council we discover our inner stories and with them our sense of calling. As we watch the activities of dream images and witness the tales that they are telling, we may even get a glimpse of our destiny. In Dream Council we see our providence in the activities of the dream images. They are the authors of our life's story. As we come to know their movements, we learn the contours of our interior landscape and the motivations for our exterior behavior. We feel placed, rooted in the knowledge of our personal mythology. Dream Council becomes a portal through which we travel to meet these embodied dream images. Here we experience first hand the makers of soul.

EXERCISE: *The Dream Council of the Soul*

Choose Images—At this level you relinquish all sense that you are the one holding Council. Rather, the figures themselves hold Council and you are an active participant. So the first step in the Dream Council of the Soul is to watch as the dream images choose themselves or each other for a seat in the proceedings. As a Council member you can lobby for the inclusion or exclusion of various images, but it is a group process. See if you can maintain the state of consciousness necessary to experience Council in this way.

Make Figures—You have already experimented quite a bit with allowing the figures to co-create themselves. Now you will witness the individuation of the figures. Here the figures *work together to create each other.* The process pushes each figure to define itself ever more distinctly. This is important in Dream Council because as the figures individuate, so do you. Follow the natural transformation of the figures, and let newly emerging forms find their way onto Council.

Select Location—Just as the figures choose themselves, the temenos too will come forward and stake its claim on this Council. Wander around until it makes itself known to you. You have had a lot of experience with doing this in other exercises, so tap into your own natural understanding of how to do this.

Once the location has found you, however, there will be an addition to this step. At this level, the temenos will not only appear as a physical location, but also as a figure on the Council. It too will actively contribute on Council. Of course, there is no need to create a figure, since the location itself is the physical representation of this image.

Place Figures—This type of Dream Council can be thought of as watching a play on stage. Here the figures will place themselves and actively participate in the placement of the other figures. But beyond that you can imagine that you and the figures are setting the stage in the theater of the deep mind. Take care to listen to all the figures involved. Here at the level of soul this can give us tremendous insight.

Listen Deeply—Now let the play begin. Sit back and listen to the story as it begins to tell itself through the activity of the figures. You are literally watching the spontaneous unfolding of your own living soul. How do you feel as you are watching the figures interact? How does your body feel? What thoughts occur to you?

Engage Council—As you continue to watch the figures holding Council, notice that you are having spontaneous insights into your life as well as into theirs. Witness not only how the figures inform your behavior in the external, everyday world, but also how they create a soul life that is independent of yours. Glimpse the ongoing story that underpins your existence. How do the struggles and evolving alliances of the soul implicate your actions in the visible world? Insights may appear quite suddenly with no effort on your part. The activity of soul informs everything you do, everything you think, everything you fear, everything you hate, and everything you love. Engagement at this level brings not just knowledge, but a deep and abiding sensitivity to the world of soul behind the material world.

Close Council—Here the closing of Council is really the unclosing of Council. You must make a commitment to stay in dialogue with the figures of soul throughout the day, a commitment to feed your soul. This is one of the most satisfying experiences a human can have—to continually remain in contact with the images at the core of being, to always be in touch with the primal energies behind those images.

The Figures Live On

Throughout this chapter, the metaphor of Hermes has helped us to understand the role of Dream Council in our lives. But at this stage I suggest that Hermes, the messenger who connects the human realm with the god realm, is no longer just a metaphor. Council has brought us to the place where we can move seamlessly between our outer lives and our inner lives, to the place where we no longer draw a sharp division between them. They overlap, they intertwine, and each informs and interacts with the other. We can reach inside ourselves to the deepest levels of the psyche and see our personal destiny as it unfolds. We can reach out into the world and participate in the manifestation of that destiny. I believe that this is what the Greeks were pointing to with the story of Hermes, and it is now the reality we embody through Dream Council.

Dream Council is my meeting place for the figures that live deep within myself. There I can have a real, embodied relationship with the figures of my dreams or the people of my past. When I go to the ocean and place my Council members in the sand, Elder Woman, Animal, Boy, The Woman with Crystal Blue Eyes, and many others come to life before me, and I can talk with them, listen to them, and interact with them. Figures come and go through the years, but there is one who always remains: great-grandfather. It is in Council that the great-grandfather of my youth, my grandmother's father, lives again.

He does not exist as some static memory there, an image frozen in a musty, hundred-year-old photograph. Instead he continues to grow, to evolve, and to instruct me in the way of the dream. In Council he lives on as a mythic image, a person of soul, a healer. From the moment Zadie first visited in a dream, telling me to look for the book that would contain my future, I have been shaped by his living presence. My work as a teacher, a therapist, a graduate school president, a father, and a husband has flourished under his loving guidance. His style, his manner, and his knowledge are always with me.

My mother recently told me an interesting fact about my great grandfather. She said that every morning he rose before dawn, walked downstairs, and went outside. Standing on the Pasadena street corner outside his home, he waited for the sun to rise. As the light lifted above the horizon, he quietly enjoyed its beauty.

When she told me this about him, it reminded me of something he said to me just before he died, when he was in his nineties and I was about six or so. He said, "When I go outside at dawn and watch the sunrise, I wonder when the sun rises years from now, if it will find anything alive on Earth or if it will find a world burnt down and destroyed by man's own hands."

I didn't understand it at the time of course, but I realize now that this story points to something essential about my great-grandfather. Everyone always remarked on how happy he was. His was not the happiness of someone who sticks their head in the sand and numbs his consciousness with the repeated affirmation that everything is going to be OK. Zadie knew from personal experience the pain of starvation, of persecution, of poverty, of injustice, and such happiness-through-denial was impossible for him. His was the happiness of a man who had a passion for social justice, who cared about the fate of the Earth, and who looked the challenges of humanity squarely in the eye.

Through Dream Tending, and in the writing of this book, I have come to understand that great-grandfather was speaking from a vision of the future he saw in his mind's eye. Watching the sunrise with his great-grandson, he saw that little boy caring for the World's Dream and all that lives within it, just as he,

Zalman the Shoemaker, did. He saw his great-grandson offering his own teachings to anyone inspired by the call of the dream. Today the teachings of a humble cobbler compel us to imagine what it would mean to live in a world where all the creatures and things in it were encountered as ensouled living images in the grand World's Dream.

LISTING OF
DREAM TENDING EXERCISES

CHAPTER THREE — APPLYING LIVING IMAGES TO MAJOR LIFE CHALLENGES

CHAPTER FOUR — THE WORLD'S DREAM

CHAPTER FIVE — MEDICINES OF THE SOUL

CHAPTER SIX — DREAM COUNCILE — A LIFE PRACTICE